Jane's HISTORIC MILITARY AIRCRAFT

Tony Holmes

HarperCollins*Publishers*

HarperCollins*Publishers*
77-85 Fulham Palace Road
Hammersmith
London W6 8JB

First published by HarperCollins*Publishers* 1998

1 3 5 7 9 10 8 6 4 2

ISBN 0 00 472140 7

Design: Rod Teasdale

Printed in Italy

Dedication

For my son Thomas. I hope that this book still has some relevance when you are old enough to distinguish the differences between a Merlin- and a Griffon-powered Spitfire.

Contents

8 Introduction

World War I Aircraft

12	Avro 504K	UK
14	Bristol F2B	UK
16	Curtiss JN-4 Jenny	USA
18	LVG C.VI	Germany
20	Morane-Saulnier Type AI	France
22	Nieuport 10.C1	France
24	Nieuport 28.C1	France
26	Royal Aircraft Factory SE5A	UK
28	Sopwith Pup	UK
30	Sopwith Triplane	UK
32	Sopwith Camel	UK
34	Spad 13.C1	France
36	Thomas-Morse S-4	USA

Inter-War Aircraft

40	Avro Tutor	UK
42	Avro Anson	UK
44	Boeing Model 100 (F4B-1)	USA
46	Boeing-Stearman Model 75	USA
48	Bücker Bü 131 Jungmann/CASA 1.131E	Germany/Spain
50	Bücker Bü 133 Jungmeister/ CASA ES-1	Germany/Spain
52	Curtiss O-52 Owl	USA
54	Curtiss SNC	USA
56	de Havilland DH 82 Tiger Moth	UK
58	de Havilland DH 89 Dominie	UK
60	Dewoitine D 26	France
62	Douglas B-23 Dragon	USA
64	Fairchild PT-19/-23/-26 Cornell	USA
66	Fleet Finch	UK
68	Focke-Wulf Fw 44 Stieglitz	Germany
70	Gloster Gladiator	UK
72	Grumman JF/J2F Duck	USA
74	Grumman F3F	USA
76	Grumman G-21A Goose	USA
78	Hawker Hind	UK
80	Junkers Ju 52/3m/CASA 352L	Germany/Spain
82	Klemm Kl 35	Germany
84	Messerschmitt Bf 108 Taifun/ Nord Pingouin	Germany/France
86	Miles Hawk Magister III/M 14 Magister	UK
88	Morane-Saulnier MS230	France
90	Naval Factory N3N	USA

Contents

92	North American BT-9/-14/Yale I	USA
94	North American NA-50/-68 and P-64	USA
96	Ryan PT-16/-22 and NR-1 Recruit	USA
98	Republic (Seversky) AT-12 Guardsman	USA
100	Stampe SV4	Belgium/France
102	Vultee BT-13/-15 and SNV-1/-2 Valiant	USA

World War II Aircraft

106	Aeronca O-58 and L-3/-16 Grasshopper	USA
108	Avro Lancaster	UK
110	Beech UC-43/GB-2 Traveller	USA
112	Beech Model 18	USA
114	Bell P-39 Airacobra	USA
116	Bell P-63 Kingcobra	USA
118	Boeing B-17 Flying Fortress	USA
120	Boeing B-29 Superfortress	USA
122	Bristol Blenheim IV/Bolingbrooke IVT	UK
124	British Taylorcraft Auster I-V	UK
126	Bücker Bü 181/Zlin C.6/C.106	Germany/ Czechoslovakia
128	CASA 2.111/Heinkel He 111H	Germany/Spain
130	Cessna Model T-50	USA
132	CAC Wirraway	Australia
134	CAC CA-12 Boomerang	Australia
136	Consolidated PBY Catalina	USA
138	Consolidated B-24 Liberator	USA
140	Consolidated PB4Y-2 Privateer	USA
142	Culver PQ-14	U
144	Curtiss P-40 Warhawk	U
146	Curtiss C-46 Commando	USA
148	Curtiss SB2C Helldiver	USA
150	de Havilland Mosquito	UK
152	Douglas SBD Dauntless	USA
154	Douglas C-47 Skytrain	USA
156	Douglas C-54 Skymaster	USA
158	Douglas A-20 Havoc	USA
160	Douglas A-26 Invader	USA
162	Fairchild Argus	USA
164	Fairey Swordfish	UK
166	Fieseler Fi 156 Storch/ Morane Saulnier 500	Germany/France
168	Fleet Fort	UK
170	Grumman F4F Wildcat	USA
172	Grumman G-44 Widgeon/Super Widgeon	USA
174	Grumman TBF/TBM Avenger	USA
176	Grumman F6F Hellcat	USA
178	Grumman F7F Tigercat	USA

180	Hawker Hurricane	UK
182	Lockheed P-38 Lightning	USA
184	Lockheed Model 18 Lodestar	USA
186	Lockheed B-34/PV Ventura/Harpoon	USA
188	Martin B-26 Marauder	USA
190	Messerschmitt Bf 109G	Germany
192	Miles M 38 Messenger	UK
194	Mitsubishi A6M Zero-Sen	Japan
196	Noorduyn UC-64 Norseman	Canada
198	North American T-6 Texan/SNJ/Harvard	USA
200	North American B-25 Mitchell	USA
202	North American A-36/P-51A Mustang	USA
204	North American P-51C/D Mustang	USA
206	Percival Proctor	UK
208	Piper O-59/L-4/L-19 Grasshopper	USA
210	Polikarpov Po-2	USSR
212	Republic P-47 Thunderbolt	USA
214	Saab B17A	Sweden
216	Stinson AT-19 Reliant	USA
218	Stinson O-49/L-1 Vigilant	USA
220	Stinson O-62/L-5 Sentinel	USA
222	Taylorcraft O-57/L-2 Grasshopper	USA
224	Vickers-Supermarine Spitfire (Merlin)	UK
226	Vickers-Supermarine Spitfire (Griffon)	UK
228	Vought F4U/Goodyear FG-1 Corsair	USA
230	Westland Lysander	UK
232	Yakovlev Yak-3UA	USSR
234	Yakovlev Yak-9UM	USSR

Postwar Aircraft

238	Aermacchi MB-326	Italy
240	Aero L-29 Delfin	Czechoslovakia
242	Aero L-39 Albatros	Czechoslovakia
244	Aerospace Airtrainer CT-4	New Zealand
246	Antonov An-2	USSR/Poland
248	Armstrong-Whitworth Argosy	UK
250	Auster AOP 6/9/11	UK
252	Avro Shackleton	UK
254	BAC Jet Provost	UK
256	BAC Strikemaster	UK
258	BAC Buccaneer	UK
260	Beech T-34 Mentor	USA/Japan
262	Boeing C-97 Stratofreighter/Stratotanker	USA
264	CAC CA-25 Winjeel	Australia
266	Cavalier F-51D Mustang Mk 2	USA
268	Cessna O-1 Birdog	USA
270	Cessna O-2 Super Skymaster	USA

Contents

272	Cessna Model 185/U-17 Skywagon	USA
274	Convair C-131	USA
276	Dassault MD.311/312 Flamant	France
278	de Havilland Vampire	UK
280	de Havilland Venom/Sea Venom	UK
282	de Havilland Devon/Sea Devon	UK
284	de Havilland Canada DHC-1 Chipmunk	Canada/UK
286	de Havilland Canada DBC-2 Beaver	Canada
288	de Havilland Canada DHC-4 Caribou	Canada
290	Douglas A-1 Skyraider	USA
292	Douglas A-4 Skyhawk	USA
294	Douglas C-133 Cargomaster	USA
296	Douglas A-3 Skywarrior	USA
298	Douglas R4D-8	USA
300	English Electric Canberra	USA
302	Fairchild C-119 Flying Boxcar	USA
304	Fairchild C-123 Provider	USA
306	Fairey Firefly AS 5/6	UK
308	Fairey Gannet	UK
310	Fiat G.46	Italy
312	Fiat G.59	Italy
314	Fokker S.11 Instructor	The Netherlands
316	Folland Gnat T1	UK
318	Fouga CM178 Magister	France
320	Gloster Meteor	UK
322	Grumman F8F Bearcat	USA
324	Grumman AF-2 Guardian	USA
326	Grumman F9F Panther	USA
328	Grumman Albatross	USA
330	Grumman S-2 Tracker/C-1 Trader	USA
332	Grumman OV-1 Mohawk	USA
334	Hawker Fury/Sea Fury	USA
336	Hawker Sea Hawk	UK
338	Hawker Hunter	UK
340	Helio AU-24 Stallion	USA
342	Hispano HA-1112 Buch	USA
344	Hispano HA-200/-220 Saetta/Super Saetta	Spain
346	Hunting Percival Provost	UK
348	Lockheed C-69/C-121	USA
350	Lockheed T-33/Canadair CL-30	USA/Canada
352	Lockheed P-2 Neptune	USA
354	Lockheed F-104 Starfighter	USA
356	Lockheed P-3 Orion	USA
358	Martin JRM-3 Mars	USA
360	Max Holste M.H.1521M Broussard	France
362	McDonnell Douglas F-4 Phantom II	USA
364	Mikoyan-Gurevich MiG-15/-15UTI	USSR/Poland
366	Mikoyan-Gurevich MiG-17	USSR

368 Mikoyan-Gurevich MiG-21 USSR
370 Morane-Saulnier MS.760 France
372 North American Aviation F-86 Sabre USA
374 North American Aviation F-100D/F Super Sabre USA
376 North American Aviation T-28 Trojan/Fennec USA/France
378 North American (Rockwell) OV-10 Bronco USA
380 North American Aviation T-2 Buckeye USA
382 North American Aviation L-17A Navion USA
384 Northrop T-38 Talon/F-5 Freedom Fighter USA
386 Percival Prentice UK
388 Percival Pembroke/Sea Prince UK
390 Piaggio P.149D Italy
392 Pilatus P-2 Switzerland
394 PZL-104 Wilga Poland
396 PZL TS-11 Iskra Poland
398 Saab J 29 Tunnan Sweden
400 Saab J 32 Lansen Sweden
402 Saab J 35 Draken Sweden
404 Saab 91 Safir Sweden
406 Scottish Aviation Twin Pioneer UK
408 Shorts Skyvan 3M UK
410 Soko G2A Galeb Yugoslavia
412 Vickers-Supermarine Spitfire Mks XVIII and XIX UK
414 Yakovlev Yak-11 USSR/Czechoslovakia
416 Yakovlev Yak-18/Nanchung CJ-5/6 USSR/China
418 Yakovlev Yak-52 USSR/Romania

Helicopters

422 Aérospatiale Alouette II France
424 Bell Model 47/H-13 Sioux USA/UK/Japan/Italy
426 Bell UH-1 Iroquois USA/Japan/Taiwan/Germany/Italy
428 Hiller UH-12 Raven USA
430 Kellet YG-1B Autogyro USA
432 Piasecki (Vertol) HUP/HU-25 Retriever USA
434 Piasecki (Vertol) H-21C Shawnee/Work horse USA
436 Saro (Saunders Roe) Skeeter UK
438 Sikorsky S-55/Westland Whirlwind USA/Japan/UK
440 Sikorsky CH-54 Tarhe (Skycrane) USA
442 Westland AH 1 Scout UK

Introduction

As aeroplane enthusiasts, we live in fortunate times. I am 30 years of age, and in my lifetime the growth of the warbird scene has been truly astounding. In the late 1960s the number of true warbirds actually flying in Britain was infinitesimal, with the few survivors residing either with the government-funded RAF Battle of Britain Memorial Flight (BBMF) or with the Shuttleworth Collection. Things were little better in the USA, with only warbird pioneers like the Confederate Air Force (CAF) and Ed Maloney at The Air Museum bothering to preserve historic military aircraft types that were being summarily sold for scrap.

In 1968 the first seeds of the now burgeoning warbird movement in the UK were sown with the making of the epic celluloid flop *The Battle of Britain*. Many formerly static Spitfires and Hurricanes were removed from storage in RAF hangars or pulled off of poles at various bases and made either airworthy, or at least capable of ground taxying. They were joined by over two-dozen Spanish 'Bf 109s' in the form of Merlin-engined Hispano HA-1112 Buchcanes were removed from storage in RAF hangars or pulled off of poles at various bases and made either airworthy, or at least capable of ground taxying. They were joined by over two-dozen Spanish 'Bf 109s' in the fUK.

Since then, impressive collections of privately-owned military aircraft – predominantly from the World War 2 period – have grown principally at Duxford (The Fighter Collection and The Old Flying Machine Company being the largest), which has become the Mecca for warbird enthusiasts not only in the UK, but across the globe. In the past decade the sheer number, and variety, of aircraft types flying in British skies alone has drastically increased. Flightlines crammed with in excess of 20 Spitfires, 10 Mustangs and numerous Corsairs, Hurricanes and Sea Furies have become the norm at big summer airshows like Duxford's *Flying Legends*.

'Across the pond', the warbird movement has easily kept apace in both the USA and Canada, with long-established organisations like the CAF and Ed Maloney's now renamed Planes of Fame Museum being joined by groups such as the Museum of Flying, Cavanaugh Flight Museum, Lone Star Flight Museum, Frasca Simulation, Flights of Fantasy and the Canadian Warplane Heritage.

North America was also home to the first jet warbird collections, and their lead has been faithfully followed not only in the UK and Europe with organisations like Jet Heritage Foundation and Source Classic Jet, but also in Australia and New Zealand. In the latter countries, ex-communist hardware from South-East Asia and the former Eastern Bloc has formed the backbone of a rapidly growing warbird movement.

Turning specifically to the volume that you hold in your hands, this book provides you with a development and service history of over 200 historic aircraft types that all share one thing in common – they *are* airworthy, or have been classed as being 'airworthy', if not flown too often. For more specific details on individual warbirds I would suggest subscriptions to

Aeroplane Monthly, FlyPast, Air Enthusiast,Warbirds Worldwide, Aircraft Illustrated, American-based *Air Classics* or the Australian publication *Flightpath* as being money well spent.

The sheer scope of today's warbird scene can be judged by the thickness of this tome, which covers types ranging from the priceless Luft-Verkehrs Gesellschaft LVG C.VI at Shuttleworth, to F-4D Phantom IIs flying high-speed trials work with Tracor out of the desert airport at Mojave in California. I have provided brief notes on the current number of airworthy examples of each type where known, and would appreciate hearing from any individual who may have information updating or correcting my figures – all correspondence can be sent to me via the publisher, and will go towards updating the next volume of the *Historic Military Aircraft Recognition Guide*..

Harking back to my opening comments at the start of this introduction, I have been fortunate enough to witness the growth of the warbird community at first hand over the past decade. Who knows what the next 30 years will bring? Perhaps my newly-born son will be watching Hunters, Phantom IIs and Tornado GR 1s of the BBMF when he gets to my age!

Tony Holmes
Sevenoaks, Kent
May 1998

Acknowledgements

My first big thank you goes to my wife Katy, who has perfected the role of 'single parent' during the writing of this book. She has coped admirably with a house move, massive redecoration, child birth (I stopped for an hour or two to give her moral support at this point), postnatal depression and a veritable mountain of nappies whilst I have continued tapping away on my Mac in ignorant bliss in the basement. My second thank you goes to my long suffering editor, Ian Drury, at HarperCollins, who has shown levels of patience and understanding above and beyond the call of duty – where do we find such men. On the photographic front, this volume would be much the poorer without the excellent lens craft of Michael O'Leary, Peter March, Dave Davies, Mike Vines, Norman Pealing and Jim Winchester. Finally, thanks to my chums Phil Jarrett, Richard Riding and Bill Gunston for searching out the odd obscure date or dimension . . . oh, and by the way Bill, that 'unidentified' Yugoslavian radial-engined type was a Soko Ikarus 522! I will have to put that one in the next volume . . .

World War I Aircraft

Avro 504K

UK

Type: two-seat, single-engined biplane trainer **Accommodation:** two pilots in tandem

Royal Flying Corps (RFC) / Royal Air Force (RAF) basic trainer throughout World War 1 and up to 1924, the Avro 504 was built to the tune of 8000+ airframes. Versions A to H were constructed between 1913 and 1917, and although best remembered for its work in the instructional role, the early marks were actually employed during the first months of World War 1 as reconnaissance-bombers. The definitive 504K was ushered into service in 1918, this version boasting a universal engine mounting which allowed the basic airframe to be powered by any one of several differing types of rotary engine. There are two airworthy Avro 504Ks currently in the UK, one of which is a replica built in 1994. The only other airworthy example is held in the USA, whilst a further 12 survive in museums across the globe.

Specification:

Dimensions:
Length: 29 ft 5 in (8.97 m)
Wingspan: 36 ft 0 in (10.97 m)
Height: 10 ft 5 in (3.17 m)

Weights:
Empty: (Le Rhône engine) 1231 lb (558.38 kg)
Max T/O: 1829 lb (829.63 kg)

Performance:
Max Speed: 95 mph (152.9 kmh)
Range: 250 miles (400 km)
Powerplant: Clerget, Le Rhône or Warner Scarab
Output: (Le Rhône engine) 110 hp (82.7 kW)

First Flight Date:
18 September 1913

Surviving Airworthy Variant(s):
504J, 504K and 504N, plus replica 504Ks

Right: Although a replica, this aircraft has been built using original Avro specifications. It currently flies with the Great War Display Team.

D8781

Bristol F2B Fighter

UK

Type: two-seat, single-engined biplane fighter **Accommodation:** pilot and gunner in tandem

Derived from Bristol's similarly-configured F2A, the F2B Fighter first entered service over the Western Front in June 1917. It immediately made inroads against the 'scourge' of the RFC, the Albatros DIII, the 'new' aircraft benefiting from the extra power produced by its Falcon III engine, which boasted 275 bhp. Indeed, the F2B was so effective that it began to produce aces with scores that rivalled those accrued by pilots of single-seat fighter types – the greatest exponent of the F2B, Canadian Lt Andrew McKeever, scored 30 victories whilst flying with No 11 Sqn, 8 of which fell to his observer Sgt L F Powell. The aircraft remained in production until December 1926, by which time some 5100+ had been delivered. Postwar, the F2B was used primarily in the Army Co-operation and dual-control training roles, where its durability ensured its survival in Iraq and the North-West Frontier of India until 1931. The UK-based Shuttleworth Collection are currently the only operators of an airworthy F2B, although a second British machine should be flying before the year 2000. At least three other Bristol Fighters are on static exhibition in museums.

Specification:

Dimensions:
Length: 25 ft 10 in (7.87 m)
Wingspan: 39 ft 3 in (11.96 m)
Height: 9 ft 9 in (2.97 m)

Weights:
Empty: 1930 lb (875 kg)
Max T/O: 2848 lb (1292 kg)

Performance:
Max Speed: 125 mph (202 kmh)
Range: endurance of 3 hours
Powerplant: Rolls-Royce Falcon III
Output: 275 hp (205 kW)

First Flight Date:
25 October 1916 (modified F2A)

Surviving Airworthy Variant(s): F2B

Right: D8096 was built in 1918, although it missed seeing any action during World War 1.

D
8096
D8096
D

Curtiss JN-4 Jenny

USA

Type: two-seat, single-engined biplane trainer

Accommodation: two pilots in tandem

America's most successful training aircraft of World War 1, the Curtiss JN-4 was an improved version of the JN-3. The Jenny relied heavily on the incredibly robust OX-5 engine for its success in the instructional role. The entry of America into World War 1 in April 1917 resulted in orders for the Jenny that totalled over 6000 examples by the time production ended soon after the November 1918 Armistice. Perhaps the type's greatest work, however, was done postwar when hundreds of surplus machines were sold cheaply to private buyers, thus helping to establish civil aviation in the USA. Today, the Jenny is the world's most populous genuine World War 1 type, with examples remaining airworthy in North America and the UK.

Specification:

Dimensions:
Length: 27 ft 4 in (8.34 m)
Wingspan: 43 ft 7 in (13.31 m)
Height: 9 ft 11 in (2.77 m)

Weights:
Empty: 1580 lb (716.88 kg)
Max T/O: 2130 lb (966.16 kg)

Performance:
Max Speed: 75 mph (120 kmh)
Range: 250 miles (400 km)
Powerplant: Curtiss OX-5
Output: 90 hp (67 kW)

First Flight Date:
1916

Surviving Airworthy Variant(s):
JN-4D, JN-4 (CAN) Canuck, JN-4H

Right: This JN-4H has been flying from Old Rhinebeck Aerodrome, New York, since 1969.

Luft-Verkehrs Gesellschaft LVG C.VI

Germany

Type: two-seat, single-engined biplane reconnaissance bomber

Accommodation: pilot and observer/gunner in tandem

A versatile reconnaissance bomber from Germany's most successful World War 1 bomber constructor, the C.VI was the most advanced of the C-type aircraft to see wartime service. Its lineage stretched back to the C.I of 1915, the final variant benefiting from the introduction of the new Benz BzIV engine in early 1918. Capable of carrying 240 lb of bombs, LVG had built over 1100 C.VIs by the end of the war. Three C.VIs have survived into the 1990s, although only 7198/18, operated by the Shuttleworth Collection, is currently airworthy – indeed, it is the only genuine German World War 1 type in such condition.

Specification:

Dimensions:
Length: 24 ft 5.25 in (7.47 m)
Wingspan: 42 ft 7.75 in (13.03 m)
Height: 9 ft 2.25 in (2.8 m)

Weights:
Empty: 2090 lb (948.02 kg)
Max T/O: 3036 lb (1377.12 kg)

Performance:
Max Speed: 106 mph (169.6 kmh)
Range: endurance of 3.5 hours
Powerplant: Benz BzIV
Output: 200 hp (149 kW)

First Flight Date:
Late January 1918

Surviving Airworthy Variant(s):
C.VI

Right: The LVG C.VI completed a 12-year restoration at Shuttleworth in 1972, and has remained airworthy ever since.

Morane-Saulnier Type AI

France

Type: single-seat, single-engined parasol fighter **Accommodation:** one pilot

Although highly rated at the time of its first flight in the late summer of 1917, the radically configured AI proved to be a disappointment once it reached frontline service early the following year. Although over 1000 were constructed by Morane-Saulnier, the type had been relegated to the advanced training role by mid-May 1918, being replaced by the more conventional Spad 13.C1. The official reasons for its rapid demise have remained obscure to this day, although sources at the time stated that numerous AIs had suffered structural failures in flight, and the type's rotary engine had proven temperamental in daily service. Two AIs are still regularly flown, one at Old Rhinebeck and the other (a semi-replica) with the Salis Collection in France. Several airworthy replicas are also in existence in the latter country.

Specification:

Dimensions:
Length: 18 ft 6.2 in (5.65 m)
Wingspan: 27 ft 11 in (8.51 m)
Height: 7 ft 10.5 in (2.40 m)

Weights:
Empty: 912 lb (414 kg)
Max T/O: 1486 lb (674 kg)

Performance:
Max Speed: 137 mph (221 kmh)
Range: endurance of 1.75 hours
Powerplant: Gnome Monosoupape 9Nb
Output: 150 hp (112 kW)

First Flight Date:
Early August 1917

Surviving Airworthy Variant(s):
Type AI

Right: One of the Salis Collection replica AIs taxies at La Ferté Alais.

Nieuport 10.C1

France

Type: single-seat, single-engined biplane fighter **Accommodation:** one pilot

The first in a long line of successful fighters built by Nieuport for the French *Aviation Militaire*, the 10 was reputedly derived from a one-off racing special designed by Gustave Delage for the cancelled 1914 Gordon-Bennett contest. The first examples to enter service in May 1915 were two-seaters built for the observation role, but these aircraft were quickly modified into single-place configuration through the simple expedient of fairing over the front seat. With the addition of an overwing Lewis machine gun, the Nieuport 10 became a fighter – this armament was also employed by those aircraft that remained true to the original design, the observer being forced to stand erect through a hole in the upper wing in order to fire the gun! The Nieuport 10 was also built under licence in Italy by Macchi, and today two static aircraft survive in this country. Only one other example exists, and this is maintained in an airworthy condition at Old Rhinebeck Aerodrome.

Specification:

Dimensions:

Length: 22 ft 2.5 in (7.00 m)
Wingspan: 25 ft 11 in (7.90 m)
Height: 8 ft 10.25 in (2.70 m)

Weights:

Empty: 904 lb (410 kg)
Max T/O: 1455 lb (660 kg)

Performance:

Max Speed: 91 mph (146 kmh)
Range: endurance of 3 hours
Powerplant: Gnome or Le Rhône
Output: 80 hp (59.5 kW)

First Flight Date:

Late 1914

Surviving Airworthy Variant(s):

Nieuport 10.C1

Right: French ace Charles Nungesser originally imported this Nieuport 10.C1 into the USA in 1924 to help publicise the film* The Sky Raider, *in which both he and the aircraft appeared.

Nieuport 28.C1

France

Type: single-seat, single-engined biplane fighter **Accommodation:** one pilot

The last Nieuport fighter design to reach the frontline during World War 1, the 28.C1 was also the first aircraft from this manufacturer to feature a two-spar lower wing with a chord almost equal to the upper flying surface, rather than the company's trademark sesquiplane configuration. Built to replace earlier Nieuport and Spad designs within the *Aviation Militaire*, the 28.C1 was deemed to be unsuitable by the French and issued instead to the American Expeditionary Force (AEF). The latter received 297 examples from March 1918, equipping four pursuit squadrons. However, the fighter suffered from traditional Nieuport frailty, and a number were lost when upper wing fabric was shed in extended dives. Engine fuel line fires were also a common occurrence, and by August the 28.C1s had been withdrawn. Following the Armistice, a number of aircraft were shipped to America, where they eventually wound up as 'film stars' in the Hollywood epics *The Dawn Patrol* (the aircraft seen opposite was 'N5246' in this motion picture) and *Men with Wings*. Today, at least seven 28.C1s are still in existence, with three maintained in airworthy condition.

Specification:

Dimensions:
Length: 21 ft 0 in (6.40 m)
Wingspan: 26 ft 9.25 in (8.16 m)
Height: 8 ft 2.5 in (2.50 m)

Weights:
Empty: 961 lb (436 kg)
Max T/O: 1539 lb (698 kg)

Performance:
Max Speed: 123 mph (198 kmh)
Range: endurance of 1.5 hours
Powerplant: Gnome Monosoupape 9N
Output: 150 hp (112 kW)

First Flight Date:
June 1917

Surviving Airworthy Variant(s):
Nieuport 28.C1

Right: Veteran of a number of Hollywood films, 'N5246' was returned to airworthiness in the UK, before being sold to an American collector and returned to the USA in 1993.

5

Royal Aircraft Factory SE5a

UK

Type: single-seat, single-engined biplane fighter **Accommodation:** one pilot

Derived from the SE (Scout Experimental) 5, designed in 1916 by the Royal Aircraft Factory at Farnborough, the SE5a proved to be one of the most successful fighters of World War 1. Mass-produced by five companies to the tune of 5125 examples in under 18 months up to Armistice Day, the SE5a was the staple fighter of both the RFC and the fledgling RAF. Rugged, reliable and manoeuvrable, the fighter helped the Allies wrest air supremacy over the Western Front from the Germans in early 1918. Its stability as a gun platform made the fighter a firm favourite with numerous aces during the last year of the war, with men of the calibre of Mannock, McCudden and Dallas amassing high scores in the SE5a. Postwar, examples remained in service in Australia, Canada and South Africa into the 1920s, whilst a small number were re-engined in America and flown as SE5Es. Six original aircraft are still in existence, two of which are 'flyers' – the Shuttleworth Collection SE5a F904, and the world's only SE5E, which is operated by Kermit Weeks in Florida.

Specification:

Dimensions:
Length: 20 ft 11 in (6.38 m)
Wingspan: 26 ft 11 in (8.11 m)
Height: 9 ft 6 in (2.89 m)

Weights:
Empty: 1531 lb (694 kg)
Max T/O: 2048 lb (929 kg)

Performance:
Max Speed: 120 mph (193 kmh)
Range: endurance of 2.25 hours
Powerplant: Hispano-Suiza 8B or Wolseley W.4a Viper
Output: 200 hp (149.3 kW)

First Flight Date:
12 January 1917

Surviving Airworthy Variant(s):
SE5a and SE5E

Right: Shuttleworth's SE5a has flown in the markings of a No 56 Sqn machine for over 25 years.

F
904

Sopwith Pup

UK

Type: single-seat, single-engined biplane fighter **Accommodation:** one pilot

Essentially a scaled-down, single-seat, derivative of Sopwith's 1½-Strutter (the RFC's first true two-seat fighter), the Pup was initially known as the Scout. However, due to its small size and strong family resemblance to the 'Strutter', it was quickly dubbed the 'Pup' – an appellation which eventually became official. Ordered by both the RFC and Royal Naval Air Service (RNAS), the first Pups reached the Western Front in September 1916, and remained in frontline service until rendered obsolete by the SE5a and the Camel in the late summer of the following year. Some 1770 Pups were eventually built, the type continuing to be produced well into 1918 in order to satisfy the demand for Home Defence fighters to engage marauding German bombers and Zeppelin dirigibles. Aside from operating with RNAS units on land, a number of Pups were also embarked on the Royal Navy's trio of aircraft carrier from early 1917 until war's end. Two semi-original Pups are maintained in flying order today, one of which – the Shuttleworth Collection's N6181 – was converted from a two-seat civilian Sopwith Dove. A further two replica aircraft are also regularly flown.

Specification:

Dimensions:
Length: 19 ft 3.75 in (5.89 m)
Wingspan: 26 ft 6 in (8.08 m)
Height: 9 ft 5 in (2.87 m)

Weights:
Empty: 787 lb (357 kg)
Max T/O: 1225 lb (556 kg)

Performance:
Max Speed: 111 mph (179 kmh)
Range: endurance of 3 hours
Powerplant: Le Rhône 9C
Output: 80 hp (59.6 kW)

First Flight Date:
February 1916

Surviving Airworthy Variant(s):
Pup

Right: The Shuttleworth Pup wears the distinctive scheme of a No 3 Sqn RNAS wartime aircraft.

HAPPY
THE SOPWITH AVIATION Company Ltd KINGSTON ON THAMES

Sopwith Triplane (replica) UK

Type: single-seat, single-engined triplane fighter **Accommodation:** one pilot

Built as a replacement for the Pup, the Triplane boasted a superior rate of climb and greatly improved manoeuvrability thanks to its extra wing. Indeed, when the type made its combat debut with the RNAS in February 1917, the Triplane could easily out-climb any other aircraft operated by either side. Apart from its use by the navy, the Triplane was also ordered by the RFC, but a deal struck in the early spring of 1917 saw the latter service exchange all its Sopwith fighters for Spad 7s originally destined for the RNAS. This agreement subsequently resulted in the planned production run for the Triplane being rapidly scaled down, and only 150 were completed. Nevertheless, the design had a great impact when it finally met the enemy – so much so that the German High Command immediately ordered their manufacturers to produce triplane designs to counter the Sopwith fighter, the most famous of which was the Fokker Dr I. The Triplane began to be replaced by the Camel from July 1917 onwards. Two original Triplanes are still in existence on static display, whilst two flying replicas can also be found in the UK.

Specification:

Dimensions:
Length: 18 ft 10 in (5.74 m)
Wingspan: 26 ft 6 in (8.08 m)
Height: 10 ft 6 in (3.20 m)

Weights:
Empty: 993 lb (450 kg)
Max T/O: 1415 lb (642 kg)

Performance:
Max Speed: 116 mph (187 kmh)
Range: endurance of 2.75 hours
Powerplant: Clerget 9B
Output: 130 hp (96.6 kW)

First Flight Date:
28 May 1916

Surviving Airworthy Variant(s):
Triplane

Right: Like the Pup, the Shuttleworth Triplane also honours an RNAS wartime fighter, this time from No 8 Wing.

DIXIE

Sopwith Camel

UK

Type: single-seat, single-engined biplane fighter **Accommodation:** one pilot

The most famous British fighter of World War 1, the Camel was also the most successful design to see service with either side in respect to the number of victories claimed by its pilots – 1294 aeroplanes and three airships destroyed. Designed by Herbert Smith, the Camel was the first purpose-built fighter to boast two Vickers machine guns synchronised to fire through the propeller arc. The humped fairing covering the breeches of these weapons actually provided the inspiration for the fighter's unique sobriquet which, like its predecessor the Pup, went from being an unofficial appellation to its official name. Although the Camel boasted a fearsome reputation in combat, the fighter's exacting handling characteristics took a heavy toll on poorly trained novice pilots. Nevertheless, near on 5500 Camels were eventually built, the Sopwith design seeing service not only with the RFC/RAF on the Western Front, but also on Home Defence duties in the nightfighter role and at sea with the RNAS in specially-modified 2F1 form. Six genuine Camels have survived into the 1990s, although only B6291 (now based in the USA) is a 'flyer' – there are numerous airworthy replicas, however.

Specification:

Dimensions:
Length: 18 ft 9 in (5.72 m)
Wingspan: 28 ft 0 in (8.53 m)
Height: 8 ft 6 in (2.59 m)

Weights:
Empty: 929 lb (421 kg)
Max T/O: 1453 lb (659 kg)

Performance:
Max Speed: 113 mph (182 kmh)
Range: endurance of 2.5 hours
Powerplant: Clerget 9B, Bentley B.R.1 or Le Rhône
Output: 130 hp (96.6 kW)

First Flight Date:
22 December 1916

Surviving Airworthy Variant(s):
F1 Camel

Right: The world's sole authentic airworthy Camel flew in the UK in 1993/94 before being sold to an American collector.

SOPWITH
B6291

Spad 13.C1 France

Type: single-seat, single-engined biplane fighter **Accommodation:** one pilot

Derived from the highly successful Spad 7 and limited-edition Spad 12, the 13.C1 was developed to make use of the powerful Hispano-Suiza 8B engine, which cranked out 200 hp. The extra performance offered by the motor allowed company designers to fit two 7.7 mm Vickers guns into the 13.C1, and the *Aviation Militaire* enthusiastically ordered 8470 examples to be built. However, a combination of manufacturing problems and chronic engine reliability drastically slowed the delivery process, and of the 2200 13.C1s promised by Spad for completion by March 1918, just 764 had been built, of which only 300 were in operational service. With the engine woes eventually rectified, production finally began to meet demand in the late spring of 1918, Spad churning out 11 13.C1s a day until manufacturing ceased in 1919. By this time some 8470 aircraft had been built, and aside from its use by French Escadrilles, British, Italian, Belgian and American units also saw action with the Spad. Seven 13.C1s remain today, with single examples being flown on an irregular basis at Old Rhinebeck and La Ferté Alais, in France – the latter machine is owned by the Jean Salis Collection and operated by the Meudon Memorial Flight Association.

Specification:

Dimensions:
Length: 20 ft 6 in (6.25 m)
Wingspan: 27 ft 1 in (8.25 m)
Height: 8 ft 6.5 in (2.60 m)

Weights:
Empty: 1326 lb (601 kg)
Max T/O: 1888 lb (856 kg)

Performance:
Max Speed: 135 mph (218 kmh)
Range: endurance of 1.67 hours
Powerplant: Hispano-Suiza 8B
Output: 200 hp (149 kW)

First Flight Date:
4 April 1917

Surviving Airworthy Variant(s):
13.C1

Right: The impeccably restored Spad 13.C1 of the Meudon Memorial Flight has its engine run at La Ferté Alais.

4377

Thomas-Morse S-4

USA

Type: single-seat, single-engined biplane fighter trainer **Accommodation:** one pilot

The Thomas-Morse Aircraft Corporation formed in January 1917 when the English-born Thomas brothers went into partnership with the American-based Morse Chain Co. Their chief designer was B D Thomas (no relation), who had previously worked for Curtiss on the Jenny. His first offering for his new employer was also a trainer in the form of the single-seat S-4 scout, this diminutive machine being ordered by the US Signal Corps to the tune of 100 examples for use in the advanced instructional role. Designated S-4Bs, these aircraft were powered by the Gnome Monosoupape rotary, although the engine proved to be a less than successful choice due to it being continually blighted by oil leaks. So bad was the problem that the follow-on batch of 400 S-4Cs, ordered in January 1918, utilised the less powerful, but infinitely more reliable, Le Rhône 9C. Used exclusively in America, the 'Tommy', as it was dubbed in service, was soon retired after the Armistice, and many surplus machines found gainful civilian employment as air racers or in film work. Their widespread use in private hands has ensured that at least 15 S-4s (virtually all S-4Cs) have survived into the 1990s, several of which are airworthy.

Specification:

Dimensions:
Length: 19 ft 10 in (5.82 m)
Wingspan: 26 ft 6 in (8.01 m)
Height: 8 ft 1 in (2.73 m)

Weights:
Empty: 940 lb (426.38 kg)
Max T/O: 1330 lb (603.28 kg)

Performance:
Max Speed: 97 mph (155.2 kmh)
Range: endurance of 2 hours
Powerplant: Gnome Monosoupape and Le Rhône 9C
Output: 100 hp (74.5 kW) and 80 hp (59.5 kW) respectively

First Flight Date:
June 1917

Surviving Airworthy Variant(s):
S-4B and S-4C

Right: This S-4C seems to be virtually complete except for a propeller.

Inter-War Aircraft

Avro 621 Tutor

UK

Type: single-engined biplane trainer **Accommodation:** two pilots in tandem

Created by legendary Avro designer, Roy Chadwick, the Tutor was built as a replacement for the company's veteran 504K/N, many of which were still in everyday use with RAF flying training schools as the 1920s drew to a close. Following an evaluation of the new machine at the Aircraft and Armament Experimental Establishment (A & AEE) at Martlesham Heath in December 1929, the RAF chose the Tutor as its new basic trainer. A trial batch of 21 was initially ordered, and following their successful introduction into service at the Central Flying School (CFS), a further 373 Tutors were taken on strength between 1934 and 1936. Possessing excellent handling characteristics, CFS Tutors were regularly put through their aerobatic paces at numerous air pageants and RAF displays throughout the 1930s. The aircraft also proved popular with overseas air arms too, the South African Air Force actually operating locally-built Tutors. The advent of monoplane fighters like the Hurricane and Spitfire sounded the death knell for the Avro biplane trainer as the decade drew to a close, and by 1939 most had been replaced by Miles Magisters. Just one Tutor has survived in the UK, this aircraft having been flown by the Shuttleworth Collection since 1959.

Specification:

Dimensions:

Length: 26 ft 6 in (8.08 m)
Wingspan: 34 ft 0 in (10.36 m)
Height: 9 ft 7 in (2.92 m)

Weights:

Empty: 1844 lb (836 kg)
Max T/O: 2458 lb (1115 kg)

Performance:

Max Speed: 122 mph (196.7 kmh)
Range: 250 miles (402 km)
Powerplant: Armstrong Siddeley Lynx IVC
Output: 240 hp (179 kW)

First Flight Date:

December 1929

Surviving Airworthy Variant(s):

621 Tutor

Right: Built in 1932, K3215 was used by No 1 Flying Training School (FTS) during its time with the RAF.

K
3215
K 3215

Avro Anson

UK

Type: twin-engined trainer/communications aircraft **Accommodation:** crew of up to six in training role

Derived from Avro's 652 airliner, the Anson claimed two firsts when it entered military service in March 1936 as it was not only the RAF's first monoplane design, but it also boasted a retractable undercarriage. The primary user of the Anson I pre-war was Coastal Command, whose squadrons employed the aircraft in the general reconnaissance and search and rescue roles until 1942. Soon after the outbreak of World War 2, the Anson was chosen as a standard training aircraft for the British Commonwealth Air Training Plan, and it was in this instructional role that the Anson really excelled. Indeed, it was so successful that a second production line was set up in Canada in order to satisfy the demand for new aircrew. The Anson's fuselage shape was revised with the advent of the Mk XI/XII, and its reliability and docile handling ensured that the design remained in production until May 1952 – a total of 11,020 Ansons were built. Following the final retirement of the T 21 from RAF service in June 1968, a small number of Ansons were briefly flown by civilian operators into the 1970s. Today, only two remain airworthy in the UK, with a third machine being flown in North America.

Specification:

Dimensions:

Length: 42 ft 3 in (12.88 m)
Wingspan: 56 ft 5 in (17.20m)
Height: 13 ft 1 in (3.99 m)

Weights:

Empty: 5375 lb (2438 kg)
Max T/O: 8000 lb (3629 kg)

Performance:

Max Speed: 188 mph (303 kmh)
Range: 790 miles (1271 km)
Powerplant: (Mk 19/T 21) two Armstrong Siddeley Cheetah 15s
Output: 840 hp (626.4 kW)

First Flight Date:

24 March 1935

Surviving Airworthy Variant(s):

Mk 19 and T21

Right: Finished in a postwar RAF Transport Command Scheme, Anson T 21 WD413 has recently been returned to airworthiness by Atlantic Airlines after undergoing a lengthy overhaul

ROYAL AIR FORCE TRANSPORT COMMAND

Boeing Model 100 (F4B-1/P-12B) USA

Type: single-engined biplane fighter **Accommodation:** one pilot

Built as the private venture Model 100 by Boeing in 1929, this diminutive machine was a natural successor to the company's F2B/F3B naval fighters of several years before. The new design's big advantage rested in its smaller and lighter airframe, which combined with Pratt & Whitney's latest specification Wasp radial to produce an aircraft that was 32 mph faster than the Boeing fighters then in service. After testing two prototypes, the US Navy ordered 27 F4B-1s, followed in 1931 by 46 F4B-2s, fitted with engine cowls, Frise ailerons, a tailwheel and a supercharged engine, 21 F4B-3s with an entirely new light-alloy monocoque fuselage, and finally 92 F4B-4s with a wider fin – a further 23 B-4s were exported to Brazil. In a rare display of service unity, the US Army Air Corps also ordered the Model 100, which they duly designated the P-12 – their purchases consisted of 90 P-12Bs, 96 P-12Cs, 35 P-12Ds, 110 P-12Es and 25 P-12Fs. These machines differed only in minor detail from their navy brethren. Used throughout the 1930s firstly as frontline fighters and then in the advanced training role, the last F4Bs/P-12s were phased out of service in 1941. At least two ex-civilian Model 100s are still flying today.

Specification:

Dimensions:
Length: 20 ft 1 in (6.12 m)
Wingspan: 30 ft 0 in (9.14 m)
Height: 9 ft 7 in (2.92 m)

Weights:
Empty: 1758 lb (797 kg)
Max T/O: 2536 lb (1150 kg)

Performance:
Max Speed: 171 mph (275 kmh)
Range: 371 miles (597 km)
Powerplant: Pratt & Whitney R-1340-8 Wasp
Output: 500 hp (373 kW)

First Flight Date:
6 May 1929 (F4B-1)

Surviving Airworthy Variant(s):
Model 100

Right: This aircraft is painted up as an F4B-1 of VF-5B 'Red Rippers', whilst a second Model 100 wears the scheme of the USAAC's 96th Pursuit Squadron.

E

Boeing/Stearman Model 75

USA

Type: single-engined biplane trainer **Accommodation:** two pilots in tandem

Built as a private venture by the Stearman Aircraft Company (which was bought by Boeing in 1934) utilising the firm's Model C as a base, the X70, as it was designated by the manufacturer, was submitted as a contender for the USAAC's primary trainer requirement of 1934. It was therefore rather ironic that the first service to show interest in the design was the US Navy, who ordered 61 (designated NS-1s) in early 1935. Following a prolonged evaluation of the X70, the USAAC finally bought an initial batch of just 26 airframes (which they designated PT-13s) in 1936. This small quantity reflected the paucity of the funding then available to the air corps, but all this changed with the outbreak of World War 2 – 3519 PT-17s were built in 1940 alone. A vast array of military designations were given to the basic Boeing Model 75 (as it was officially known after 1939) during its service career, these usually denoting the aircraft's engine fitment. 'North of the border', Canadian machines were given the appellation 'Kaydet', a name which is now universally applied to all Boeing/Stearman Model 75s. By the time production ceased in early 1945, over 10,000 had been built, and today more than 1000 are still flying across the globe.

Specification:

Dimensions:
Length: 25 ft 0.25 in (7.63 m)
Wingspan: 32 ft 2 in (9.80 m)
Height: 9 ft 2 in (2.79 m)

Weights:
Empty: 1936 lb (878 kg)
Max T/O: 2717 lb (1232 kg)

Performance:
Max Speed: 124 mph (200 kmh)
Range: 505 miles (813 km)
Powerplant: Continental R-670 or Lycoming R-680
Output: 220 hp (164 kW)

First Flight Date:
December 1933 (Stearman X70)

Surviving Airworthy Variant(s):
PT-13, PT-17, PT-18, PT-27 and N2S

Right: Although production ceased before the end of World War II, more Stearmans remain airworthy than almost any other warbird.

Bücker Bü 131 Jungmann/CASA 1.131E

Germany & Spain

Type: single-engined biplane trainer **Accommodation:** two pilots in tandem

The first aircraft to be built by the Bücker Flugzeugbau, the Jungmann was employed as a basic trainer by both civil and military flying schools in Germany from late 1934 onwards. The initial production version (Bü 131A) relied on the 80 hp (60 kW) Hirth Hm 60R inline engine, but a later variant (and all export models) made use of the more powerful Hm 504A-2 powerplant. Aside from its success in its own native land, the Jungmann garnered impressive foreign sales, with eight European nations obtaining aircraft in substantial quantities prior to the outbreak of war. Bücker also concluded a licence deal with Japan, where some 1037 were constructed for the army (as Ki-86As) and 200+ for the navy (designated K9W1s). The trainer remained in service with the Luftwaffe throughout World War 2, although it was eventually displaced by Bücker's Bü 181 Bestmann. The humble Jungmann also fulfilled an offensive role during the conflict, dropping light bombs on Soviet troops during nocturnal nuisance raids. Postwar, the design was resurrected in Czechoslovakia, Hungary and Spain, and many have remained airworthy into the 1990s.

Specification:

Dimensions:
Length: 21 ft 8 in (6.60 m)
Wingspan: 24 ft 3.25 in (7.40 m)
Height: 7 ft 4.5 in (2.25 m)

Weights:
Empty: 860 lb (390 kg)
Max T/O: 1499 lb (680 kg)

Performance:
Max Speed: 115 mph (185 kmh)
Range: 404 miles (650 km)
Powerplant: Hirth Hm 504A-2
Output: 105 hp (78 kW)

First Flight Date:
27 April 1934

Surviving Airworthy Variant(s):
Bü 131A/B, 1.131E and Aero C.4

Right: This aircraft is an ex-Spanish Air Force EE-3.

781
32

Bücker Bü 133 Jungmeister/CASA ES-1

Germany & Spain

Type: single-engined biplane trainer **Accommodation:** one pilot

Similar in overall configuration to the Jungmann, the Jungmeister was designed and built at Bücker's then-new Rangsdorf factory, which had been opened in order to allow the company to cope with the overwhelming demand for its earlier trainer. Whereas the Bü 131 had been designed for the basic training role, the smaller and more powerful Bü 133 was aimed at the more advanced student, being fully aerobatic. The Luftwaffe soon ordered the Jungmeister into volume production following its evaluation in 1935-36, the type being used extensively by pilots destined to fly single-seat fighters. Although the prototype and early production Bü 133As relied on the 135 hp (101 kW) Hirth Hm 6 inline engine, the major production variant (C-model) was fitted with the more powerful Siemens Sh 14a-4 radial – as were the 47 licence-built machines (designated Bü 133Bs) produced for the Swiss Air Force by Dornier-Werke. CASA of Spain also built a similar number of Bü 133Cs for the Spanish Air Force, who designated them ES-1s. Aside from the many Swiss and Spanish machines still flying today, a substantial number of 1960s-vintage Bü 133Fs can also be found in airworthy condition.

Specification:

Dimensions:
Length: 19 ft 8.25 in (6 m)
Wingspan: 21 ft 7.75 in (6.60 m)
Height: 7 ft 2.5 in (2.20 m)

Weights:
Empty: 937 lb (425 kg)
Max T/O: 1290 lb (585 kg)

Performance:
Max Speed: 137 mph (220 kmh)
Range: 311 miles (500 km)
Powerplant: Siemens Sh 14a-4 and Franklin 6A-650-C1 (Bü 133F of the 1960s)
Output: 160 hp (119 kW) and 220 hp (164 kW) respectively

First Flight Date:
1935

Surviving Airworthy Variant(s):
Bü 133B/C/F and ES-1

Right: This Bü 133 has been on the UK civil register since the early 1970s, owned and flown by* Pilot *magazine publisher, James Gilbert. It wears the colours of a* Deutsche Luftsportyérband *Jungmeister of the late 1930s.

G-AY

Curtiss O-52 Owl

USA

Type: single-engined parasol heavy observation aircraft **Accommodation:** pilot and observer in tandem

Built by Curtiss in response to a US Army requirement for a two-seat observation aircraft issued to the company in the late 1930s, the Owl was a very capable machine with good low-speed manoeuvrability and landing characteristics – both prerequisites for the army co-operation role. Designated the Model 85 by the company, the all-metal design (with fabric-covered flying surfaces) relied on full-span automatic leading edge slots working in conjunction with wide-span trailing edge flaps to achieve low-speed agility. The observer was equipped with a .30-in (7.62 mm) flexibly-mounted machine gun, whilst the pilot had a fixed weapon of a similar calibre firing through the propeller arc. Ordered into production in 1939, a total of 203 O-52 Owls were built for the US Army from 1940 onwards, although none actually saw frontline service – 19 of these machines were eventually passed on to the Soviet Union. The O-52's military career was to be a brief one, for by 1942 virtually all Owls had been retired from the training role. Despite an undistinguished service history and paucity in numbers, four Owls have survived (all in the USA) into the 1990s, two of which are airworthy.

Specification:

Dimensions:
Length: 26 ft 4 in (8.03 m)
Wingspan: 40 ft 9.50 in (12.43 m)
Height: 9 ft 3.25 in (2.83 m)

Weights:
Empty: 4231 lb (1919 kg)
Max T/O: 5364 lb (2433 kg)

Performance:
Max Speed: 220 mph (354 kmh)
Range: 700 miles (1127 km)
Powerplant: Pratt & Whitney R-1340-51 Wasp
Output: 600 hp (447 kW)

First Flight Date:
1938

Surviving Airworthy Variant(s):
O-52

Right: This O-52 is operated by the Yankee Air Corps from Chino, California.

02769

Curtiss SNC

USA

Type: single-engined advanced trainer **Accommodation:** two pilot in tandem

This rather obscure aircraft was ordered by the US Navy in 1940 to fulfil the Scout Trainer role, its layout being based on the Curtiss CW-21 fighter of 1938. Unlike the latter machine, the SNC had a tandem cockpit arrangement and a much lower-powered engine – a 420 hp (313 kW) Wright Whirlwind in place of the 1000 hp (744 kW) Cyclone from the same manufacturer – as befitted its training tasking. Unofficially named the 'Falcon', the SNC was fully equipped to undertake instrument flying, high altitude training, air gunnery and bomb delivery. An initial contract for 150 aircraft was placed with Curtiss in November 1940, followed by subsequent orders for 150 and 5 the following year. With the delivery of the 305th SNC in late 1941, the production line was terminated. A solitary example of the SNC remains airworthy.

Specification:

Dimensions:
Length: 26 ft 6 in (8.08 m)
Wingspan: 35 ft 0 in (10.67 m)
Height: 7 ft 6 in (2.29 m)

Weights:
Empty: 2610 lb (1184 kg)
Max T/O: 3626 lb (1645 kg)

Performance:
Max Speed: 201 mph (323 kmh)
Range: 515 miles (829 km)
Powerplant: Wright R-975-E3 Whirlwind 9
Output: 420 hp (313 kW)

First Flight Date:
1939

Surviving Airworthy Variant(s):
SNC

Right: Production of the SNC ceased just before the USA entered World War II and this is the only remaining airworthy example.

de Havilland DH 82 Tiger Moth

UK

Type: single-engined biplane trainer **Accommodation:** two pilots in tandem

As with the Avro 504, the Tiger Moth ranks as one of the most famous military training aircraft ever built. Derived from the highly successful civilian DH 60G Gipsy Moth, the Tiger Moth differed from its predecessor in having staggered and swept-back wings (which enabled the parachute-equipped occupant to exit the aircraft in a hurry), an inverted engine to aid visibility over the nose and strengthening to the wings and fuselage in order to allow the aircraft to operate at a higher all up weight. Designated the DH 82, the prototype completed its maiden flight on 26 October 1931 and entered service with the RAF the following month. De Havilland further improved the trainer three years later when it mated the more powerful Gipsy Major engine with a slightly modified Tiger Moth fuselage (wooden rear fuselage decking in place of fabric), the new version being designated the DH 82A. The final variant to reach series production was the winterised DH 82C, built by de Havilland Aircraft of Canada. A staple trainer for virtually all Allied air arms during World War 2, over 8500 Tiger Moths were eventually built. The aircraft remains a firm favourite today, particularly in those countries in which it was built.

Specification:

Dimensions:
Length: 23 ft 11 in (7.29 m)
Wingspan: 29 ft 4 in (8.94 m)
Height: 8 ft 9.50 in (2.68 m)

Weights:
Empty: 1115 lb (506 kg)
Max T/O: 1770 lb (803 kg)

Performance:
Max Speed: 109 mph (175 kmh)
Range: 302 miles (486 km)
Powerplant: de Havilland Gipsy III (DH 82) or Gipsy Major (DH 82B/C)
Output: DH 82 120 hp (89 kW), DH 82B 130 hp (97 kW), DH 82C 145 hp (108 kW)

First Flight Date:
26 October 1931

Surviving Airworthy Variant(s):
DH 82, DH 82A and DH 82C

Right: This immaculate DH 82A wears the K-serial of the very first Tiger Moth I delivered to the RAF on 10 November 1931 – the aircraft was issued to No 3 FTS.

K
2567
K-2567

de Havilland DH 89 Dominie

UK

Type: twin-engined biplane trainer/communications aircraft
Accommodation: crew of up to six in training role, seats for up to ten in communications configuration

The military version of the Dragon Rapide light airliner, the Dominie was initially produced to meet the same Air Ministry Specification (G.18/35) as the Avro Anson. As previously mentioned, the monoplane design was chosen for the general reconnaissance task, and de Havilland had to be satisfied with selling a handful of DH 89Ms (as the military Rapide was designated) to the Spanish government for use in Morocco. However, all was not lost for the elegant Rapide as it was selected by the RAF to fill the role of communications aircraft – several DH 89s were purchased in 1937-38, whilst in 1939, a further 17 were acquired for wireless training. At this time the trainer variant – which boasted a direction-finding loop on the cabin roof – was designated the Dominie Mk I, whilst the communications version was christened Dominie Mk II. The type remained in production until July 1946, some 475 Dominies being built for the RAF and FAA (plus a handful issued to the USAAF in the UK). Aside from the eight Dragon Rapides/Dominies that remain airworthy in the UK today, a number of others are also kept in flying condition in Europe, Australia and New Zealand.

Specification:

Dimensions:
Length: 34 ft 6 in (10.52 m)
Wingspan: 48 ft 0 in (14.63 m)
Height: 10 ft 3 in (3.12 m)

Weights:
Empty: 3230 lb (1465 kg)
Max T/O: 5500 lb (2945 kg)

Performance:
Max Speed: 157 mph (253 kmh)
Range: 570 miles (917 km)
Powerplant: two de Havilland Gipsy Queens
Output: 400 hp (298.2 kW)

First Flight Date:
17 April 1934 (civilian Dragon Rapide)

Surviving Airworthy Variant(s):
DH 89A and DH 89B

Right: Dominie Z7260 flew for a number of years in this air ambulance scheme, inspired by one of two such aircraft subscribed for by the Silver Thimble Fund in the spring of 1941. Tragically, this machine was lost in a fatal accident at Audley End, UK, in June 1991.

Dewoitine D 26

France and Switzerland

Type: single-engined parasol fighter trainer **Accommodation:** one pilot

Based on the Dewoitine D 27 III parasol fighter, which entered service with the Swiss Air Force in 1931, the D 26 was a dedicated training variant built in limited numbers (11) under licence by EKW of Switzerland. Whilst the frontline fighter was fitted with a 500 hp (372.6 kW) Hispano-Suiza 12Mb V12, the D 26 was equipped with a radial engine from the same manufacturer that produced exactly half the horsepower. The Dewoitine proved to be the perfect training tool for future *Fliegertruppe* fighter pilots, and despite the D 27 IIIs being replaced in 1940 (and finally scrapped in 1944) by Bf 109Es bought from Germany, the D 26s remained in service until late in the decade. Of the eleven originally built, six survived military service to be sold into private hands in Switzerland between 1949 and 1951. Examples have since appeared in the UK and France, and several have had their original engines replaced by the more powerful, and reliable, US-built Jacobs R-755-A2 radial.

Specification:

Dimensions:
Length: 21 ft 6 in (6.40 m)
Wingspan: 33 ft 9.5 in (10.30 m)
Height: 9 ft 1.5 in (2.78 m)

Weights:
Empty: 2046 lb (930 kg)
Max T/O: 2350 lb (1065.96 kg)

Performance:
Max Speed: 120 mph (192 kmh)
Range: 230 miles (368 km)
Powerplant: originally a Hispano 9QA, now a Jacobs R-755-A2
Output: 250 hp (186.3 kW) and 300 hp (224 kW) respectively

First Flight Date:
1928

Surviving Airworthy Variant(s):
D 26

Right: French registered D 26 F-AZJD currently masquerades as an* Armée de l'Air *D 27.

D-27
N°290
F-AZJD
DEWOITINE

Douglas B-23 Dragon

USA

Type: twin-engined medium bomber **Accommodation:** four/five-man crew

The B-23 Dragon was essentially a reworked and improved version of Douglas's B-18 Bolo of 1934. Produced as a result of the success of the multi-engined B-17, which had been built at the same time as the B-18, the Dragon boasted a new, more aerodynamic, fuselage, greater wingspan and taller vertical tail unit – it was also the first US bomber with a tail gunner's position. All of these modifications were meant to make the bomber a better performer, and when married to the greater power of the twin Wright R-2600s, Douglas felt sure that they had an aircraft to rival the Flying Fortress. However, trials flown soon after the prototype had completed its first flight on 27 July 1939 revealed less than inspiring performance figures, particularly in light of combat information reaching America from Europe in relation to bomb load and range. The B-23 was quickly passed over in favour of newer medium bombers under development, and only 38 were eventually delivered. These machines saw limited service as coastal patrol aircraft along the Pacific seaboard, whilst 12 were later converted into utility transports (designated UC-67s). Despite being built in modest numbers, over a dozen have survived, with several being kept in airworthy condition.

Specification:

Dimensions:
Length: 58 ft 4 in (17.78 m)
Wingspan: 92 ft 0 in (28.04 m)
Height: 18 ft 6 in (5.64 m)

Weights:
Empty: 19 059 lb (8645 kg)
Max T/O: 30 475 lb (13 823 kg)

Performance:
Max Speed: 282 mph (454 kmh)
Range: 1455 miles (2342 km)
Powerplant: two Wright R-2600-3 Cyclones
Output: 3200 hp (2366 kW)

First Flight Date:
27 July 1939

Surviving Airworthy Variant(s):
B-23 and UC-67

Right: This Dragon was rebuilt in the mid-1980s by a team led by Ascher Ward at Mojave. It was traded to the USAF Museum soon after the restoration was completed, and today resides in the Heritage Museum at McChord Air Force Base, Washington state.

US

Fairchild PT-19/-23/-26 Cornell

USA

Type: single-engined trainer **Accommodation:** two pilots in tandem

Procured by the USAAC in order to prepare trainee pilots destined to fly monoplane aircraft in the frontline, the Fairchild PT-19 started life as the private-venture M-62. Evaluated by the army in 1939, the diminutive trainer was ordered into series production in 1940 and entered service as the PT-19 Cornell later that same year – some 270 were constructed before the re-engined PT-19A came on line in 1941. Over 3700 PT-19As were built, but by 1942 production was being seriously affected by a shortage of Ranger inline engines. With engineless airframes backing up at three assembly lines in the Mid-West, a solution to the problem was needed quickly, so Fairchild simply mated an uncowled Continental R-670 radial to a standard PT-19A and produced the PT-23 – a further 6000 were delivered before production finally ceased in 1944. North of the border, the Canadians found the Fairchild design ideal for the Commonwealth Air Training Scheme, Fleet building substantial quantities of the PT-23 (Cornell I – 93 examples) and PT-26A/B (Cornell II – 1057 examples) under licence. Many remain airworthy in North America today, whilst several 'flyers' can also be found in the UK.

Specification:

Dimensions:
Length: 27 ft 8.5 in (8.45 m)
Wingspan: 36 ft 0 in (10.97 m)
Height: 7 ft 7.5 in (2.32 m)

Weights:
Empty: 2022 lb (917 kg)
Max T/O: 2736 lb (1241 kg)

Performance:
Max Speed: 122 mph (196 kmh)
Range: 400 miles (644 km)
Powerplant: Ranger L-440 or Continental R-670
Output: 200 hp (149 kW) and 220 hp (164 kW) respectively

First Flight Date:
March 1939

Surviving Airworthy Variant(s):
PT-19, PT-19A, PT-19B, PT-23A, PT-26A, PT-26B and Cornell I/II

Right: Radial-engined PT-23 42-49307 is finished in an authentic mid-war USAAF training scheme.

73
249307
73

Fleet Finch

Canada

Type: single-engined biplane trainer **Accommodation:** two pilots in tandem

The Fleet Model 16 Finch was a progressive development of the original Consolidated Fleet primary trainer, the manufacture of which was initiated in Canada by Fleet Aircraft in 1930. Its origins can be traced back to Consolidated's then President, Major Reuben H Fleet, who believed that there was a gap in the civil market in North America for a basic trainer. However, with the first prototype built and tested, Consolidated's management decided not to enter the field of light aviation, so the Major decided to establish Fleet Aircraft and build the trainer independently. Six months later, Consolidated yet again changed its mind and bought Fleet out, duly setting up a factory for trainer construction in Canada. Sold in modest numbers throughout the 1930s on both sides of the border, the aircraft was finally evaluated by the RCAF in Model 10 form in September 1938. Following the trials, the air force stipulated that certain strengthening modifications must be carried out to enable the aircraft to perform aerobatics when fully equipped with military equipment. Known as the Model 16, and christened the Finch I in RCAF service, 606 were eventually built between 1939 and 1941 – this figure includes the later Mk II, which was fitted with an enclosed cockpit. The trainer remained in RCAF service until 1947, and a number saw further employment with civilian flying schools into the late 1950s. Several remain airworthy today.

Specification:

Dimensions:

Length: 21 ft 8 in (6.6 m)
Wingspan: 28 ft 0 in (8.53 m)
Height: 7 ft 9 in (2.36 m)

Weights:

Empty: 1122 lb (509 kg)
Max T/O: 2000 lb (908 kg)

Performance:

Max Speed: 104 mph (167.3 kmh)
Range: 320 miles (512 km)
Powerplant: Kinner B-5
Output: 125 hp (93.25 kW)

First Flight Date:

September 1938

Surviving Airworthy Variant(s):

Fleet 16B and 16R

Right: Finch N16BR shares ramp space at Midland Airport, Texas, with other more warlike types operated by the Confederate Air Force.

N16BR
X FT
CONFEDERATE AIR FORCE
EXPERIMENTAL

Focke-Wulf Fw 44 Stieglitz

Germany

Type: single-engined biplane trainer **Accommodation:** two pilots in tandem

The most prolific design to appear from Focke-Wulf aside from the Fw 190, the humble Fw 44 Stieglitz (goldfinch) basic trainer first took to the skies in the late summer of 1932. Despite its conventional appearance, the prototype aircraft proved to be extremely difficult to fly, and it was left to recently-arrived designer, Kurt Tank, to sort the trainer out. This he duly did, and the revised Fw 44 was subsequently ordered into series production not only for the newly-born Luftwaffe, but also for the ostensibly civilian-run *Deutsche Verkehrsfliegerschule* and the *Deutsche Luftsportverband.* Focke-Wulf followed up the radial-powered Fw 44 with the Argus As 8 inline-engined B- and E-models, small numbers of which were also issued to Luftwaffe training units. However, the company returned to the Siemens Sh 14a radial again for the remaining variants, with the C-, D-, F-, and J-models being built in substantial quantities until the end of the war. Licence production was also undertaken in a number of foreign countries, whilst numerous other air arms bought Fw 44s directly from Focke-Wulf. Today, only a handful remain, this particular example being an ex-Finnish Air Force aircraft now flown by the Confederate Air Force in Texas.

Specification:

Dimensions:
Length: 23 ft 11.5 in (7.30 m)
Wingspan: 29 ft 6.5 in (9.00 m)
Height: 8 ft 10.25 in (2.70 m)

Weights:
Empty: 1157 lb (525 kg)
Max T/O: 1985 lb (900 kg)

Performance:
Max Speed: 115 mph (185 kmh)
Range: 419 miles (675 km)
Powerplant: Siemens Sh 14a
Output: 150 hp (112 kW)

First Flight Date:
Late Summer 1932

Surviving Airworthy Variant(s):
Fw 44J

Right: The Confederate Air Force's very rare Fw 44 performed its military service with the Finnish Air Force.

RF
N2497
AIR FORCE

Gloster Gladiator

UK

Type: single-engined biplane fighter **Accommodation:** one pilot

The last British biplane fighter, the Gladiator started life as a company private venture, Gloster basing their new SS.37 (as the Gladiator was designated) very much on its predecessor, the Gauntlet. Although boasting four guns, the design still embraced the 'old' technology of doped fabric over its wood and metal ribbed and stringered fuselage and wings. Following its first flight in September 1934, the Gladiator I was swiftly put into production, with Glosters eventually building 231 examples. It made its service debut in January 1937, and went on to serve with 27 RAF fighter squadrons. The later Mk II was fitted with the Bristol Mercury VIIIA engine, and 252 new-build machines were delivered, plus a number of Mk Is upgraded to this spec through the fitment of the later powerplant. Sixty arrestor-hooked Sea Gladiators were also delivered to the Royal Navy, plus a further 165 Mk Is and IIs for foreign export customers. A considerable number of Gladiators were still in service when war broke out in September 1939, and although virtually obsolete, they gave a good account of themselves in France, the Middle East, over Malta and in East Africa. Today, only one Gladiator is currently airworthy – Mk II L8032 of the Shuttleworth Trust – although a second Mk II is being restored to fly by The Fighter Collection at Duxford.

Specification:

Dimensions:
Length: 27 ft 5 in (8.36 m)
Wingspan: 32 ft 3 in (9.83 m)
Height: 11 ft 7 in (3.53 m)

Weights:
Empty: 3444 lb (1562 kg)
Max T/O: 4864 lb (2206 kg)

Performance:
Max Speed: 257 mph (414 kmh)
Range: 440 miles (708 km)
Powerplant: Bristol Mercury IX
Output: 830 hp (619 kW)

First Flight Date:
12 September 1934

Surviving Airworthy Variant(s):
Gladiator II

***Right: Although L8032 never actually served with a frontline RAF Fighter Command Unit, it was flown for many years firstly in the all-silver scheme of premier Gladiator operators, No 72 Sqn, then in brown/green camouflage of No 247 Sqn. It was returned to all-silver in 1997, and presently wears the markings of a Gladiator II of the Norwegian* Haerens Flyveaben.**

L
8032
B.O.A.C

Grumman JF/J2F Duck

USA

Type: single-engined biplane utility amphibian **Accommodation:** crew of up to three

The first amphibian designed by the legendary naval manufacturer Grumman, the Duck was heavily influenced by the company's premier production aircraft, the FF-1 and F2F carrier-based fighters of the early 1930s. Grumman also borrowed ideas from the navy's then current amphibian, the Loening OL-9, with the end result being a proposal for the XJF-1. The navy evaluated Grumman's 'paper project', and duly agreed to fund the prototype. Flight testing revealed no serious problems with the new amphibian, and the navy duly ordered an initial production run of 27 Ducks, the first of which was delivered in late 1934. The J2F was vastly superior to the OL-9, possessing a better rate of climb, greater maximum speed and increased service ceiling. Fulfilling both the general utility role and observation mission, the Duck was procured in steady numbers for almost a decade from 1934 onwards, with the Coast Guard and Marine Corps also receiving examples. Grumman built its last Ducks (J2F-5s) in 1941, after which a further 330 (J2F-6s) were constructed by the Columbia Aircraft Corporation. Although a dozen Ducks have survived into the 1990s, only Weeks Air Museum's J2F-6 BuNo 33549 is currently airworthy.

Specification:

Dimensions:
Length: 34 ft 0 in (10.36 m)
Wingspan: 39 ft 0 in (11.89 m)
Height: 13 ft 11 in (4.24 m)

Weights:
Empty: 4400 lb (1996 kg)
Max T/O: 7700 lb (3493 kg)

Performance:
Max Speed: 190 mph (306 kmh)
Range: 750 miles (1207 km)
Powerplant: Wright R-1820-54 Cyclone 9
Output: 900 hp (671 kW)

First Flight Date:
4 May 1933

Surviving Airworthy Variant(s):
J2F-6

Right: J2F-6 BuNo 33549 was damaged when Hurricane Andrew struck Tamiami in August 1992, although the amphibian has since been restored to airworthiness.

J2F-6
N1214N
CANDY CLIPPER

Grumman F3F (replica)

USA

Type: single-engined biplane fighter **Accommodation:** one pilot

The third in the long line of Grumman fighters that have created a dynasty of frontline service with the US Navy that has lasted over 60 years, the portly F3F was the last biplane interceptor to operate from the deck of an American carrier. Built as an improved F2F, with a longer fuselage, greater wingspan and more powerful Pratt & Whitney (F3F-1) or Wright Cyclone (F3F-2/-3) engine, some 162 F3Fs served with frontline Navy and Marine Corps units between 1936 and 1941. During this time the Grumman design proved both rugged and highly manoeuvrable, and many of the US Navy's most influential fighter leaders of World War 2 (Butch O'Hare and Jimmy Thach, to name but two) 'cut their teeth' operationally with the F3F in the years leading up to 1941. This particular F3F-2 is an exact replica of the original Grumman biplane fighter, being built in the early 1990s by Herb Tischler's Texas Airplane Factory from original plans supplied by the company. One of four 'made to order', the aircraft is powered by a period Wright Cyclone engine and painted in a US Navy frontline fighter scheme as worn by the F3F in 1940.

Specification:

Dimensions:
Length: 23 ft 0 in (7.01 m)
Wingspan: 32 ft 0 in (9.75 m)
Height: 9 ft 4 in (2.84 m)

Weights:
Empty: 3254 lb (1476 kg)
Max T/O: 4750 lb (2155 kg)

Performance:
Max Speed: 234 mph (376 kmh)
Range: 1130 miles (1818 km)
Powerplant: Wright R-1820-22 Cyclone (F3F-2)
Output: 950 hp (708 kW)

First Flight Date:
20 March 1935 (XF3F-1)

Surviving Airworthy Variant(s):
F3F-2 (replica) and G-32 (replica)

Right: Cinema Air Jet Center own three of the four replica Grumman biplanes built in Texas, this machine being based at The Air Museum facility at Chino. It presently wears a hybrid VF-6/-7 scheme.

1033 F3F-2
N20FG

Grumman G-21A Goose

USA

Type: twin-engined utility amphibian flying-boat **Accommodation:** crew of two and up to five passengers

Initially built as a private venture for the civil market of the late 1930s, Grumman's G-21 Goose evoked immediate interest from within the US military, with the navy ordering one for evaluation in 1938. Designated the XJ3F-1, the prototype was subsequently followed by 20 JRF-1As in 1939 after its successful flight test programme. The first examples were employed as general transports, in the target tug role and as photographic platforms by both the navy and Marine Corps. The next batch of ten, designated JRF-4s, could carry bombs or depth charges, and these were followed by variants for the Coast Guard and USAAC (where they were designated OA-9/-13s). The build up to war in 1941 resulted in Grumman introducing the improved JRF-5, of which 184 examples were eventually built. At least 56 of these were supplied as Goose I/IAs to the RAF in 1943, the air force using them for navigational training, air-sea rescue and general ferrying duties. After the war the surviving JRFs were sold into civilian hands, and many were re-engined with turbine powerplants to increase their longevity. A small number of ex-navy JRFs are still flying commercially today, whilst a handful of others have been restored to their wartime configuration.

Specification:

Dimensions:
Length: 38 ft 6 in (11.73 m)
Wingspan: 49 ft 0 in (14.94 m)
Height: 16 ft 2 in (4.93 m)

Weights:
Empty: 5425 lb (2461 kg)
Max T/O: 8000 lb (3629 kg)

Performance:
Max Speed: 201 mph (323 kmh)
Range: 640 miles (1030 km)

Powerplant: two Pratt & Whitney R-985-AN-6 Wasp Juniors or two Pratt & Whitney PT6A turboprops (McKinnon Goose)
Output: 900 hp (670 kW) and 1430 shp (1067.16 kW) respectively

First Flight Date:
June 1937

Surviving Airworthy Variant(s):
G-21A/E/G and JRF-5

Right: Freshly resprayed in 1943-period US Navy markings, this JRF-5 sits outside one of The Air Museum's hangars at Chino in September 1996.

Hawker Hind

UK

Type: single-engined biplane light bomber/trainer **Accommodation:** pilot and observer/gunner in tandem

The Hawker family of Rolls-Royce Kestrel powered fighters and bombers of the 1930s were some of the most stylish aircraft ever to wear the RAF roundel. The first in this distinguished line of military aircraft to emerge from Hawker's Kingston factory in 1928 was the Hart day bomber. So advanced was this machine that it actually outpaced the RAF's main fighter of the day, the Bristol Bulldog, by 2 mph. However, by 1934 a replacement was needed, so Hawkers swiftly produced the equally elegant Hind. Essentially an interim machine to 'tide' the RAF over until the new generation of monoplane bombers entered service in the late 1930s, the Hind benefited from having the more powerful 640 hp Kestrel V fitted within its shapely engine nacelle. Production aircraft entered RAF service in 1935, and within two years Bomber Command had received 338 Hinds, and the Auxiliary Air Force a further 114. However, within 12 short months the Hawker biplane had been all but replaced in the frontline by the Battle and the Blenheim. Although obsolete in the frontline, surplus Hinds proved to be capable trainers, and they served in this role until 1939. Hinds were also exported, including 20 to the Royal Afghan Air Force in 1939 – today, the only two survivors of the 527 built come from this obscure source. The sole airworthy Hind is part of the Shuttleworth Collection.

Specification:

Dimensions:
Length: 29 ft 7 in (9.02 m)
Wingspan: 37 ft 3 in (11.35 m)
Height: 10 ft 7 in (3.23 m)

Weights:
Empty: 3251 lb (1475 kg)
Max T/O: 5298 lb (2403 kg)

Performance:
Max Speed: 186 mph (299 kmh)
Range: 430 miles (692 km)
Powerplant: Rolls-Royce Kestrel V
Output: 640 hp (477 kW)

First Flight Date:
12 September 1934

Surviving Airworthy Variant(s):
Hind

Right: Shuttleworth's Hind currently wears a No 15 Sqn scheme, although the aircraft never actually served with the RAF. The original K5414 also served with No 611 Sqn, before being struck off charge in April 1940 after the latter unit re-equipped with Spitfire Is.

K
5414
XV
K5414

Junkers Ju 52/3m/CASA 352L

Germany & Spain

Type: three-engined bomber/transport **Accommodation:** crew of two and seating for up to 17 passengers

The German equivalent of the DC-3/C-47, Junkers' Ju 52 tri-motor boasted rugged construction thanks principally to its manufacturer's trademark corrugated skinning technique. The aircraft started life as a single-engined airliner in late 1930, but after a production run of just six Ju 52s, Junkers decided to evaluate a three-engined version, powered by 550 hp (410 kW) Pratt & Whitney Hornet radials. The results were so successful that the single-engined variant was immediately superseded by the Ju 52/3mce. Chief customer for the civilian tri-motor was Deutsche Lufthansa, who had 230+ on strength by 1939. The Luftwaffe was also an early recipient of the Ju 52/3mge, initially operating it as a stop-gap bomber after Junkers had re-engined the aircraft with more powerful BMW 132A-3 radials. By the eve of World War 2 near on 1000 Ju 52/3ms were either in military service or ready for call up from Lufthansa, the type going on to become the 'workhorse' of the Luftwaffe during the conflict – it performed all manner of missions from troop transport to mine-sweeping on all war fronts. An estimated 4845 were built between 1932 and 1944, and postwar construction continued in France and Spain. Five remain airworthy today.

Specification:

Dimensions:
Length: 62 ft 0 in (18.90 m)
Wingspan: 95 ft 11.5 in (29.25 m)
Height: 18 ft 2.5 in (5.55 m)

Weights:
Empty: 12 610 lb (5720 kg)
Max T/O: 23 149 lb (10 500 kg)

Performance:
Max Speed: 171 mph (275 kmh)
Range: 808 miles (1300 km) with auxiliary tanks

Powerplant: three BMW 132Ts (Ju 52/3m) or ENMA Betas (CASA 352L)
Output: 2490 hp (1856.7 kW) and 2250 (1677 kW) respectively

First Flight Date:
April 1931

Surviving Airworthy Variant(s):
Ju 52/3mg2e, Ju 52/3mg4e, Ju 52/3mg7e and CASA 352L

Right: Lufthansa's Ju 52/3mg2e breaks through the Los Angeles overcast during its US tour in the early 1990s. Prior to being owned by the German flag carrier, this veteran airliner had spent time on floats in Norway and handling all manner of cargo over the Ecuadorian jungle.

D-AQUI

Klemm Kl 35

Germany

Type: single-engined trainer **Accommodation:** two pilots in tandem

Formed in 1926, Klemm Leichtflugzeugbau GmbH's first aircraft was the Kl 25 two-man monoplane trainer/tourer, released soon after the company's establishment. This highly successful machine was built to the tune of 600 airframes over the next decade, inspiring the company to eventually produce a successor in the mid-1930s. Christened the Kl 35, the first prototype completed its maiden flight in 1935. Again, the new Klemm design was a tandem two-seater of wooden construction, although this time the aircraft was fitted with an inverted gull wing and an inline engine. The first production version was the Kl 35B, which was built between 1935 and 1938, and also provided the basis for a floatplane variant, designated the Kl 35BW. The principal model used by the Luftwaffe was the Kl 35D, which had had the spatted undercarriage of the civil Klemm replaced with a strengthened unit that could be adapted for use with wheels, floats or skis. It remained in service as a primary trainer with numerous Luftwaffe pilot training schools right up to the end of World War 2, and was also used by the air forces of Sweden, Hungary, Romania and Czechoslovakia. Several civilian-owned Kl 35s are still regularly flown in Europe.

Specification:

Dimensions:

Length: 24 ft 7.25 in (7.50 m)
Wingspan: 34 ft 1.5 in (10.40 m)
Height: 6 ft 8.75 in (2.05 m)

Weights:

Empty: 1014 lb (460 kg)
Max T/O: 1654 lb (750 kg)

Performance:

Max Speed: 132 mph (212 kmh)
Range: 413 miles (665 km)
Powerplant: Hirth Hm 60R
Output: 80 hp (60 kW)

First Flight Date:

1935

Surviving Airworthy Variant(s):

Kl 35D

Right: This Swiss-registered Kl 35 is a D-model.

HB-UBK

Germany & France

Messerschmitt Bf 108 Taifun/Nord Pingouin

Type: single-engined utility **Accommodation:** one pilot and three passengers

Built to compete in the prestigious Fourth Challenge de Tourisme International held in 1934, the Willy Messerschmitt-designed Bf 108 was streets ahead of its contemporaries thanks to features like its retractable undercarriage and all-metal construction. Although the sleek Messerschmitt was unsuccessful at the competition, over 30 aircraft were subsequently ordered in 1935 for private use, predominantly in Germany. Its high performance made the Bf 108 a natural choice for record flights, and within months of production aircraft leaving the Augsburg factory, several had captured the headlines with stunning feats of endurance. One such machine was a Bf 108A christened 'Taifun' (typhoon), flown by German aviatrix Elly Beinhorn from Berlin to Constantinople in a single day. In honour of this success, Messerschmitt subsequently named all its Bf 108s Taifun. The Luftwaffe was quick to appreciate the performance of the Bf 108, and the aircraft was acquired in substantial quantities for the communications role. By 1942 the Taifun assembly line had moved to the SNCAN factory near Paris, and it was this French connection which kept the aircraft in production after the German defeat. Re-engined with a Renault powerplant, some 285 Nord 1001 and 1002s were built to add to the 885 completed between 1934 and 1945. Of the handful that remain airworthy today, almost all are Nord-built machines.

Specification:

Dimensions:
Length: 27 ft 2.5 in (8.29 m)
Wingspan: 34 ft 10 in (10.62 m)
Height: 7 ft 6.5 in (2.30 m)

Weights:
Empty: 1941 lb (880 kg)
Max T/O: 2987 lb (1355 kg)

Performance:
Max Speed: 186 mph (300 kmh)
Range: 621 miles (1000 km)
Powerplant: Argus As 10C (Bf 108B) or Renault 60-11 (Nord 1002)
Output: both 240 hp (179 kW)

First Flight Date:
June 1934

Surviving Airworthy Variant(s):
Bf 108B Taifun, Nord 1001, 1002 and 1101

Right: This glossy Pingouin is one of several Nord Bf 108's flying in North America today.

TAIFUN
4

Miles Hawk Trainer III/M 14 Magister

UK

Type: single-engined trainer **Accommodation:** two pilots in tandem

Like most RAF trainers of the inter-war period, the Magister was a military development of a civilian design – in this case the Miles Hawk trainer. To meet Air Ministry Specification T40/36, which covered the acquisition of a monoplane elementary trainer for the RAF, Miles had to increase the size of the Hawk's tandem cockpits and make provision for the fitment of blind flying equipment. Christened the Magister, the first examples of the all-wooden trainer were delivered to the air force in May 1937, but within months of their arrival a number had been lost as a result of their failure to recover from spinning. Following extensive trials with the A & AEE, Miles not only redesigned the rear fuselage and decking of the aircraft, but also fitted a larger rudder, raised tailplane and anti-spin strakes. The new machine was redesignated the M 14A, and it went on to enjoy a healthy production run that lasted from 1937 to 1941. Some 1229 were built (plus 100 under licence in Turkey), and they served with many Elementary Flying Training Schools and the Central Flying School. Finally retired from the RAF in 1948, a large number of Magisters continued to fly as civilian trainers (redesignated Hawk Trainer IIIs) well into the 1950s. Today, three examples remain airworthy in the UK.

Specification:

Dimensions:
Length: 24 ft 7.5 in (7.51 m)
Wingspan: 33 ft 10 in (10.31 m)
Height: 6 ft 8 in (2.03 m)

Weights:
Empty: 1286 lb (583 kg)
Max T/O: 1900 lb (862 kg)

Performance:
Max Speed: 132 mph (212 kmh)
Range: 380 miles (612 km)
Powerplant: de Havilland Gipsy Major I
Output: 130 hp (96.9 kW)

First Flight Date:
20 March 1937

Surviving Airworthy Variant(s):
M 14A Magister and Hawk Trainer III

Right: The Shuttleworth Collection's Magister I P6382 was delivered to the RAF in the summer of 1939. During its service career it flew with Nos 16 and 3 EFTSs, before being sold into civilian hands on 10 March 1947.

P
6382
P6382
C

Morane-Saulnier MS 230

France

Type: single-engined parasol advanced trainer **Accommodation:** two pilots in tandem

This distinctively Gallic-looking aircraft was designed by Morane-Saulnier to meet a French Air Ministry requirement, issued in 1928, for a basic training aircraft that boasted a decent performance. The end result was the MS 230, which mated the manufacturer's trademark parasol configuration (as seen on its fighter designs of the period) with a 250 hp (186.4 kW) Salmson radial engine. Warmly received by the French, more than 1000 were built during the 1930s, with the *Armée de l'Air* using the MS 230 not only for advanced pilot training, but also as a platform for general observation and gunnery work. The MS 230 was superseded by the generally similar (although both larger and lighter) MS 315 in 1932, and aside from those examples operated in France, a number were exported to Romania, Greece, Belgium and Brazil. Airworthy examples of the MS 230/315 can be found in France, Belgium, Switzerland and the UK.

Specification:

Dimensions:
Length: 22 ft 9 in (6.93 m)
Wingspan: 35 ft 2 in (10.72 m)
Height: 9 ft 9.33 in (2.98 m)

Weights:
Empty: 1835 lb (832.35 kg)
Max T/O: 2558 lb (1160.30 kg)

Performance:
Max Speed: 127 mph (204 kmh)
Range: 350 miles (560 km)
Powerplant: Salmson 9Ab
Output: 250 hp (186.4 kW)

First Flight Date:
February 1929

Surviving Airworthy Variant(s):
MS 230 and MS 315

Right: This aircraft has been based at Wycombe Air Park since 1969.

01
№157
Mo S
230 Et2
№157
01

Naval Aircraft Factory N3N

USA

Type: single-engined biplane trainer **Accommodation:** two pilots in tandem

The Naval Aircraft Factory (NAF) was created in 1918 to give the US Navy the ability to design and manufacture aircraft uniquely tailored to its needs, and during the inter-war years it did just that by producing a series of flying-boats and a carrier-based fleet fighter. The final NAF design to be mass-produced was the N3N primary trainer, which was built to replace the Consolidated NY-2s and -3s of the 1920s. The prototype XN3N-1 took to the skies for the first time in August 1935, and following successful trials in both land- and seaplane configurations, an order for 179 production N3N-1s was placed with the NAF. Power was initially provided by the Wright J-5 radial, but this obsolescent powerplant was replaced towards the end of the first production run by the R-760 Whirlwind from the same source. This engine change resulted in a designation change to N3N-3, and a further 816 trainers were procured from 1938 onwards. The N3N remained in the primary training role with the navy until 1945, when all but a handful of the survivors were promptly declared surplus and sold to civilian operators. A small number can still be found in airworthy condition in the USA, their population continuing to grow thanks primarily to the restoration efforts of the Yankee Air Corps at Chino.

Specification:

Dimensions:
Length: 25 ft 6 in (7.77 m)
Wingspan: 34 ft 0 in (10.36 m)
Height: 10 ft 10 in (3.30 m)

Weights:
Empty: 2090 lb (948 kg)
Max T/O: 2792 lb (1266 kg)

Performance:
Max Speed: 126 mph (203 kmh)
Range: 470 miles (756 km)
Powerplant: Wright J-5 and Wright R-760-96 Whirlwind
Output: 220 hp (164 kW) and 240 hp (179 kW) respectively

First Flight Date:
August 1935

Surviving Airworthy Variant(s):
N3N-1 and N3N-3

Right: This Belgian-based N3N-3 wears a striking pre-war naval training scheme, although it appears to be devoid of a US national insignia.

69
OO JUS

North American BT-9/-14/Yale I

USA

Type: single-engined trainer **Accommodation:** two pilots in tandem

The BT-9 was the USAAC version of North American Aviation's (NAA) private-venture NA-16 basic trainer. Flown in prototype form for the first time in April 1935, the NA-16 revealed performance figures near equal to the USAAC's frontline combat aircraft of the time. It was immediately ordered into production as the BT-9, and the USAAC duly took delivery of its first example in April 1936. A total of 226 BT-9s were delivered in three different variants (A-, B- and C-models), whilst the US Navy received 40 NJ-1s, fitted with a 600 hp (447 kW) Pratt & Whitney R-1340 Wasp radial in place of the 400 hp (298 kW) Wright unit. NAA then produced the BT-14, which had a fuselage covered in metal instead of fabric and a more powerful 450 hp (336 kW) Wright R-985. Some 251 were built for the USAAC, and export orders for the trainer were received from several nations, including France, which bought 230 (designated NA-57s). When the latter country fell to the Germans in June 1940 some 119 undelivered aircraft were acquired by Britain and issued to the Canadians as Yale Is. Several BT-9s/-14s and Yale Is are still flying in North America today, their fixed landing gear being a distinctive recognition feature.

Specification:

Dimensions:
Length: 27 ft 7 in (8.39 m)
Wingspan: 42 ft 0 in (12.80 m)
Height: 13 ft 7 in (4.13 m)

Weights:
Empty: 3314 lb (1500 kg)
Max T/O: 4471 lb (2030 kg)

Performance:
Max Speed: 170 mph (274 kmh)
Range: 882 miles (1420 km)
Powerplant: Wright R-975-7 (BT-9) and Wright R-985-11 (BT-14)
Output: 400 hp (298 kW) and 450 hp (336 kW) respectively

First Flight Date:
April 1935

Surviving Airworthy Variant(s):
BT-9, BT-14 and Yale I

Right: Painted in authentic RCAF trainer yellow, this preserved Yale I is just one of several still flying in Canada.

North American NA-50/-68 and P-64 USA

Type: single-engined fighter **Accommodation:** one pilot

With a long history of building successful fighter types like the Mustang and Sabre, it is therefore rather ironic that NAA's first effort in this sphere was the humble NA-50. Essentially a low-cost fighter derived from the company's successful NA-16 trainer, the single-seat machine was aimed at smaller air forces who had neither the cash or the technical expertise to operate the latest monoplane fighters emerging from Europe and the USA. Using the tandem trainer as a base, NAA designers reduced the seating to one, made the undercarriage retractable, fitted a more powerful Wright R-1820 engine in place of the R-985-11 unit and armed the fighter with two 0.3-in (7.62 mm) machine guns. Only seven NA-50s were ever built in response to an order placed by Peru in January 1938. Used in combat against Ecuador in 1941, the last examples were finally retired some 20 years later. The NA-68 variant was very similar to the NA-50 (the former had a longer chord cowling, redesigned wingtips and tail surfaces, and two 20 mm cannon as well as the 0.3-in guns), the Royal Thai Air Force ordering six in 1939 for delivery in 1941. However, Thailand was invaded by Japan before it could take delivery of the aircraft, and they were impressed into service instead by the USAAC (as P-64s) in the advanced fighter trainer role. A solitary P-64 has survived into the 1990s, and is occasionally flown from its Oshkosh base.

Specification:

Dimensions:
Length: 27 ft 0 in (8.23 m)
Wingspan: 37 ft 3 in (11.35 m)
Height: 9 ft 0 in (2.74 m)

Weights:
Empty: 4660 lb (2114 kg)
Max T/O: 5990 lb (2717 kg)

Performance:
Max Speed: 270 mph (435 kmh)
Range: 630 miles (1014 km)
Powerplant: Wright R-1820-77 Cyclone 9
Output: 870 hp (649 kW)

First Flight Date:
1939

Surviving Airworthy Variant(s):
NA-68 (original) and P-64 replicas

Right: A number of T-6 Texans have also been converted into P-64 configuration over the years, although as this example reveals, most have retained the trainer's second seat.

74
74

Ryan PT-16/-20/-21/-22 and NR-1 Recruit USA

Type: single-engined trainer **Accommodation:** two pilots in tandem

The USAAC's first ever monoplane primary trainer, the PT (in its various guises) can trace its ancestry to the Ryan Aeronautical Company's S-T two-seater design of 1933-34. Highly successful in its numerous civil forms, the Ryan first garnered military interest in 1939 when the USAAC began looking around for a new primary trainer. Initially a sole example of the S-T-A was acquired (redesignated the XPT-16), and it was thoroughly tested. A further 15 were then purchased to allow a wider evaluation to be completed more speedily, and in 1940 an order for 30 was received. After taking delivery of these machines, the USAAC decided that the more powerful Kinner radial would endure the rigours of training better than the Menasco inline engine, and the 100 PT-21s ordered in 1941 were duly delivered with the former powerplant in place. So successful was the new airframe/engine combination that Ryan subsequently received an order for 1023 examples, which were designated PT-22 Recruits. The navy also ordered 125 (designated NR-1s) which were near identical to the PT-22, whilst an export order for 25 N-R-3s from the Netherlands was also received. Operated primarily by civilian-run flying training schools, the last PTs were retired towards the end of World War 2. Ryan trainers can still be found flying in North America today, whilst others remain airworthy in both the UK and Australia.

Specification:

Dimensions:
Length: 22 ft 5 in (6.83 m)
Wingspan: 30 ft 1 in (9.17 m)
Height: 6 ft 10 in (2.08 m)

Weights:
Empty: 1313 lb (596 kg)
Max T/O: 1860 lb (844 kg)

Performance:
Max Speed: 131 mph (211 kmh)
Range: 352 miles (566 km)

Powerplant: Menasco L-365-1 (PT-16 and -20), Kinner R-440-3 (PT-21 and NR-1) and R-540-1 (PT-22 and S-T-3)
Output: 125 hp (93 kW), 132 hp (98 kW) and 160 hp (119 kW) respectively

First Flight Date:
3 February 1939

Surviving Airworthy Variant(s):
PT-16, PT-20, PT-21 and PT-22 Recruit, NR-3 and S-T-3

Right: This immaculate PT-22 is one of several still flying in the UK today.

I-492

Republic (Seversky) AT-12 Guardsman USA

Type: single-engined advanced trainer **Accommodation:** pilot and instructor/gunner in tandem

Built as a two-seat development of the USAAC's P-35 fighter of 1937, the privately-funded 'Convoy Fighter' was designated the 2PA by its manufacturer. Like the single-seater, this machine had two 0.3-in (7.62 mm) or 0.5-in (12.7 mm) guns fitted in the wings, plus a flexibly-mounted 0.3-in weapon in the rear cockpit. Two 2PAs were sold to the Soviet Union in 1938, together with a manufacturing licence, but no further aircraft were built by the communists. Some 52 examples were ordered by Sweden the following year in the wake of a European tour conducted by Major Alexander P de Seversky himself, whilst 20 were also clandestinely bought by the Japanese Imperial Navy for use over China. However, the 2PA's lack of manoeuvrability and poor rate of climb saw it swiftly relegated from the role of escort fighter to reconnaissance mount over central China. The 2PA eventually joined the ranks of the USAAC in 1941, when all bar two of the fifty-two aircraft ordered by Sweden were hastily requisitioned by the air corps and pressed into service following events in the Pacific. Designated AT-12s, these aircraft saw limited flying as advanced trainers and general communications hacks. The sole airworthy example is operated by the Planes of Fame Museum at Chino.

Specification:

Dimensions:
Length: 26 ft 11 in (8.20 m)
Wingspan: 36 ft 0 in (10.97 m)
Height: 9 ft 9.5 in (2.99 m)

Weights:
Empty: 4581 lb (2078 kg)
Max T/O: 7658 lb (3474 kg)

Performance:
Max Speed: 316 mph (508 kmh)
Range: 1150 miles (1850 km)
Powerplant: Pratt & Whitney R-1830-S3C Twin Wasp
Output: 1100 hp (820.6 kW)

First Flight Date:
1936

Surviving Airworthy Variant(s):
AT-12 Guardsman

Right: This ultra-rare AT-12 Guardsman is operated from Chino by the Planes of Fame Museum. Prior to its acquisition by warbird visionary Ed Maloney, this aircraft had been based in Latin America.

SPIRIT OF BATAAN

Stampe SV4

Belgium & France

Type: single-engined biplane trainer **Accommodation:** two pilots in tandem

Designed by Belgian agent for de Havilland Jean Stampe, it is therefore not surprising to find that the SV4 bears more than a passing resemblance to the DH 82 Tiger Moth. First flown in May 1933, the biplane trainer also shares a similar powerplant with its British contemporary in the ever-reliable de Havilland Gipsy Major 10. The SV4 was ordered by both the Belgian and French air forces in the mid-1930s, but before large-scale production commenced, the Stampe factory was seized by the invading German army in May 1940. In 1944 French manufacturer Nord resurrected the design once again, and over the next two years some 70 examples were built with the designation SV4C. These machines differed from the pre-war Stampe primarily through the fitment of the Renault 4 Pei engine in place of the Gipsy Major, the bulk of the Nord-built aircraft being shared between the *Armeé de l'Air* and numerous French flying clubs. Jean Stampe returned to business soon after the end of the war in Europe when he formed Stampe et Renard in Belgium, his new company completing an order for 65 SV4Bs for the Belgian air force. Unlike the French aircraft, these machines featured an enclosed cabin for both cockpits. Many ex-air force SV4s passed into civilian hands in the 1960s, and the survivors of these can still be found throughout Europe today – there are over 40 on the UK register alone.

Specification:

Dimensions:
Length: 22 ft 10 in (6.96 m)
Wingspan: 27 ft 6 in (8.38 m)
Height: 9 ft 1 in (2.77 m)

Weights:
Empty: 1056 lb (480 kg)
Max T/O: 1716 lb (780 kg)

Performance:
Max Speed: 112 mph (180 kmh)
Range: 300 miles (480 km)
Powerplant: de Havilland Gipsy Major 10 (SV4/SV4B), Renault 4 Pei (SV4C)
Output: 130 hp (97 kW) and 140 hp (104.9 kW)

First Flight Date:
May 1933

Surviving Airworthy Variant(s):
SV4, B and C

Right: The enclosed cockpit and national roundels denote that this civilianised Stampe SV4B is an ex-Belgian Air Force example.

60
OPA
60

Vultee BT-13/-15 and SNV-1/-2 Valiant USA

Type: single-engined trainer **Accommodation:** two pilots in tandem

The most populous basic trainer produced in the USA during World War 2, the Valiant family can trace its lineage back to Vultee's BC-3 basic combat trainer. Tested by the USAAC in 1938, the BC-3 was initially fitted with a retractable landing gear and powerful 600 hp (447 kW) Pratt & Whitney Wasp engine. The evaluation showed that the aircraft had perfect handling characteristics for the training role, but that the landing gear need not be retractable or the powerplant so big. Vultee duly fitted oleo-pneumatic shock-struts in place of the stowable landing gear and bolted a Pratt & Whitney Wasp Junior 'up front'. The end result was the BT-13 Valiant, and the USAAC duly ordered 300 in September 1939. A follow-on variant fitted with a different version of the Wasp Junior engine, plus other detail changes, was then procured (designated the BT-13A) to the tune of 6407 examples. Indeed, the rapidity at which these airframes were built resulted in a shortage of Pratt & Whitney engines, thus forcing Vultee to build the BT-15 with the Wright R-975-11 Whirlwind 9 radial fitted instead – the US Navy also procured well over 1500 Valiants, which it designated the SNV-1/-2, depending on the engine specification. By the time production ceased in 1944, well over 11,000 Valiants had been built, and today in excess of 100 potential 'flyers' still appear on the US civil register.

Specification:

Dimensions:
Length: 28 ft 10 in (8.79 m)
Wingspan: 42 ft 0 in (12.80 m)
Height: 11 ft 6 in (3.51 m)

Weights:
Empty: 3375 lb (1531 kg)
Max T/O: 4496 lb (2039 kg)

Performance:
Max Speed: 180 mph (290 kmh)
Range: 725 miles (1167 km)
Powerplant: Pratt & Whitney R-985-AN-1 Wasp Junior (BT-13 and SNV-1/-2) and Wright R-975-11 Whirlwind 9 (BT-15)
Output: both 450 hp (336 kW)

First Flight Date:
24 March 1939 (BT-13)

Surviving Airworthy Variant(s):
BT-13, BT-15, SNV-1 and SNV-2

Right: In order not to spoil the whole period effect of the aircraft, the pilot of this US-registered BT-13 has even donned an A-1 leather jacket and crush cap – although his headphones are most definitely not 1942 issue!

141

World War II Aircraft

Aeronca O-58 and L-3/-16 Grasshopper USA

Type: single-engined high-wing liaison/observation aircraft **Accommodation:** pilot and observer/passenger in tandem

In an effort to acquire a light aircraft for observation/liaison duties in the frontline in the final months of peace in 1941, the US Army evaluated four readily available designs from three established American manufacturers – namely Piper, Taylorcraft and Aeronca. The latter company's offering was the Model 65, which was modified from its two-seat trainer configuration and designated the O-58 by the USAAC. Over 400 were purchased in three different versions, and in 1942 their designation was changed from O (for Observation) to L (for Liaison). A further 1030 were built before production ceased in 1944, these aircraft seeing action across the globe. Postwar, further aircraft were built both for the civil and military markets, with the US Army designating their version the L-16 – this aircraft was based on the civil Model 7BC Champion, and utilised the more powerful Continental O-205-1 engine. Many ex-military Grasshoppers are still flown in North America, whilst at least seven currently appear on the British civil register.

Specification:

Dimensions:
Length: 21 ft 0 in (6.40 m)
Wingspan: 35 ft 0 in (10.67 m)
Height: 7 ft 8 in (2.34 m)

Weights:
Empty: 835 lb (379 kg)
Max T/O: 1300 lb (590 kg)

Performance:
Max Speed: 87 mph (140 kmh)
Range: 200 miles (322 km)
Powerplant: Continental O-170-3 (O-58/L-3) and Continental O-205-1 (L-16)
Output: 65 hp (48.9 kW) and 90 hp (67 kW) respectively

First Flight Date:
1941

Surviving Airworthy Variant(s):
O-58, L-3 and L-16

Right: This UK-based Grasshopper wears an early-war O-58 scheme.

FAT BULLET
42-78044

Avro Lancaster

UK

Type: four-engined heavy bomber **Accommodation:** seven-man crew

Avro's superlative heavy bomber was literally the 'phoenix that rose from the ashes' of the disastrous Manchester programme of 1940/41. The latter machine was powered by two Rolls-Royce Vultures and boasted a layout near-identical to the Lancaster, but was plagued from the start by grave engine reliability problems. Avro realised that their airframe design was essentially correct, however, and turned to Rolls-Royce and demanded access to the company's proven Merlin powerplant. The Manchester had also been chronically underpowered, so Avro's chief designer, Roy Chadwick, ensured that its replacement would suffer no such problems by installing four Merlin Xs beneath the Lancaster's wing. The prototype (a converted Manchester airframe) first flew on 9 January 1941, and its potential was soon realised during extensive flight trials. An order for 1070 bombers was quickly placed with Avro in mid-1941, and the first production machines emerged that October. No 44 Sqn carried out the first operational sorties with the type in March 1942, and a further 58 Bomber Command units went on to see active service with the Lancaster, flying 156,000 sorties and dropping 608,612 tons of high explosive bombs and 51 million incendiaries. Some 7377 airframes were built by the six factories devoted to Lancaster production, this number being split between five distinctive marks. Postwar, a number of bombers survived in maritime patrol, transport and test trials roles until the late 1950s, and today single airworthy examples are operated in Canada and the UK.

Specification:

Dimensions:
Length: 69 ft 6 in (21.18 m)
Wingspan: 102 ft 0 in (31.09 m)
Height: 20 ft 0 in (6.10 m)

Weights:
Empty: 36 900 lb (16 738 kg)
Max T/O: 70 000 lb (31 751 kg)

Performance:
Max Speed: 287 mph (462 kmh)
Range: 2530 miles (4072 km)
Powerplant: four Rolls-Royce Merlin 24 engines
Output: 5120 hp (3849.6 kW)

First Flight Date:
9 January 1941

Surviving Airworthy Variant(s):
B I and B 10MR

Right: B I PA474 is the centrepiece of the RAF Battle of Britain Memorial Flight.

PA474
M

Beech UC-43/GB-2 Traveller

USA

Type: single-engined biplane liaison/communications aircraft **Accommodation:** pilot and three/four passengers

The first design put into production by Walter Beech following his departure from Travel Air, the distinctive Model 17 Staggerwing quickly established itself in the growing US civil market of the 1930s. At least six different variants were built between 1934 and 1939, each utilising a new powerplant, but all offering both comfort and performance to their occupants. These attributes also appealed to senior US military officers, and the US Navy duly acquired a handful (which it designated GB-1s) for the VIP transportation role in 1939 – with the outbreak of war two years later, the navy would go on to purchase a further 300+ examples (GB-2s), 105 of which were in turn supplied to the Royal Navy. The USAAC also purchased three D17Ss in 1939, which were designated YC-43 Travellers. Three years later a production order for 27 UC-43s was placed with Beech, followed by two subsequent requests for 75 and 105 Travellers, which brought total USAAF procurement to 207 aircraft. A large number of civilian Staggerwings (434 had been built by Beech up to 7 December 1941) were also impressed into military service. Production of civil Staggerwings recommenced with the cessation of hostilities in August 1945, and the last example left the Beech assembly line in 1948. A large number of civilian Staggerwings have remained airworthy into the 1990s, as have a sizeable quantity of ex-military UC-43s/GB-2s.

Specification:

Dimensions:

Length: 26 ft 2 in (7.98 m)
Wingspan: 32 ft 0 in (9.75 m)
Height: 10 ft 3 in (3.12 m)

Weights:

Empty: 3085 lb (1399 kg)
Max T/O: 4700 lb (2123 kg)

Performance:

Max Speed: 198 mph (319 kmh)
Range: 500 miles (805 km)
Powerplant: Pratt & Whitney R-985-AN-1 Wasp Junior
Output: 450 hp (335.3 kW)

First Flight Date:

4 November 1932 (civilian Beech 17 Staggerwing)

Surviving Airworthy Variant(s):

YC-43, UC-43, GB-2 and civilian Beech 17s

Right: This aircraft is an ex-navy GB-2 and was formerly operated by Planes of Fame East.

U.S.NAVY

Beech Model 18

USA

Type: twin-engined light transport, and trainer

Accommodation: pilot and seven passengers in transport role

Like the Model 17, the Beech Model 18 started life as a transport aimed squarely at the American civil market of the late 1930s. Similarities between the two Beech designs did not stop there, however, for like the Staggerwing, the first examples of the Model 18 ordered by the USAAC in 1940 operated in the staff transport role. Designated the C-45, over 250 were procured by the army air corps, who also used them as utility transports. Some of these aircraft were duly passed on to the RAF/Fleet Air Arm/RCAF under Lend-Lease, the British naming them Expediter I/II/IIIs, depending on their variant state. The final transport version built for the USAAF was the C-45F, which was produced to the tune of 1137 examples – all army air force C-45s were redesignated UC-45s in 1943. Two years earlier Beech had produced the navigation trainer optimised AT-7, and the USAAC took delivery of 549. Following in the AT-7's footsteps was the AT-11 Kansan bombing/gunnery trainer, of which some 1582 were built. Finally, the US Navy/Marine Corps also procured in excess of 1500 Model 18s, which it designated JRBs (equivalent to the USAAF's C-45) and SNBs (AT-7/-11). US military use of the venerable aircraft lasted until the late 1960s, and today many ex-military Beech 'twins' are still regularly flown across the globe.

Specification:

Dimensions:
Length: 34 ft 3 in (10.4 m)
Wingspan: 47 ft 8 in (14.5 m)
Height: 9 ft 8 in (2.95 m)

Weights:
Empty: 6175 lb (2801 kg)
Max T/O: 8727 lb (3959 kg)

Performance:
Max Speed: 215 mph (346 kmh)
Range: 850 miles (1368 km)
Powerplant: two Pratt & Whitney R-985-AN-1 Wasp Junior engines
Output: 900 hp (670.6 kW)

First Flight Date:
15 January 1937 (civilian Beech 18)

Surviving Airworthy Variant(s):
C-45, UC-45, AT-7 Navigator, AT-11 Kansan, JRB, SNB and civilian Beech 18s

Right: An Oshkosh award winner in 1991, this rare SNB-2P photo-recce aircraft was totally rebuilt by owner Eric Clifford during the late 1980s.

NAVY
UNITED STATES NAVY
EXPERIMENTAL
NAVY
GTMO BAY
EC
N72409
PROPELL
09

Bell P-39 Airacobra

USA

Type: single-engined fighter **Accommodation:** pilot

Bell's revolutionary P-39 introduced the concept of both the centrally-mounted powerplant and the tricycle undercarriage to single-engined fighters, the aircraft's unusual configuration stemming from its principal armament, the propeller hub-mounted T9 37 mm cannon. In order to allow the weapon to be housed in the nose the P-39's engine was moved aft to sit virtually over the rear half of the wing centre-section. This drastically shifted the aircraft's centre of gravity, thus forcing designers to adopt a tricycle undercarriage. Unfortunately, the P-39's radical design was not matched by stunning performance figures particularly at heights exceeding 14,000 ft, its normally-aspirated Allison V-1710 struggling in the 'thinner' air at these altitudes – following a service evaluation of the YP-39 in 1938-39, Bell was told by USAAC and NACA officials that a turbocharged version of the V-1710 then available for the Airacobra was not needed! Once the fighter entered service in 1941 the wisdom of this decision was quickly called into question. Indeed, so compromised was the aircraft's 'combatability' in its designated role that it was soon relegated to close air support duties in theatres where other aircraft could be employed as fighters. Operating at much lower altitudes over the Eastern Front, the Soviet air force did, however, achieve great aerial success with the Bell fighter, utilising some 5000 from 1942 onwards. Today, two airworthy P-39s can still be found in the USA, whilst a third is under restoration to fly in the UK.

Specification:

Dimensions:
Length: 30 ft 2 in (9.19 m)
Wingspan: 34 ft 0 in (10.36 m)
Height: 11 ft 10 in (3.61 m)

Weights:
Empty: 5610 lb (2545 kg)
Max T/O: 8400 lb (3810 kg)

Performance:
Max Speed: 386 mph (621 kmh)
Range: 650 miles (1046 km)
Powerplant: Allison V-1710-83
Output: 1200 hp (895 kW)

First Flight Date:
6 April 1938 (XP-39)

Surviving Airworthy Variant(s):
P-39N, P-39Q and TP-39Q

Right: Rescued from the Papua New Guinean jungles and stored firstly in New Zealand, and then Australia, P-39Q 42-19993 is now part of The Fighter Collection at Duxford.

219993
Brooklyn
BUM

Bell P-63 Kingcobra

USA

Type: single-engined fighter **Accommodation:** pilot

Although the P-63 looked like an enlarged Airacobra, it was in fact an all-new design that had a superior turn of speed at all altitudes. Dubbed the Kingcobra, the fighter drew heavily on modifications incorporated into the P-39's original replacement, the cancelled XP-39E. However, unlike the latter design, the P-63 was more than just an Airacobra fuselage with new semi-laminar flow wings – the fighter was appreciably larger, and boasted an Allison V-1710-93 engine (P-63A) that could be boosted to 1500 hp in flight in the event of an emergency. Although some 3300 were built in several different versions, by the time the first production examples began to reach the USAAF in October 1943, the P-51B, P-38H and P-47C had successfully filled the air force's requirement for a frontline fighter. Most P-63s were therefore made available for lend-lease purchase, and the Soviet air force happily snapped up 2400 examples. A further 300 went to Free French units in the Mediterranean, but the primary customer – the USAAF – restricted their use of the Kingcobra to training squadrons in America. The final variant in production at war's end was the P-63E, of which only 13 out of an order for 2930 had been delivered when the contract was cancelled in the wake of VJ-Day. Six have remained airworthy into the 1990s, five of which are flown in the USA and one in the UK.

Specification:

Dimensions:
Length: 32 ft 8 in (9.96 m)
Wingspan: 38 ft 4 in (11.68 m)
Height: 12 ft 7 in (3.84 m)

Weights:
Empty: 6375 lb (2892 kg)
Max T/O: 10 500 lb (4763 kg)

Performance:
Max Speed: 410 mph (660 kmh)

Range: 2200 miles (3540 km) with maximum internal/external fuel load
Powerplant: Allison V-1710-93
Output: 1325 hp (988 kW)

First Flight Date:
7 December 1942

Surviving Airworthy Variant(s):
P-63A/F and RP-63A/C

Right: The oldest surviving Kingcobra, P-63A 42-68864 was formerly operated by Planes of Fame East.

864
NX163BP

Boeing B-17 Flying Fortress

USA

Type: four-engined heavy bomber **Accommodation:** ten-man crew

First flown on 28 July 1935, the prototype B-17 was immediately dubbed the 'Flying Fortress' by the press corps in attendance. The USAAC was impressed by the new bomber, and ordered an initial batch of 13 YB-17s, followed by the signing of a second contract for 39 near-identical B-17Bs. By mid-1940 the Flying Fortress had been further improved with the addition of two extra guns and the fitment of more powerful engines. Designated the B-17C, 20 were exported to Britain for service with the RAF. Lessons learned from the European conflict saw Boeing 'beef up' the armour fitted to future models of B-17, plus fit extra guns and self-sealing fuel tanks. The result of these changes was the B-17E, 512 of which were built in 1941/42, followed by the B-17F, which had a redesigned nose to incorporate a 0.50-in gun, a strengthened undercarriage to cope with increased bomb loads and Wright R-1820-97 engines. The final version to see mass-production was the chin-turreted B-17G, some 8680 examples of which were built. Postwar, the Flying Fortress was used as both a fire-bomber and aerial survey platform, before finally being retired in the early 1970s. A handful have since been restored to wartime configuration by enthusiasts in the USA and Europe, and 12 are currently airworthy (ten in the USA and one in both the UK and France).

Specification:

Dimensions:
Length: 74 ft 4 in (22.66 m)
Wingspan: 103 ft 9 in (31.62 m)
Height: 19 ft 1 in (5.82 m)

Weights:
Empty: 36 135 lb (16 391 kg)
Max T/O: 65 500 lb (29 710 kg)

Performance:
Max Speed: 287 mph (462 kmh)
Range: 2000 miles (3219 km)
Powerplant: four Wright R-1820-97 Cyclone engines
Output: 4800 hp (3580 kW)

First Flight Date:
28 July 1935

Surviving Airworthy Variant(s):
B-17F/G

Right: B-17G (ex-USCG PB-1G) 44-85829 is part of the Yankee Air Force at Willow Run.

YANKEE
L
485829
Y
GD

Boeing B-29 Superfortress

USA

Type: four-engined heavy bomber **Accommodation:** ten-man crew

Boeing's timely response to the USAAC's request for a long-range strategic bomber to replace the B-17, the B-29 concept was devised soon after the Flying Fortress entered service in the mid-1930s. Initially hindered by the lack of a suitable powerplant, the very long-range bomber project was resurrected in 1940 when five US manufacturers were invited to tender proposals. Eventually only Consolidated and Boeing would produce flyable prototypes, and although the former's XB-32 Dominator flew first, it was plagued by development problems. Boeing, however, was able to convince the USAAC that they could deliver production versions of their Model 345 (designated the XB-29 by the military) by 1943, and they duly won the contract for 1500+ bombers *before* the prototype had even flown. Boasting incredible advances in technology, the first production B-29s were delivered to the 58th Very Heavy Bomb Wing in the autumn of 1943. By the spring of 1944 the Superfortress was bombing targets in the Pacific, and by war's end the aircraft had played as great a part as any weapon in ending the conflict with the Japanese. By the time production finally ceased in May 1946, some 3970 B-29s had been built. Postwar, the type enjoyed a long career in the USAF (including seeing further action over Korea between 1950-53), with some 19 different variants fulfilling a variety of roles into the early 1960s. Only one B-29 remains airworthy today, 44-62070 being flown by the Confederate Air Force.

Specification:

Dimensions:

Length: 99 ft 0 in (30.18 m)
Wingspan: 141 ft 3 in (43.05 m)
Height: 29 ft 7 in (9.02 m)

Weights:

Empty: 70 140 lb (31 815 kg)
Max T/O: 124 000 lb (56 245 kg)

Performance:

Max Speed: 358 mph (576 kmh)
Range: 3250 miles (5230 km)
Powerplant: four Wright R-3350-23 Duplex Cyclone engines
Output: 8800 hp (6564 kW)

First Flight Date:

21 September 1942

Surviving Airworthy Variant(s):

B-29A

Right: The Texas-based Confederate Air Force operates the last remaining airworthy Superfortress, B-29A 44-62070.

"FIFI"
A

Bristol Blenheim IV/Bolingbroke IVT UK/Canada

Type: twin-engined light bomber/fighter **Accommodation:** three-man crew

Bristol's venerable Blenheim was the result of a speculative private venture on the part of the manufacturers. Unencumbered by restrictions on the aircraft's weight, powerplants, general layout or radius of action, the Bristol design team produced a sleek twin-engined machine known as the Type 142. First flown at Filton on 12 April 1935, the aircraft's performance sent ripples through the RAF when it was discovered that its top speed was 30 mph greater than Fighter Command's then new biplane fighter, the Gloster Gauntlet I. The Air Ministry ordered 150 airframes, which they christened the Blenheim, and the first of these entered service with the RAF in March 1937. By September 1939 most UK-based Blenheim squadrons had replaced their Mk Is with the improved Mk IV, the latter having grown out of an Air Ministry requirement for a reconnaissance type with greater crew accommodation and an increased range. The backbone of Bomber Command at the start of hostilities, it fell to the Mk IV to make both the first armed reconnaissance incursion into German airspace and the first bombing raid. The Blenheim went on to see action across the globe, remaining in the frontline well into 1943 in North Africa and the Far East. Most British-based aircraft were scrapped after VE-Day, but a number of Canadian-built examples have survived into the 1990s. Indeed, the world's only 'flyer', RCAF 10201, which is owned and operated by The Aircraft Restoration Company at Duxford, is a Bolingbroke IVT.

Specification:

Dimensions:
Length: 42 ft 7 in (12.98 m)
Wingspan: 56 ft 4 in (17.17 m)
Height: 9 ft 10 in (3.00 m)

Weights:
Empty: 9790 lb (4441 kg)
Max T/O: 14 400 lb (6532 kg)

Performance:
Max Speed: 266 mph (428 kmh)
Range: 1460 miles (2350 km)
Powerplant: two Bristol Mercury XV engines
Output: 1810 hp (1350 kW)

First Flight Date:
12 April 1935 (Blenheim I)

Surviving Airworthy Variant(s):
Bolingbroke IVT

Right: Ex-RCAF Bolingbroke IVT 10201 has been extensively flown by The Aircraft Restoration Company since May 1993.

WM
Z5722

British Taylorcraft Auster I-V

UK

Type: single-engined high-wing liaison/observation aircraft **Accommodation:** pilot and observer/passenger seated side-by-side

Taylorcraft was originally formed in the USA in 1936 with the express purpose of constructing lightplanes for private use. The company enjoyed so much success with their Models B, C and D that in 1938 a subsidiary firm was formed in England to build these machines under licence. Of braced high-wing configuration and with side-by-side seating, the Taylorcraft design garnered more modest orders in the UK, however, and by September 1939 just 32 had been built. Twenty of these (Plus Cs and Ds, which were UK-built Model Cs) were impressed into RAF service upon the outbreak of war in order to assess their suitability for use in the observation and liaison roles. So successful was the aircraft that a further 100 were ordered, these being duly given the military designation Auster I when they entered service in August 1942. The RAF's aircraft were little modified from the original Taylorcraft design, although split trailing-edge flaps were soon added to improve short-field performance. Some 1600+ Austers were delivered up to the end of the war, with the Mk V proving to be the most successful – roughly 800 of this variant alone were constructed. At its peak, the humble Auster equipped 19 squadrons within the 2nd Tactical Air Force and the Desert Air Force. Numerous civilian and ex-military Austers remain airworthy in the UK, Europe, Australasia and North America.

Specification:

Dimensions:
Length: 22 ft 5 in (6.83 m)
Wingspan: 36 ft 0 in (10.97 m)
Height: 8 ft 0 in (2.44 m)

Weights:
Empty: 1100 lb (499 kg)
Max T/O: 1850 lb (839 kg)

Performance:
Max Speed: 130 mph (209 kmh)
Range: 250 miles (402 km)

Powerplant: Blackburn Cirrus Minor I (Auster I), de Havilland Gipsy Major I (Auster III) and Lycoming O-290 (Auster II, IV and V)
Output: 90 hp (67 kW) Cirrus Minor I, 130 hp (97 kW) Gipsy Major I and Lycoming O-290

First Flight Date:
May 1942 (Auster I)

Surviving Airworthy Variant(s):
Auster III/IV/V

Right: This Auster III was built in mid 1943 and initially saw service with the Malaya Communications Squadron – hence its present Far East Command scheme.

MT 438

Bücker Bü 181/Zlin C.6/C.106 Germany/Czechoslovakia

Type: single-engined primary trainer **Accommodation:** two pilots side-by-side

Although only modestly powered, Bücker's Bü 181 proved to be the ideal primary trainer for the Luftwaffe, and it was produced in its thousands during the war years. Based on the company's Bü 180 of similar configuration, the Bestmann was the first design from Bücker to incorporate side-by-side seating for the instructor and his student. First flown in early 1939, the Bü 181 was ordered into production following successful flight testing by the Luftwaffe. Once sufficient quantities of Bü 181As had been delivered to training units, a considerbale number of airframes were then allocated to the communication/liaison role, whilst others became glider tugs. Aside from those airframes built by Bücker, 708 were constructed by Fokker in the Netherlands during German occupation and 125 produced under licence in Sweden. The Germans also opened a production line in Czechoslovakia at the Zlin works, and aircraft continued to be built here long after VE-Day. A number of Zlin C.6/C.106s are still flying in Europe today, whilst a handful of genuine Bücker-built aircraft also remain airworthy in North America and Europe.

Specification:

Dimensions:
Length: 25 ft 9 in (7.85 m)
Wingspan: 34 ft 9.25 in (10.60 m)
Height: 6 ft 8.75 in (2.05 m)

Weights:
Empty: 1058 lb (480 kg)
Max T/O: 1653 lb (750 kg)

Performance:
Max Speed: 134 mph (215 kmh)
Range: 497 miles (800 km)
Powerplant: Hirth Hm 504
Output: 105 hp (78 kW)

First Flight Date:
Early 1939

Surviving Airworthy Variant(s):
Bü 181A/D and Zlin C.6/C.106

Right: This Bücker-built Bü 181 has been restored in a wartime Luftwaffe training scheme.

AM

CASA 2.111 (Heinkel He 111H)

Spain

Type: twin-engined medium bomber/transport **Accommodation:** five-man crew

The original Heinkel He 111 was the staple medium bomber of the Luftwaffe's *Kampfgeschwader* throughout World War 2, some 5400+ being built during its nine-year production life which spanned the years 1935 to 1944. Developed from the He 70 Blitz airliner, which had entered service with Luft Hansa in 1934, the He 111 retained the former's characteristic elliptical wings and tail surfaces. As with the Blitz, Luft Hansa also received a small number of airliner-optimised He 111s, designated He 111C/Gs, in 1936. Whilst the transport variant was proving itself over Europe, the bomber version was also being developed by Heinkel. Squadron deliveries began in late 1936, and the following year 30 He 111B-1s saw action during the Spanish Civil War. By the eve of World War 2, the redesigned H- and P-models had begun to enter service, the new variants having the distinctive fully-glazed nose area and revised ventral gondola. These versions would go on to see action in every theatre of war in which the Luftwaffe was involved. In 1941 Spain acquired a licence to build the He 111H-16, and some 236 were duly constructed up to 1956. Of this number, 136 were fitted with Junkers Jumo 211F-2 engines (2.111A) whilst the remainder received Rolls-Royce Merlins (2.111B/D). Retired from the Spanish Air Force in 1976, a number were sold to collections in Europe and North America and one of these remains airworthy.

Specification:

Dimensions:
Length: 54 ft 6 in (16.60 m)
Wingspan: 74 ft 1.75 in (22.60 m)
Height: 13 ft 1.25 in (4.00 m)

Weights:
Empty: 19 136 lb (8680 kg)
Max T/O: 30 865 lb (14 000 kg)

Performance:
Max Speed: 258 mph (415 kmh)
Range: 1212 miles (1950 km)
Powerplant: two Rolls-Royce Merlin 500-29 engines
Output: 3200 hp (2386 kW)

First Flight Date:
24 February 1935 (He 111a)

Surviving Airworthy Variant(s):
CASA 2.111D

Right: This aircraft (2.111D ET.8B-124) is operated by the Confederate Air Force in Arizona.

G

Cessna Model T-50

USA

Type: twin-engined trainer/light transport

Accommodation: two pilots seated side-by-side in the training role or one pilot and four passengers when in the transport configuration

The T-50 was the first twin-engined aircraft produced by the company, being built as a five-seater for the civilian market. Chosen by the RCAF for the conversion of pilots from single- to twin-engined aircraft within 12 months of the prototype flying, 550 Crane 1As – as they were duly designated – were supplied under Lend-Lease for the Commonwealth Joint Air Training Plan. Following the Canadian lead, the USAAC also acquired 33 T-50s for service evaluation (designated AT-8s) in late 1940, and after exhaustive trials, an order for 450 was placed. These aircraft differed from the AT-8s in having less powerful Jacobs R-755-9 radials (245 hp) fitted in place of R-680-9s (295 hp) from the same manufacturer. Designated the AT-17, the trainer was ordered in further batches of 223 (AT-17A), 466 (AT-17B) and 60 (AT-17C), with each having slightly different equipment fits. In 1942 the USAAF decided that the Cessna would also be useful in the original role intended for it by the manufacturer, and so 1287 C-78 (changed later to UC-78) Bobcats were also bought – over 2100 surplus AT-17C/Ds were also completed in transport configuration from late 1942 onwards. Finally, the US Navy also procured 67 examples of the utility variant primarily for the transportation of ferry pilots, designating these aircraft JRC-1s. A small number of airworthy ex-USAAF/RCAF T-50s can still be found in North America today.

Specification:

Dimensions:
Length: 32 ft 9 in (9.98 m)
Wingspan: 41 ft 11 in (12.78 m)
Height: 9 ft 11 in (3.02 m)

Weights:
Empty: 3500 lb (1588 kg)
Max T/O: 5700 lb (2585 kg)

Performance:
Max Speed: 195 mph (314 kmh)
Range: 750 miles (1207 km)
Powerplant: two Jacobs R-755-9 engines
Output: 490 hp (366 kW)

First Flight Date:
1939 (civilian T-50)

Surviving Airworthy Variant(s):
Crane IA, AT-17 and UC-78

Right: This US-registered UC-78 wears the short-lived red-outlined 'stars and bars' on its fuselage and wings.

415
2644

CAC CA-25 Wirraway

Australia

Type: single-engined trainer/dive-bomber **Accommodation:** two pilots or pilot and a rear-gunner

Essentially a licence-built North America BC-1 incorporating Australian modifications, the Commonwealth Aircraft Corporation (CAC) Wirraway served not only as the RAAF's primary trainer throughout World War 2, but also as a makeshift fighter-bomber over New Guinea and Rabaul during 1942-43. The major changes carried out to the basic North American Aviation design centred around the fitment of a three-bladed propeller, the installation of two 0.303-in guns in the upper engine cowling and a third weapon on a flexible mounting in the rear cockpit, and underwing stores racks for up to 500 lb (226.8 kg) of bombs. The first production Wirraway was rolled out in March 1939, and by June 1942 620 had been delivered to the RAAF. The high point the Wirraway's frontline career occurred on 26 December 1942 when an aircraft from No 4 Army Co-operation Squadron shot down a Japanese navy A6M Zero-sen – this machine (A20-103) is preserved today in the Australian War Memorial in Canberra. Construction of the Wirraway continued after VJ-Day (some 755 were eventually built by CAC), the trainer remaining in RAAF service until finally being retired in 1959. There are at least six Wirraways flying in Australia today, with a number of others under restoration to airworthiness.

Specification:

Dimensions:
Length: 29 ft 6 in (8.99 m)
Wingspan: 43 ft 0 in (13.10 m)
Height: 12 ft 3 in (3.74 m)

Weights:
Empty: 3980 lb (1805 kg)
Max T/O: 6450 lb (2925 kg)

Performance:
Max Speed: 205 mph (328 kmh)
Range: 720 miles (1152 km)
Powerplant: Pratt & Whitney R-1340-47 Wasp
Output: 600 hp (447 kW)

First Flight Date:
27 March 1939

Surviving Airworthy Variant(s):
CA-25

Right: A20-688 has been an exhibit in the RAAF Association Museum at Bullcreek, in Western Australia, since 1973.

688

CAC CA-12 Boomerang

Australia

Type: single-engined fighter **Accommodation:** pilot

The only Australian-designed fighter aircraft ever to see combat, the Boomerang was designed and built in record time in the wake of the Japanese raid on Pearl Harbor. Realising that neither the British or American governments could spare valuable fighter aircraft to stem the Japanese tide in south-east Asia, the Australians set about producing their own home-built machine. The result was the Commonwealth Aircraft Corporation (CAC) CA-12 Boomerang, which took to the skies for the first time just 16 weeks and three days after its design had been approved. Constructed around the largest engine then built in Australia (the Twin Wasp), and incorporating as many components from the semi-indigenous Wirraway trainer/dive-bomber as possible, the Boomerang boasted marvellous manoeuvrability but poor straightline speed. It was therefore relegated to the army support role when it reached the frontline in mid-1943, the USAAF having since arrived in-theatre with vastly superior P-38s, P-40s and P-47s. Some 250 Boomerangs were eventually built by the CAC, and the aircraft performed valuable work over the mountainous terrain of New Guinea, usually operating under army control. A number of Boomerang hulks have come to light in Australia over the past 30 years, and two have been restored to airworthiness in the USA with the help of numerous T-6 Texan parts – one has since returned to Australia (CA-19 A46-206).

Specification:

Dimensions:
Length: 25 ft 6 in (7.77 m)
Wingspan: 36 ft 0 in (10.97 m)
Height: 9 ft 7 in (2.92 m)

Weights:
Empty: 5373 lb (2437 kg)
Max T/O: 7699 lb (3492 kg)

Performance:
Max Speed: 302 mph (486 kmh)
Range: 930 miles (1497 km)
Powerplant: Pratt & Whitney R-1830-S3C4-G Twin Wasp
Output: 1200 hp (894 kW)

First Flight Date:
29 May 1942

Surviving Airworthy Variant(s):
CA-13 and CA-19

Right: CA-13 A46-139 is based at Chino following its restoration by Dennis Sanders and Dale Clarke in the late 1980s

PHOOEY
A46-139
NX32CS

Consolidated PBY Catalina

USA

Type: twin-engined high-wing maritime patrol bomber, amphibian and flying boat **Accommodation:** seven- to nine-man crew

It is extremely unlikely that the PBY Catalina's record of being the most extensively-built flying boat in aviation history will ever be surpassed, Consolidated constructing (or granting the licence to build in Canada and the USSR) over 4000 examples of the robustly simple twin-engined high-winged aircraft over a ten-year period starting in 1935. Used by virtually all the Allied nations during World War 2, the humble PBY flew more hours on combat patrols than any other American warplane of the period. The US Navy's VP-11F was the first unit to receive the new floatplane, taking on strength its premier PBY-1 in October 1936. Such was the pace of re-equipment that by mid-1938 14 squadrons were operating PBYs, and many more were scheduled to receive them. Further improvements to the engine spec resulted in new variants entering service over the next four years, with the PBY-5A finally introducing the tricycle undercarriage to the Catalina, and thus making it a far more versatile design. Consolidated continued to update, re-engine and generally improve its tried and trusted PBY throughout the years of conflict, the final wartime variant being the PBY-6A, which was designated the OA-10B in USAAF service. Postwar, the Catalina remained in military service well into the 1970s, whilst in North America the last civilian fire-bombers have only recently been retired. On the warbird scene, there are five airworthy Catalinas currently based in Europe and over two-dozen in North America.

Specification:

Dimensions:
Length: 63 ft 10.5 in (19.47 m)
Wingspan: 104 ft 0 in (31.70 m)
Height: 20 ft 2 in (6.5 m)

Weights:
Empty: 20 910 lb (9485 kg)
Max T/O: 35 420 lb (16 066 kg)

Performance:
Max Speed: 179 mph (288 kmh)

Range: 2545 miles (4096 km)
Powerplant: two Pratt & Whitney R-1830-92 Twin Wasp engines (PBY-5A)
Output: 2400 hp (1790 kW)

First Flight Date:
21 March 1935

Surviving Airworthy Variant(s):
PBY-5A, PBY-6A, PBV-1A and OA-10A

Right: PBY-5A (BuNo 46633) has been operated by Plane Sailing Air Displays in the UK since its arrival from South Africa in 1985.

S. ORSOLA
ASTI

Consolidated B-24 Liberator

USA

Type: four-engined heavy bomber **Accommodation:** ten-man crew

Born out of an approach made by the USAAC to Consolidated for a bomber with superior performance to the B-17, the Liberator was built in near record time. Designated the Model 32 by its manufacturer, the bomber was designed around the then-new long-span/low-drag Davis wing. The army was so impressed with how the project was shaping up that it ordered 36 production examples well before the prototype XB-24 had taken to the skies – a French purchasing mission also committed to buying 120 bombers, these aircraft later being issued to Britain following France's capitulation in 1940. Indeed, it was the British who coined the name 'Liberator', RAF Coastal Command aircraft being the first of the type to see action over the Atlantic in mid-1941. USAAF production began to get into full swing with the advent of the B-24D, and it was this variant which was sent to the Middle East and Europe in 1942/43. It was superceded on all five production lines by the most successful B-24 of them all, the J-model, which was built to the tune of 6678 airframes. The Liberator was also used by the US Navy in PB4Y form and the RAAF in the Far East. By the time production ceased on 31 May 1945, 18,475 Liberators had been built, making it the most produced American aircraft of World War 2. Three remain airworthy today, all of these in the USA.

Specification:

Dimensions:
Length: 67 ft 2 in (20.47 m)
Wingspan: 110 ft 0 in (33.53 m)
Height: 18 ft 0 in (5.49 m)

Weights:
Empty: 36 500 lb (16 556 kg)
Max T/O: 71 200 lb (32 296 kg)

Performance:
Max Speed: 290 mph (467 kmh)
Range: 2100 miles (3380 km)
Powerplant: four Pratt & Whitney R-1830-65 Twin Wasp engines
Output: 4800 hp (3580 kW)

First Flight Date:
29 December 1939

Surviving Airworthy Variant(s):
LB-30A and B-24J

Right: B-24J 44-44052 (ex-RAF Liberator B VII KH191) is operated by the Florida-based Collings Foundation.

J
All American
LEAD CREW
PLANE SPONSORS
HONOR CREW

Consolidated PB4Y-2 Privateer

USA

Type: four-engined maritime patrol bomber **Accommodation:** 11-man crew

Although the US Navy had made much use of its B-24D-derived PB4Y-1 Liberators from August 1942 onwards in the Pacific and over the Atlantic, these aircraft had all been configured for USAAF service when originally built . It was therefore decided in early 1943 that a navalised variant would be most beneficial, and a contract was placed to this end in May for a dedicated long-range patrol bomber based on the Liberator. Three B-24Ds were duly taken off the San Diego production line and rebuilt with lengthened fuselages (7 ft - 2.14 m), navalised interiors, greater defensive armament, modified engine cowlings and a distinctive vertical tail similar to that fitted to the final Liberator transport variant. The navy ordered 739 aircraft in a single production run, 286 of which were delivered in 1944 and the remainder the following year. Few had reached the frontline by VJ-Day, although VP-24 did achieve operational status with the Bat anti-ship cruise missile in the weeks prior to Japan's surrender. Indeed, the Privateer went on to perform its best work in the Cold War as a radar and electronic countermeasures platform, having been redesignated the P4Y in 1951. After further service with the US Coast Guard, the final examples were retired in the early 1960s, and a handful are still flown today in the USA as fire-bombers.

Specification:

Dimensions:
Length: 74 ft 7 in (22.73 m)
Wingspan: 110 ft 0 in (33.53 m)
Height: 30 ft 1 in (9.17 m)

Weights:
Empty: 37 485 lb (17 003 kg)
Max T/O: 65 000 lb (29 484 kg)

Performance:
Max Speed: 237 mph (381 kmh)
Range: 2800 miles (4506 km)
Powerplant: four Pratt & Whitney R-1830-94 Twin Wasp engines
Output: 5400 hp (4028 kW)

First Flight Date:
20 September 1943

Surviving Airworthy Variant(s):
PB4Y-2 and PB4Y-2G

Right: PB4Y-2G BuNo 66260 presently flies as Tanker #123 with Hawkins & Powers Aviation of Greybull, Wyoming.

N7620C
123

Culver PQ-14

USA

Type: single-engined radio-controlled target aircraft **Accommodation:** pilot, although usually flown unmanned

Culver cornered the market for unmanned aerial gunnery targets in 1940 when its LCA Cadet lightplane was selected by the USAAC for conversion into a radio-controlled drone. Some 600 were eventually built, 200 of which were issued to the navy as training aids for anti-aircraft gunners. As the performance of manned combat aircraft increased, so the need for a more powerful gunnery target grew. To answer this demand Culver created a purpose-built machine, which entered service in 1943 as the PQ-14. Some 65 mph faster than its predecessor, the new design was also more manoeuvrable thanks to its larger control surfaces and retractable gear. A total of 1348 PQ-14As were built, 1201 of which were transferred to the US Navy, where they were duly designated TD2C-1s. The final version to enter USAAF service was the heavier PQ-14B, a number of which survived after the war to be registered on the civil market. At least six 'flyers' can still be found on the US civil register today.

Specification:

Dimensions:
Length: 19 ft 6 in (5.94 m)
Wingspan: 30 ft 0 in (9.14 m)
Height: 7 ft 11 in (2.41 m)

Weights:
Empty: 1500 lb (680.4 kg)
Max T/O: 1830 lb (830 kg)

Performance:
Max Speed: 180 mph (290 kmh)
Range: 512 miles (824 km)
Powerplant: Franklin O-300-11
Output: 150 hp (112 kW)

First Flight Date:
1942

Surviving Airworthy Variant(s):
PQ-14A/B

Right: This PQ-14A was issued to the US Navy as a TD2C-1 and given the BuNo 79573. It is presently owned by The Air Museum at Chino.

Curtiss P-40 Warhawk

USA

Type: single-engined fighter **Accommodation:** pilot

Overshadowed by other more successful USAAF fighter types like the P-38, P-47 and P-51, the Curtiss P-40 was nevertheless the primary USAAF fighter at the time of the Japanese fleet's surprise attack on Pearl Harbor on 7 December 1941. The Warhawk was responsible for 'holding the line' in the Pacific for much of 1942, vainly attempting to blunt the aerial onslaught unleashed by the Japanese. The last in a long line of fighters to carry the appellation 'Hawk', the P-40 family was born out of the marriage of an early-production P-36A fuselage with the all-new Allison V-1710-19 liquid-cooled inline engine. When first flown as the Hawk 81, Curtiss engineers could never have imagined that roughly 13,800 aircraft would be built between early 1939 and December 1944, and used in virtually every theatre of conflict during World War 2. Although the Allison engine was initially the P-40's strong point, it soon became its Achilles' heel, as it quickly 'ran out of steam' above 15,000 ft due to it lacking a turbo or supercharger. This made the Warhawk inferior to virtually all other Axis fighters above certain ceilings, and reduced it to a life of ground attack work, where its durability and crisp handling made it a favourite with Allied pilots. Roughly 20 airworthy P-40s (covering several marks) have survived into the 1990s, with all bar a handful of these residing in the USA.

Specification:

Dimensions:
Length: 33 ft 4 in (10.16 m)
Wingspan: 37 ft 4 in (11.38 m)
Height: 12 ft 4 in (3.76 m)

Weights:
Empty: 6200 lb (2903 kg)
Max T/O: 11 500 lb (5216 kg)

Performance:
Max Speed: 343 mph (552 kmh)
Range: 750 miles (1207 km)

Powerplant: Allison V-1710-39 (P-40E), V-1710-73 (P-40K) and V-1710-81/-99/-115 (P-40M/N)
Output: 1150 hp (857.33 kW), 1325 hp (1106 kW) and 1200 hp (895 kW) respectively

First Flight Date:
14 October 1938

Surviving Airworthy Variant(s):
P-40E, P-40K, P-40M, P-40N and TP-40N

Right: P-40N 42-105192 was built for the RCAF as Kittyhawk Mk IV 858 in the spring of 1943. It has been part of the The Air Museum/Planes of Fame collection since 1960.

Curtiss C-46 Commando

USA

Type: twin-engined transport **Accommodation:** two-man crew and up to sixty passengers

Built by Curtiss-Wright in an effort to recover airliner sales that had been lost to modern monoplane designs from Boeing, Douglas and Lockheed, the C-46 started life as the CW-20 project in 1936. With the prototype flying by the early spring of 1940, its performance figures impressed civil and military operators alike – the USAAC placed an order for 200 examples in September of that year. To fulfil its military role, the CW-20's pressurised interior was gutted and replaced by canvas seating in an unpressurised environment. Large double cargo doors were built into the fuselage, the floor strengthened and uprated engines fitted. Production examples began to reach the USAAC's Air Transport Command in the autumn of 1942, the type almost immediately proving itself on long-range flights transporting men and equipment to North Africa in the wake of the *Torch* landings. The C-46's 'finest hour' came in the Far East where the India-China Wing's aircraft formed the backbone of the 'Hump' airlift across the Himalayas in 1943-44. The Commando's towing capability was also put to good use in Europe during the Rhine crossing, the C-46 towing two CG-4 gliders at a time. Over 3000 were built in five different variants, the aircraft continuing to serve with the USAF during both the Korean and Vietnam Wars. Many ex-military C-46s were sold off to civilian cargo haulers particularly in Central and South America, and today over 50 examples are still gainfully employed predominantly in these locations.

Specification:

Dimensions:
Length: 76 ft 4 in (23.27 m)
Wingspan: 108 ft 1 in (32.92 m)
Height: 21 ft 9 in (6.63 m)

Weights:
Empty: 29 483 lb (13 373 kg)
Max T/O: 56 000 lb (25 400 kg)

Performance:
Max Speed: 269 mph (433 kmh)
Range: 1200 miles (1931 km)
Powerplant: two Pratt & Whitney R-2800-51 Double Wasp engines
Output: 2000 hp (1491 kW)

First Flight Date:
26 March 1940

Surviving Airworthy Variant(s):
C-46A/D and F

Right: Commando 47-8663 is operated from Camarillo Airport by the Southern California Wing of the Texas-based Confederate Air Force.

478663
DOLL

Curtiss SB2C Helldiver

USA

Type: single-engined dive-bomber **Accommodation:** pilot and rear-gunner

The most numerous Allied dive-bomber of World War 2, the Curtiss Helldiver endured a prolonged gestation period to mature into one of the most effective aircraft of its type. Some 7200 were built between 1942 and 1945, the Helldiver making its service debut over Rabaul in November 1943 flying from the deck of USS *Bunker Hill*. At that time, the aircraft was still inferior in many respects to the Douglas SBD Dauntless, the very aircraft it was meant to replace! Despite being drastically improved over the next two years (some 880 major design changes had to be made to the SB2C-1 before production could even get underway), the Helldiver retained an unenviable reputation 'around the boat', with more aircraft being lost in deck landing accidents than to enemy action – its unpleasant flying characteristics near to the stall earned it the nickname 'The Beast', whilst aircrews who flew the type in combat grimly joked that its designation (SB2C) stood for 'Son of a Bitch, 2nd Class'. Although passionately disliked by many of the crews sent into combat flying it, the Helldiver was responsible for the destruction of more Japanese targets than any other US dive-bomber. Postwar, a small number of aircraft saw further use with the French, Italian, Greek and Portuguese navies and the Royal Thai air force, whilst its US Navy career lingered on until the end of the 1940s. Few Helldivers escaped the scrapper's torch, and today only the Confederate Air Force's SB2C-5 BuNo 83589 remains airworthy.

Specification:

Dimensions:
Length: 36 ft 8 in (11.20 m)
Wingspan: 49 ft 9 in (15.20 m)
Height: 16 ft 11 in (5.10 m)

Weights:
Empty: 11 000 lb (4990 kg)
Max T/O: 16 607 lb (7550 kg)

Performance:
Max Speed: 281 mph (452 kmh)
Range: 1110 miles (1786 km)
Powerplant: Wright R-2600-8 Cyclone
Output: 1700 hp (1267.67 kW)

First Flight Date:
18 December 1940

Surviving Airworthy Variant(s):
SB2C-5

Right: The Confederate Air Force's extremely rare SB2C-5 is adorned with the distinctive 'G' marking as worn by CVG-5's VB-5 aboard USS **Franklin** ***(CV 13) in March 1945.***

32
32
32
NX92879

de Havilland Mosquito UK

Type: twin-engined fighter-bomber and photo-recce aircraft **Accommodation:** pilot and navigator

Built to replace the ageing Blenheim, the Mosquito flew very much in the face of convention by utilising a wooden fuselage and wings. Initially rejected by the Air Ministry in the autumn of 1938 on the grounds of its unorthodox construction, the aircraft's wooden structure actually ensured its series production with the outbreak of war due to the fear that the supply of light alloys from abroad would be affected by the conflict. An order for 50 aircraft was received on 1 March 1940, and the prototype Mosquito took to the skies eight months later. The sleek Merlin-powered design soon proved its worth during flight trials, possessing the manoeuvrability of a fighter and the payload of a medium bomber. The first Mosquito to see operational service was the photo-recce variant on 20 September 1941, whilst bomber optimised B Mk IVs began to reach the frontline two months later. Whilst the Mosquito was being successfully blooded as a bomber, the nightfighter version was also making its mark, having been developed from the second prototype of 1941. Numerous variant modifications were made to the overall design during its production life, which also saw the Mosquito built under-licence in Australia and Canada. Some 7781 examples were eventually built, and later versions of the aircraft remained in service with the RAF until 1961. Today, just a solitary Mosquito is maintained in airworthy condition.

Specification:

Dimensions:
Length: 40 ft 10.75 in (12.47 m)
Wingspan: 54 ft 2 in (16.51 m)
Height: 15 ft 3 in (4.65 m)

Weights:
Empty: 14 300 lb (6486 kg)
Max T/O: 22 300 lb (10 115 kg)

Performance:
Max Speed: 362 mph (583 kmh)
Range: 1650 miles (2655 km)
Powerplant: two Rolls-Royce Merlin 113/114 engines
Output: 3380 hp (2520 kW)

First Flight Date:
25 November 1940

Surviving Airworthy Variant(s):
B 35

Right: Following the crash of British Aerospace's T III in 1996, the sole remaining airworthy Mosquito is the infrequently flown B 35 of the Weeks Air Museum, which is currently on loan to the Experimental Aircraft Association Museum at Oshkosh, Wisconsin.

Douglas SBD Dauntless

USA

Type: single-engined dive-bomber **Accommodation:** two-man crew

The SBD Dauntless was the scourge of the Japanese Imperial Fleet in the crucial years of the Pacific war. Almost single-handedly, 54 SBDs from the carriers *Enterprise* and *Yorktown* won the pivotal Battle of Midway on 4 June 1942, destroying four Japanese 'flat tops' in the course of just 24 hours. The SBD of 1942 could trace its origins back to rival designs penned by gifted engineers John Northrop and Ed Heinemann in the mid 1930s. Northrop produced the BT-1 for the US Navy in the spring of 1938, its revolutionary all-metal stressed-skin design exhibiting airframe strength that made it an ideal candidate for adoption as a dive-bomber. By the time the BT-1 had evolved into the BT-2, Northrop had been acquired by Douglas, and the type was redesignated the SBD-1. Production aircraft began to reach the Marine Corps in 1940, and by the spring of the following year the definitive SBD-3 was in service, this version boasting self-sealing tanks, a bullet-proof windscreen, armour protection, an uprated engine and improved armament. 584 SBD-3s were built, and it was these machines that became the key combat aircraft in the Pacific in 1942/43. The USAAC also procured nearly 900 Dauntlesses, which it designated the A-24 – production of all variants of SBD/A-24 finally totalled 5936. Five SBDs/A-24s remain airworthy in the USA today, and the recent recovery of a number of airframes from Lake Michigan may bolster this number in time.

Specification:

Dimensions:
Length: 33 ft 0 in (10.06 m)
Wingspan: 41 ft 6 in (12.65 m)
Height: 12 ft 11 in (3.94 m)

Weights:
Empty: 6535 lb (2964 kg)
Max T/O: 9519 lb (4318 kg)

Performance:
Max Speed: 255 mph (410 kmh)
Range: 773 miles (1244 km)
Powerplant: Wright R-1820-66 Cyclone 9
Output: 1350 hp (1007 kW)

First Flight Date:
July 1935 (XBT-1)

Surviving Airworthy Variant(s):
SBD-5 and A-24A/B

Right: SBD-5 BuNo 28536 is operated by the Planes of Fame Museum at Chino.

39
39

Douglas C-47 Skytrain

USA

Type: twin-engined transport aircraft **Accommodation:** three-man crew and up to 28 paratroopers

An improved version of Douglas's revolutionary DC-1 of 1933, the C-47 was the military descendent of the Douglas Sleeper Transport, which was itself an enlarged DC-2. When the DC-3 entered civilian service in 1936, the army immediately contacted Douglas and advised the company of changes that needed to be made in order to render the airliner suitable for military use – these included the fitment of more powerful engines, the reinforcement of the cabin floor and the inclusion of large cargo doors. Therefore, when the USAAC issued contracts in 1940 for the first C-47s, Douglas was able to get production immediately underway. Some 963 examples of the basic C-47 were built, the first aircraft entering USAAC service in 1941. Follow-on variants of the Skytrain included the A- and B-models, which differed primarily in electrical systems and powerplant from the basic C-47. The Douglas transport was a key factor in the global success of the Allied war effort, fulfilling the critical 'air bridge' role by transporting men and material to virtually all theatres of conflict. Some 10,926 examples were eventually built in the USA, plus a further 2000 Lisunov Li-2s in the USSR and 485 Japanese Nakajima L2Ds. More than 200 C-47/DC-3s remain in military service with 31 air forces today, whilst a large number (300+) are also flown by civilian operators.

Specification:

Dimensions:
Length: 64 ft 5.50 in (19.64 m)
Wingspan: 95 ft 0 in (28.96 m)
Height: 16 ft 11 in (5.16 m)

Weights:
Empty: 16 970 lb (7700 kg)
Max T/O: 26 000 lb (11 793 kg)

Performance:
Max Speed: 229 mph (369 kmh)
Range: 2125 miles (3420 km)
Powerplant: two Pratt & Whitney R-1830-93 Twin Wasp engines
Output: 2400 hp (1790 kW)

First Flight Date:
17 December 1935 (Douglas Sleeper Transport)

Surviving Airworthy Variant(s):
C-47, C-47A, C-47B, C-53, R4D, DC-3 and Li-2

Right: VC-47D 0-50972 has been restored in its USAF VIP transport configuration of the 1950s.

U.S. AIR FORCE
0-50972

Douglas C-54 Skymaster

USA

Type: four-engined strategic transport aircraft **Accommodation:** three-man crew and up to forty-nine troops

Like its more famous Douglas forebear, the C-54 was a military derivative of a civilian airliner, in this case the DC-4A. Designed specifically to fulfil a specification drawn up by United Air Lines for a long-range pressurised airliner, the aircraft was ordered to the tune of 61 airframes by the US operators, followed by a further buy of 71 for the USAAC – in the event, most of the civilian DC-4As were also requistioned into military service. The first production C-54 made its maiden flight on 26 March 1942, and by the following October 24 were in service with the Air Transport Command's Atlantic Wing. The A-model was introduced early in 1943, this aircraft having a cargo door, stronger floor, cargo boom hoist and larger wing tanks. The design was further modified during the remaining war years to suit different USAAF requirements, some 1242 C-54s of varying marks eventually being built. Included in this number were 183 examples for the US Navy, who operated them in the Pacific as R4Ds. Postwar, the C-54/R4D enjoyed a long career with both the USAF and US Navy, the final examples not being retired until the late 1960s. Ex-military aircraft also proved popular with civilian freight and fire bomber operators, and today a number of aircraft are still in gainful employment across the globe. A handful of ex-military 'flyers' have also recently appeared within the warbird fraternity in the USA.

Specification:

Dimensions:
Length: 93 ft 11 in (28.63 m)
Wingspan: 117 ft 6 in (35.81 m)
Height: 27 ft 6.25 in (8.39 m)

Weights:
Empty: 38 000 lb (17 237 kg)
Max T/O: 73 000 lb (33 112 kg)

Performance:
Max Speed: 274 mph (441 kmh)
Range: 3900 miles (6276 km)
Powerplant: four Pratt & Whitney R-2000-7 Twin Wasp engines
Output: 5400 hp (4028 kW)

First Flight Date:
7 June 1938 (Civilian DC-4E)

Surviving Airworthy Variant(s):
C-54A/B/D/E/G, VC-54, R5D and DC-4

Right: The immaculately restored C-54 seen opposite is owned by Atlantic Warbird in the USA.

56498
AIR TRANSPORT COMMAND
Atlantic Division

Douglas A-20 Havoc

USA

Type: twin-engined light bomber **Accommodation:** three-man crew

One of the most widely-used light/medium bombers of World War 2, the A-20 evolved from a Douglas design built to meet a USAAC attack specification issued in 1938. Initially known as the Model 7A, the prototype was drastically reworked soon after its first flight trials in order to make the aircraft more suitable for use in Europe, and indeed the first order for the new bomber (100 examples) came from France, not the USAAC. Redesignated the DB-7, production of the new bomber commenced in late 1939, and some 60 aircraft reached France prior to the start of the *Blitzkrieg* on 10 May 1940. A handful of undelivered DB-7s were duly issued to the RAF, who christened them Boston Is and used them in both the training and nightfighter roles. The performance of the Douglas 'twin' was far in advance of anything the British were then operating, and the Boston went on to become one of the mainstays of the RAF – well over 1000 aircraft were supplied through Lend-Lease. The USAAC committed to the DB-7 (redesignated the A-20) in May 1939, and by the time production ended in September 1944, no less than 7385 Havoc/Bostons had been built. The type saw combat across the globe, its rugged build quality proving particularly attractive to the Soviet air forces, who used a vast quantity (3125) of A-20s. Despite being built in huge numbers, few A-20s have survived into the 1990s, and only one example remains airworthy (in the USA).

Specification:

Dimensions:
Length: 48 ft 0 in (14.63 m)
Wingspan: 61 ft 4 in (18.69 m)
Height: 17 ft 7 in (5.36 m)

Weights:
Empty: 15 984 lb (7250 kg)
Max T/O: 27 200 lb (12 338 kg)

Performance:
Max Speed: 317 mph (510 kmh)
Range: 1025 miles (1650 km) with 725 US gallons (2744 litres) of fuel and 2000 lb (907 kg) of bombs
Powerplant: two Wright R-2600-23 Cyclone 14 engines (A-20G)
Output: 3200 hp (2386 kW)

First Flight Date:
26 October 1938 (Douglas 7B)

Surviving Airworthy Variant(s): A-20G

Right: This A-20G was part of the Confederate Air Force from October 1965 until October 1988, when it was destroyed in a crash near its Harlingen, Texas, home.

T
322210
N67 921

Douglas A-26 Invader

USA

Type: twin-engined attack bomber **Accommodation:** three-man crew

The A-26 Invader was designed as a natural successor to Douglas's hugely successful A-20. Harnessing the power of Pratt & Whitne then new Double Wasp radial engine, prototype XP-26s were ordered by the USAAC in May 1941 in three different forms – one wit a 75 mm gun, a second with a solid radar nose and armed with a quartet of 20 mm forward-firing weapons plus four guns in an upper turret, and the third with optical sighting equipment in the nose and two defensive turrets. The latter machine was ordered first as the A-26B, production aircraft being capable of carrying twice the bombload originally specified. Making its combat debut c 19 November 1944, some 1355 A-26Bs were eventually built, followed by 1091 C-models (which had a transparent nose fitted with navigational and radar bombing equipment). The aircraft enjoyed a more active postwar career with the USAF than any of its twin-engined contemporaries, more than 450 B-26s (the Invader was redesignated in 1948 following the retirement of the last Marauder seeing combat in the Korean War, whilst the French also used them over Indo-China. After the latter's lead, the USAF employed specially converted On Mark B-26Ks in Vietnam too. Following decades of service, some surviving Invaders found an equally hazardous occupation in retirement as civilian fire-bombers in North America – 21 still fly today in this role. A further 25+ are also flown purely as warbirds in North America, whilst a solitary example is operated in north-west Europe.

Specification:

Dimensions:
Length: 51 ft 3 in (15.62 m)
Wingspan: 70 ft 0 in (21.34 m)
Height: 18 ft 3 in (5.56 m)

Weights:
Empty: 22 850 lb (10 365 kg)
Max T/O: 35 000 lb (15 876 kg)

Performance:
Max Speed: 373 mph (600 kmh)
Range: 1400 miles (2253 km)
Powerplant: two Pratt & Whitney R-2800-79 Double Wasp engines
Output: 4000 hp (2982 kW)

First Flight Date:
10 July 1942

Surviving Airworthy Variant(s):
A-26A/B/C, B-26B/C/K, RB-26C, TB-26C, On Mark, Monarch and Marksman conversions

Right: Aside from wearing an authentic Korean War scheme, this B-26C also carries a full warload of 'dummy' 0.5-in rockets on its underwing rails.

FEEDING FRENZY
T
U.S. AIR FORCE
BC-538

Fairchild Argus

USA

Type: single-engined high-wing liaison/communications and instrument training aircraft

Accommodation: one pilot and three passengers

A product of the Fairchild Aircraft Corporation, the humble Argus could trace its lineage back to the Model 24C three-seater civilia tourer of 1933. The company enlarged the high-wing design in 1937 with the introduction of the four-seat Model 24J, which cam the choice of either a Warner radial or Ranger inline engine. With the general enlarging of the US military in the late 1930s, the M 24 was one of the numerous civilian types which suddenly found itself a role within the rapidly exapanding USAAC. However, of th UC-61 Forwarders (as the militarised Fairchild was designated), all bar two were passed on to the British under lend-lease. Christen Argus Is, the first examples arrived in the UK in 1941 and were duly issued to both the RAF and the Air Transport Auxiliary (ATA), w used them as 'aerial taxis' for the carriage of ferry pilots. A further 364 Mk IIs followed soon after, these machines having new radi a 24-volt electrical system fitted – the USAAC also acquired 148 examples to this specification, which it designated UC-61As. The f variant built was the Ranger-engined Argus III (UC-61K), some 306 being issued to the British. Aside from USAAC and RAF/ATA use, handful of Fairchild 24s were also supplied to the US Navy, who designated them J2Ks. A healthy quantity of civilian and ex-milita machines have survived into the 1990s, with six flyable Argus IIIs currently appearing on the UK civil register.

Specification:

Dimensions:
Length: 23 ft 9 in (7.24 m)
Wingspan: 36 ft 4 in (11.07 m)
Height: 7 ft 7.5 in (2.32 m)

Weights:
Empty: 1613 lb (732 kg)
Max T/O: 2562 lb (1162 kg)

Performance:
Max Speed: 132 mph (212 kmh)
Range: 640 miles (1030 km)
Powerplant: Warner R-500 Super Scarab or Ranger L-440-7
Output: 165 hp (123 kW) and 200 hp (149 kW) respectively

First Flight Date:
1933 (civilian Model 24C)

Surviving Airworthy Variant(s):
UC-61A and Argus III

Right: Painted up as a D-Day striped UC-61K, this Argus III is based at Liverpool's Speke Airport.

314887

Fairey Swordfish

UK

Type: single-engined biplane torpedo-bomber/reconnaissance aircraft **Accommodation:** pilot, observer and gunner

Looking sadly out-dated by 1939 when compared with its sleek monoplane contemporaries, the Fairey Swordfish somehow remained a viable weapon of war in its primary torpedo-bomber role right through to mid-1942. Indeed, the aircraft continued to be produced for a further two years after that, and was only phased out of frontline service with the Royal Navy's Fleet Air Arm (FAA) in May 1945! It could trace its lineage back to a private-venture biplane design known as the T.S.R.I, which had been originated by Fairey in 1933 in the hope of soliciting interest from the Air Ministry. The ploy worked, and Specification S.15/33 was duly issued calling for a carrier-based torpedo-spotter-reconnaissance aircraft. The prototype T.S.R.II successfully completed its flight testing, and in 1935 a contract was placed with Fairey for 86 airframes. The standard weapon of choice for the Swordfish was the 18-in/1610-lb torpedo, which was slung beneath the fuselage. No 825 Sqn was the first unit to receive the Swordfish in July 1936, and over the next three years a further dozen squadrons re-equipped with the Fairey biplane. Aside from being the FAA's primary torpedo bomber for the first two-and-a-half years of World War 2, the Swordfish was also used offensively by the RAF's Coastal Command. Some 2391 were built over four different mark numbers, and today, four Swordfish remain airworthy – two each in both the UK and Canada.

Specification:

Dimensions:
Length: 35 ft 8 in (10.87 m)
Wingspan: 45 ft 6 in (13.87 m)
Height: 12 ft 4 in (3.76 m)

Weights:
Empty: 4700 lb (2132 kg)
Max T/O: 7510 lb (3406 kg)

Performance:
Max Speed: 138 mph (222 kmh)
Range: 1030 miles (1658 km)
Powerplant: Bristol Pegasus XXX
Output: 750 hp (559 kW)

First Flight Date:
17 April 1934

Surviving Airworthy Variant(s):
Mks II and IV

Right: The oldest surviving Swordfish in the world, Mk II W5856 was originally operated by the Royal Canadian Navy. Following an extensive restoration by British Aerospace, the aircraft has 'served' with the Royal Navy's Historic Flight since 1993.

A2A
W5856
5856

Fieseler Fi 156 Storch MS 500

Germany and France

Type: single-engined high-wing army co-operation/reconnaissance aircraft **Accommodation:** pilot and two passengers

Arguably the best army co-operation aircraft used by either side during World War 2, the Storch was the most successful product to emanate from the company founded by World War 1 ace, (and the world's greatest inter-war aerobatic pilot), Gerhard Fieseler. The Fi 156 boasted astounding STOL performance thanks to its unique high-lift wing devices – a fixed slot extending the span of the wing leading edge and slotted ailerons and camber-changing flaps along the length of the trailing edge. Beating off rival designs from Messerschmitt, Siebel and Focke-Wulf, Fieseler placed the Fi 156A-1 in production in late 1937. The Storch would subsequently see action wherever the *Wehrmacht* was committed to battle, and despite its seemingly fragile appearance, the aircraft reportedly had a frontline 'life expectancy' ten times longer than that enjoyed by a Bf 109! Indeed, it was licence-production of the latter type by Fieseler that forced the company to transfer the Fi 156's construction to factories in France and Czechoslovakia in 1942. By war's end 2000+ had been delivered to the Luftwaffe, with the C-series being the most common variant. Postwar, production of the Fi 156 continued in both France and Czechoslovakia, aircraft in the former country being built by Morane-Saulnier and powered by either a Renault 6Q inverted inline engine or Salmson 9AB radial. Over 30 Storchs have survived into the late 1990s in Europe (as well as a handful in North America), with two-thirds of these remaining airworthy.

Specification:

Dimensions:
Length: 32 ft 5.75 in (9.90 m)
Wingspan: 46 ft 9 in (14.25 m)
Height: 10 ft 0 in (3.05 m)

Weights:
Empty: 2050 lb (930 kg)
Max T/O: 2921 lb (1325 kg)

Performance:
Max Speed: 109 mph (175 kmh)
Range: 239 miles (385 km)
Powerplant: Argus As 10C-3 (Fi 156) or Salmson 9AB (MS502)
Output: 240 hp (179 kW) and 250 hp (186.4 kW) respectively

First Flight Date:
24 May 1936

Surviving Airworthy Variant(s):
Fi 156C, MS 500/502/505 and Benes-Mráz K.65 Cáp

Right: This Duxford-based 'Fi 156C' is in fact a re-engined MS 500.

Fleet Fort

Canada

Type: single-engined trainer **Accommodation:** two pilots in tandem

Built by Fleet as a private-venture trainer which could fulfil a variety of roles when fitted with different powerplants, the Fort was, in the event, only produced in the intermediate trainer version (the 60K). The prototype was evaluated by the RCAF in mid 1940, and following flight trials, an order for 200 examples was placed. Although the first production Fort was flown on 18 April 1941, the RCAF subsequently changed its mind in respect to the aircraft's ability to prepare pilots for the transition from basic to advanced types - the air force duly scaled its order down to just 100 aircraft. In 1942 the RCAF decided to convert its surviving Forts into dedicated wireless trainers, installing equipment in the rear cockpit and switching the seat in this space to face aft. Most, if not all, Forts were so converted, and remained in service until 1945. Today, just one Fort survives, this aircraft being maintained in airworthy condition by the Canadian Warplane Heritage, based at Hamilton, Ontario.

Specification:

Dimensions:
Length: 26 ft 10.30 in (8.18 m)
Wingspan: 36 ft 0 in (10.97 m)
Height: 8 ft 3 in (2.51 m)

Weights:
Empty: 2530 lb (1149 kg)
Max T/O: 3500 lb (1589 kg)

Performance:
Max Speed: 162 mph (260.60 kmh)
Range: not specified
Powerplant: Jacobs L-6MB
Output: 330 hp (246.18 kW)

First Flight Date:
22 March 1940

Surviving Airworthy Variant(s):
60K Fort

Right: The very rare 60K Fort is maintained in flying condition in Ontario, Canada, by Canadian Warplane Heritage.

Marilyn

Grumman F4F Wildcat

USA

Type: single-engined fighter **Accommodation:** pilot

Derived from a biplane design offered in competition to the more modern Brewster F2A Buffalo monoplane, the Wildcat was the result of a study undertaken by Grumman into the feasibility of a single wing naval fighter. Designated the XF4F-2, the fighter lost out to the rival Brewster in the fly-off due to the latter's superior handling qualities. However, Grumman reworked its prototype into the vastly improved XF4F-3 of March 1939, fitting a more powerful Twin Wasp engine with a two-stage supercharger, increasing the fighter's wing span and redesigning its tail surfaces. After flight trials, the Navy immediately ordered 78 F4F-3s, which they christened the Wildcat. Entering US Navy service at the end of 1940, the Wildcat proved to be a worthy opponent for the Japanese A6M Zero-sen during the great carrier battles at Coral Sea and Midway in 1942, followed by the Guadalcanal invasion. By this stage in the war General Motors (GM) had commenced building F4F-4s, which they duly designated FM-1s. In late 1943 GM switched production to the FM-2, which utilised a turbocharged Wright R-1820-56 Cyclone in place of the now venerable Twin Wasp. This swap made for a higher top speed and an optimum altitude some 50 per cent greater than that achieved with the FM-1 – by the time production was terminated in August 1945, no fewer than 4467 FM-2s had been built. Of the 19 Wildcats that remain airworthy today, all bar two of these aircraft are based in the USA.

Specification:

Dimensions:
Length: 28 ft 9 in (8.76 m)
Wingspan: 38 ft 0 in (11.58 m)
Height: 9 ft 2.5 in (2.81 m)

Weights:
Empty: 5758 lb (2612 kg)
Max T/O: 7952 lb (3607 kg)

Performance:
Max Speed: 318 mph (512 kmh)
Range: 770 miles (1239 km)
Powerplant: Pratt & Whitney R-1820-86 Twin Wasp (F4F-4/FM-1) or Wright R-1820-56 Cyclone (FM-2)
Output: 1200 hp (895 kW) and 1350 hp (1007.10 kW)

First Flight Date:
2 September 1937

Surviving Airworthy Variant(s):
F4F-3 and FM-2/-2P

Right: Painted up as the VF-3 F4F-3 of Medal of Honor winner Lt 'Butch' O'Hare, FM-2 BuNo 55627 was formerly operated by Planes of Fame East of Minneapolis, Minnesota.

3
F-3

Grumman G-44 Widgeon/Super Widgeon USA

Type: twin-engined high-wing utility/ASW amphibian flying-boat **Accommodation:** crew of two and three passengers

The Widgeon was built by Grumman as a smaller and cheaper version of their successful Goose amphibian again for the ever expanding US civil market. However, less than 40 had reached private hands when Grumman was ordered to focus production on a militarised version of the amphibian, which the USAAC designated the OA-14 and the US Navy and Coast Guard the J4F. The latter service enjoyed its first success against the U-boat menace in August 1942 when a J4F-1 of Coast Guard Squadron 212 sunk U-166 off the Passes of the Mississippi. Grumman received its biggest production order (131) for the J4F-2 version in early 1942, the final example of which was not delivered to the navy until 26 February 1945. The Royal Navy also received 15 J4F-2s under Lend-Lease, these aircraft fulfilling the communications role primarily in the West Indies. Grumman further improved the design in 1944 with the introduction of the G-44A, which boasted a deeper keel for improved hydrodynamic performance. This variant remained in production until January 1949, by which time 76 had been built – a further 41 were constructed under-licence in France in 1948-49. Over 70 of these machines were later modified into Super Widgeons by McKinnon Enterprises of Oregon through the fitment of more powerful Lycoming engines and improvements to both the hull and the cabin interior. Today, most surviving airworthy Widgeons (less than 20 in total) have had the 'McKinnon treatment' at some point in their long lives.

Specification:

Dimensions:
Length: 31 ft 1 in (9.47 m)
Wingspan: 40 ft 0 in (12.19 m)
Height: 11 ft 5 in (3.48 m)

Weights:
Empty: 3189 lb (1447 kg)
Max T/O: 4500 lb (2041 kg)

Performance:
Max Speed: 153 mph (246 kmh)
Range: 920 miles (1481 km)
Powerplant: two Ranger L-440C-5 or Lycoming GO-480-B1D engines
Output: 200 hp (149 kW) and 270 hp (201.42 kW) respectively

First Flight Date:
28 June 1940

Surviving Airworthy Variant(s):
G-44/-44A, J4F-2 and Super Widgeon

***Right:** Although originally built with inline Ranger L-440C-5 engines, this US-registered aircraft has since benefited from a full McKinnon Super Widgeon conversion, and now boasts uprated Lycoming GO-480-B1Ds.*

N-32BB

Grumman TBF/TBM Avenger USA

Type: single-engined torpedo-bomber **Accommodation:** three-man crew

Produced as a replacement for the Douglas TBD Devastator, two prototype XTBF-1s were ordered from Grumman in April 1940, along with the rival XTBU-1 design from Consolidated. The XTBF-1 was distinctly 'rotund' due to its capacious internal bomb bay, which was large enough to contain the biggest (22-in) torpedo in the Navy arsenal. The Avenger quickly completed its flight test programme, and by the end of January 1942 the first production TBF-1s were issued to the US Navy. As its name suggested, the TBF/TBM meted out severe retribution on the Japanese over the next three years in the Pacific, the aircraft participating in every major engagement from Midway onwards. One of the astounding features of the Avenger story is that the basic design of the aircraft changed very little during the course of its production life, allowing it to be built in vast quantities over a very short time scale. The US Navy's demand for the aircraft soon outstripped Grumman's production capacity, so General Motors was contracted to build the near identical TBM-1 from September 1942 onwards. By the time production finally ceased in June 1945, GM had built 7546 (out of a production run of 9836) TBMs of various marks. Over 1000 Avengers also saw action with the Fleet Air Arm in both the Atlantic and the Pacific through to VJ-Day. Postwar, the Avenger remained in naval service well into the 1950s, and today over 30 are still airworthy, the majority of these being based in North America.

Specification:

Dimensions:
Length: 40 ft 0 in (12.19 m)
Wingspan: 54 ft 2 in (16.51 m)
Height: 16 ft 5 in (5.00 m)

Weights:
Empty: 10 700 lb (4853 kg)
Max T/O: 18 250 lb (8278 kg)

Performance:
Max Speed: 267 mph (430 kmh)
Range: 1130 miles (1819 km)
Powerplant: Wright R-2600-20 Double Cyclone
Output: 1750 hp (1305 kW)

First Flight Date:
1 August 1941

Surviving Airworthy Variant(s):
TBF-1C, TBM-3/-3E/-3R/-3S/-3U

Right: TBM-3S BuNo 53818, operated by Amjet Aircraft Corporation of Minnesota, currently wears the colours of a TBM-1 of VT-17, embarked on USS* Hornet *(CV 12) in 1945.

17
17

Grumman F6F Hellcat

USA

Type: single-engined fighter **Accommodation:** pilot

The F6F embodied the early lessons learnt by users of Grumman's previous fleet fighter, the F4F Wildcat, in the Pacific, as well as general pointers from the air war in Europe. Following receipt of the US Navy's order for the fighter in June 1941, Grumman modified the 'paper' aircraft by lowering the wing centre section to enable the undercarriage to be wider splayed, fitted more armour-plating around the cockpit to protect the pilot and increased the fighter's ammunition capacity. Less than a year after being ordered, the prototype XF6F-1 made its first flight, and it was soon realised that a more powerful engine was needed to give the fighter a combat edge – a Pratt & Whitney R-2800-10 was duly installed, resulting in the F-1 being redesignated an F-3. The aircraft made its combat debut in August 1943, and from that point on, the question of aerial supremacy in the Pacific was never in doubt. Hellcats served aboard most US Navy's fleet carriers, being credited with the destruction of 4947 aircraft up to VJ-Day. Amazingly, only three major variants were produced – the -3, of which 4423 were built between October 1942 and April 1944, the improved -5 and the -3N/-5N nightfighters. The Fleet Air Arm was also a great believer in the Hellcat, procuring almost 1200 between 1943-45. The Hellcat saw only limited service postwar, being replaced by the Bearcat. Of the nine F6Fs believed to be airworthy today, seven are based in the USA and two in the UK.

Specification:

Dimensions:
Length: 33 ft 7 in (10.24 m)
Wingspan: 42 ft 10 in (13.06 m)
Height: 13 ft 6 in (4.11 m)

Weights:
Empty: 9153 lb (4152 kg)
Max T/O: 15 413 lb (6991 kg)

Performance:
Max Speed: 380 mph (612 kmh)
Range: 1040 miles (1674 km)
Powerplant: Pratt & Whitney R-2800-10W Double Wasp
Output: 2000 hp (1491 kW)

First Flight Date:
26 June 1942

Surviving Airworthy Variant(s):
F6F-3/-5/-5K/-5N

Right: F6F-5 BuNo 93879 is owned by The Air Museum at Chino.

Grumman F7F Tigercat USA

Type: twin-engined fighter-bomber **Accommodation:** pilot (and radar operator in nightfighter variant)

The radical F7F Tigercat had only just begun to enter service when Japan sued for peace following the dropping of the A-bombs in August 1945. Ordered in 1941, the fighter's long gestation period reflected the demanding Navy spec that stipulated the aircraft must have engines that, combined, produced in excess of 4000 hp, and a weight of fire double that of the F4F. Of all-metal construction with a cantilever shoulder-mounted wing, the Tigercat was a fast and well armed fighter of considerable dimension – so much so that it appeared that only the proposed 45,000-ton *Midway* class 'supercarriers' would be able to operate them. Most of the 500 F7F-1s initially built were allocated to the Marine Corps for use from island bases in the Pacific. However, just as the first 'Corps units were working up for deployment Japan surrendered, leaving the Tigercat untested in World War 2. Aside from the initial production -1, Grumman also produced the uprated -3 and the specialised F7F-3N/-4N, which was optimised for the nightfighter role through the provision of radar (fitted in a lengthened nose fairing) that was manipulated by a second crewman. It was as a nocturnal predator that the Tigercat won its 'battle spurs' over Korea in 1951. Phased out of military service soon after the end of the Korean War, many surplus F7Fs were subsequently modified into fire-bombers by US- and Canadian-based operators. Indeed, all six F7Fs currently maintained in airworthy condition were previously owned by fire-bombing companies.

Specification:

Dimensions:
Length: 45 ft 4.5 in (13.83 m)
Wingspan: 51 ft 6 in (15.70 m)
Height: 16 ft 7 in (5.05 m)

Weights:
Empty: 16 270 lb (7380 kg)
Max T/O: 25 720 lb (11 666 kg)

Performance:
Max Speed: 435 mph (700 kmh)
Range: 1200 miles (1931 km)
Powerplant: two Pratt & Whitney R-2800-34W Double Wasp engines
Output: 4200 hp (3132 kW)

First Flight Date:
3 November 1943

Surviving Airworthy Variant(s):
F7F-3/-3N/-3P

Right: Painted in the colours of a Korean War VMF(N)-513 Tigercat, F7F-3N BuNo 80503 is operated by the Lone Star Flight Museum in Galveston, Texas.

RW
MARINES
VMFN 513
PROPELLER
BOSSMAN
80503

Hawker Hurricane UK

Type: single-engined fighter **Accommodation:** pilot

The Hurricane's arrival in the frontline in December 1937 saw the RAF finally make the jump from biplane to monoplane fighters. Th aircraft owed much to Hawker's ultimate biplane design, the Fury, both types being built around an internal 'skeleton' of four wire-braced alloy and steel tube longerons – this structure was renowned for both its simplicity of construction and durability. The Hurric also benefited from Hawker's long-standing partnership with Rolls-Royce, whose newly developed Merlin I engine proved to be the powerplant. Official trials saw the aircraft exceed all performance predictions, and an order for 600 aircraft was duly placed. Toting .303-in machine guns, and capable of speeds in excess of 300 mph, the Hurricane I was the world's most advanced fighter when issu to the RAF. Although technically eclipsed by the Spitfire come the summer of 1940, Hurricanes nevertheless outnumbered the forme type during the Battle of Britain by three to one, and actually downed more Luftwaffe aircraft than the Vickers-Supermarine fighte Even prior to its 'finest hour', Hurricanes provided the first RAF aces of the war in France during the *Blitzkrieg*. In 1941 the type was used in the Mediterranean and North Africa, before being flung into action in the Far East against the Japanese. It remained in the frontline in the latter theatre until VJ-Day, despite production having ceased in September 1944 following the delivery of 14,670 Hurricanes. Six Hurricanes remain airworthy (four in the UK and two in North America).

Specification:

Dimensions:
Length: 32 ft 2.5 in (9.82 m)
Wingspan: 40 ft 0 in (12.19 m)
Height: 13 ft 1 in (3.99 m)

Weights:
Empty: 5500 lb (2495 kg)
Max T/O: 7300 lb (3311 kg)

Performance:
Max Speed: 342 mph (550 kmh)
Range: 600 miles (965 km)
Powerplant: Rolls-Royce Merlin II (Mk I) or Merlin XX (Mk II)
Output: 1030 hp (768 kW) and 1280 hp (954 kW) respectively

First Flight Date:
6 November 1935

Surviving Airworthy Variant(s):
Sea Hurricane Mk IB, Hurricane Mk IIC and Hurricane Mk XII

Right: Canadian-built Hurricane Mk XIIA 5711 is operated by The Fighter Collection at Duxford in the colours of No 71 'Eagle' Sqn.

KR
T

Lockheed P-38 Lightning

USA

Type: twin-engined fighter **Accommodation:** pilot

The P-38 Lightning was Lockheed's first venture into the world of high performance military aircraft. Keen to break into the lucrative military marketplace, the company had eagerly responded to the USAAC's 1937 Request for Proposals pertaining to the acquisition of a long-range interceptor. Aside from its novel twin-boom and central nacelle layout, the prototype XP-38, as it was designated by Lockheed, utilised butt-joined and flush-riveted all-metal skins (and flying surfaces) – a first for a US fighter. The XP-38's test programme progressed well, and aside from some minor adjustments to the flying surfaces, frontline P-38s differed little from the prototype throughout the aircraft's six-year production run. The appellation 'Lightning' was bestowed upon the P-38 by the RAF when the type was ordered in 1940, and duly adopted by the Americans the following year. In the event the RAF was so disappointed in the performance of the unsupercharged aircraft it received in 1941 that their order for 667 was cancelled – the supercharger fitted to the V-1710 engine was still designated a classified item by the US government at this point in the war, and thus restricted from overseas sale. However, the definitive P-38 models – namely the E, F, H, J and L – fitted with supercharged engines, improved Fowler flaps and extra fuel, proved more than a match for Axis fighters across the globe. Postwar, a number of F-5G photo-recce variants saw service with civil operators, and today eight Lightnings remain airworthy in the USA.

Specification:

Dimensions:

Length: 37 ft 10 in (11.53 m)
Wingspan: 52 ft 0 in (15.85 m)
Height: 9 ft 10 in (3.00 m)

Weights:

Empty: 12 780 lb (5797 kg)
Max T/O: 21 600 lb (9798 kg)

Performance:

Max Speed: 414 mph (666 kmh)
Range: 2600 miles (4184 km)
Powerplant: two Allison V-1710-89/91 (P-38J) or V-1710-111/113 (P-38L/M) engines
Output: 2850 hp (2126 kW) and 3200 hp (2387.20 kW)

First Flight Date:

27 January 1939

Surviving Airworthy Variant(s):

TP-38J, P-38L, P-38M and F-5G

Right: TP-38J 44-2314 was formerly part of the Planes of Fame East collection in Minneapolis.

Lockheed Model 18 Lodestar

USA

Type: twin-engined transport aircraft **Accommodation:** three-man crew and fourteen passengers

The final twin-engined commercial transporter designed by Lockheed, the Model 18 Lodestar was basically a larger version of the Model 14, the latter aircraft having also served as the basis for the Hudson maritime patrol bomber. Capable of accommodating up to 14 passengers in high-speed comfort in civilian guise, the Lodestar was produced in a number of versions which differed primarily in the power of the Wright or Pratt & Whitney engines fitted. The first military interest in the aircraft took the form of a series of orders placed by the US Navy in 1940 for three distinct versions of Lodestar, which were duly designated R5O-4 (executive transport), R5O-5 (personnel transport) and R5O-6 (troop transport). The following year Lockheed built 13 Lodestars for the USAAC, these machines being designated C-57s. A number of civilian Lodestars were also requisitioned by the army air corps in the wake of the Pearl Harbor raid, and these were given the designation C-56. The USAAC made further purchases in 1942/43, acquiring almost 350 C-60s, some of which were in turn passed on to the RAF and Commonwealth air forces who operated them as Lodestar Is, IAs and IIs. Postwar, many surplus Lodestars reverted to their civilian role of airliner/cargo hauler, whilst a few were also converted into executive transports. Only a handful of Lodestars have survived into the 1990s, with several being maintained in an airworthy state in North America.

Specification:

Dimensions:
Length: 49 ft 10 in (15.19 m)
Wingspan: 65 ft 6 in (19.96 m)
Height: 11 ft 1 in (3.38 m)

Weights:
Empty: 11 650 lb (5284 kg)
Max T/O: 17 500 lb (7938 kg)

Performance:
Max Speed: 253 mph (407 kmh)
Range: 1600 miles (2575 km)
Powerplant: two Wright R-1820-71 engines
Output: 2400 hp (1790 kW)

First Flight Date:
21 September 1939

Surviving Airworthy Variant(s):
Model 18 and C-60

Right: This US-registered C-60 wears a spurious RAF early-war scheme.

Lockheed B-34/PV Ventura/Harpoon USA

Type: twin-engined bomber/reconnaissance aircraft **Accommodation:** four/five-man crew

Spurred on by the success enjoyed by the RAF with the Hudson, Lockheed designed a more advanced 'bombing twin' for the same customer based on the Model 18 Lodestar. The new aircraft (designated the Ventura I by the RAF) was not only larger than its predecessor, but it had more powerful engines, a ventral gun position and could carry a greater bomb load. The first examples of 675 ordered by the British tasted combat with Bomber Command on 3 November 1942. Serious losses during subsequent daylight raids revealed the Ventura's vulnerability in this role, so the survivors were passed onto Coastal Command and the balance of 350+ airframes still on order cancelled. Surplus aircraft were snapped up by the USAAF, however, entering service with the designation B-34, again in the maritime patrol role. The US Navy also showed interest in the aircraft at this point, which it operated as the PV-1 – no fewer than 1600 navalised Venturas would be delivered up until the end of the war. The improved PV-2 Harpoon version was ordered in June 1943, 500 being delivered from March 1944 onwards. Like the PV-1, most PV-2s saw action in the Pacific, with a number remaining in service with the Navy Reserve until the late 1940s. Many surplus PV-1s and -2s were subsequently converted into executive transports by Howard Aero Services, or employed as bug/crop sprayers. About a dozen airworthy survivors can still be found in North America (and one in Australia).

Specification:

Dimensions:
Length: 51 ft 5 in (15.67 m)
Wingspan: 65 ft 6 in (19.96 m)
Height: 11 ft 11 in (3.63 m)

Weights:
Empty: 17 275 lb (7836 kg)
Max T/O: 27 250 lb (12 360 kg)

Performance:
Max Speed: 315 mph (507 kmh)
Range: 950 miles (1529 km)
Powerplant: two Pratt & Whitney R-2800-31 Double Wasp engines
Output: 4000 hp (2982 kW)

First Flight Date:
31 July 1941

Surviving Airworthy Variant(s):
PV-1, PV-2, PV-2D, PV-2T and Howard 350/400/500,

Right: Rare PV-2D BuNo 84061 was lost in a fatal crash in California in June 1990.

FP
FP
178
78

Martin B-26 Marauder

USA

Type: twin-engined bomber **Accommodation:** five/seven-man crew

Martin relied heavily on its previous experience as a successful 'bomber builder' for the USAAC when it entered its Model 179 in the air corps' widely contested 1939 Medium Bomber competition. Built around a wing optimised for high-speed cruising rather than moderate landing approach velocity, the new Martin bomber won the competition and was ordered into production 'off the drawing board'. However, the manufacturers' decision to plumb for high wing loading resulted in an aircraft that initially proved too difficult for novice pilots to fly safely. The B-26 (as is was designated by the USAAC upon its entry into service in the spring of 1941) soon earned an unenviable reputation as a 'widow maker', and despite Martin improving the aircraft's handling characteristics (from the 641st B-model onwards) through the fitment of a greater wingspan and taller tail, the sobriquet remained with the bomber throughout its service career. In light of its reputation, it is ironic that the Marauder actually enjoyed the lowest loss rate of any USAAF bomber to see action in the European theatre, B-26s equipping eight bomb groups between 1943-45. The Marauder also saw widespread use in the Pacific, the type having actually made its combat debut in this theatre in April 1942. The RAF also operated 522 out of the 5157 that were eventually built. Replaced by the A-26 soon after the war, few B-26s have survived into the 1990s, with only one early B-26 currently airworthy in the USA.

Specification:

Dimensions:
Length: 56 ft 0 in (17 m)
Wingspan: 65 ft 0 in (19.80 m)
Height: 19 ft 10 in (6.04 m)

Weights:
Empty: 23 000 lb (10 433 kg)
Max T/O: 32 000 lb (14 515 kg)

Performance:
Max Speed: 310 mph (500 kmh)

Range: 1150 miles (1850 km)
Powerplant: two Pratt & Whitney R-2800-5 Double Wasp engines
Output: 3700 hp (2760.20 kW)

First Flight Date:
25 November 1940

Surviving Airworthy Variant(s):
B-26

Right: Early-build B-26 40-1464 is owned by Kermit Weeks and was recently returned to airworthiness by Carl Scholl and his team at Chino-based Aero Trader.

ARMY

Messerschmitt Bf 109G

Germany

Type: single-engined fighter **Accommodation:** pilot

Numerically the most abundant fighter produced by either side during World War 2, the Messerschmitt Bf 109 formed the backbone of the *Jagdwaffe* on both the Eastern and Western Fronts, as well as in the Mediterranean and North Africa. The prototype Bf 109 V1 flew for the first time in September 1935 powered by a 695 hp Rolls-Royce Kestrel engine, but by the time initial production-standard fighters were issued to the Luftwaffe in the spring of 1937, the Messerschmitt had been re-engined with the Junkers Jumo 210 inline powerplant. Another 18 months, and two sub-types, were to pass before the originally specified Daimler-Benz DB 601 engine was at last made available in sufficient quantities to allow Messerschmitt to commit the outstanding E-model to production in mid-1938. From that moment on, the Bf 109 and the DB 600 series engine would prove to be inseparable. Of the eight distinct sub-types within the huge Bf 109 family, the most populous was the G-model, of which over 30,000 were built between 1941/45. Designed around the 1475 hp DB 605 engine, the G-model introduced cockpit pressurisation, which was crucial from late 1942 onwards in light of high-altitude USAAF daylight bomber raids. Despite its production run, only a handful of genuine German Bf 109s have survived into the 1990s, and with the serious damaging of the RAF's G-2 at Duxford in October 1997, only the German-based MBB G-6 and Hans Dittes G-10 (both composites) are currently airworthy.

Specification:

Dimensions:
Length: 29 ft 7 in (9.02 m)
Wingspan: 32 ft 6.5 in (9.92 m)
Height: 8 ft 6 in (2.59 m)

Weights:
Empty: 5952 lb (2700 kg)
Max T/O: 7055 lb (3200 kg)

Performance:
Max Speed: 385 mph (620 kmh)
Range: 621 miles (1000 km) with 66-Imp gal (300-litre) drop tank
Powerplant: Daimler-Benz DB 605D-1
Output: 1475 hp (1100 kW)

First Flight Date:
September 1935

Surviving Airworthy Variant(s):
Bf 109G-6/G-10 (composites)

Right: This Bf 109G-10 is an amalgàmation of fuselage, undercarriage, propeller and cowling parts from Wk-Nr 151591, married to the wings of a G-6 instructional airframe supplied to Spain during World War 2, and powered by a DB 605D-1 engine found in a bricked-up room in a swimwear factory near Turin! The rare fighter has been restored in the colours of 30-kill nightfighter ace Major Friedrich-Karl Müller of NJG 11.

Miles M 38 Messenger

UK

Type: single-engined liaison and VIP communications aircraft **Accommodation:** pilot and three passengers

Designed and built at the request of a number of senior army officers to fulfil the air observation post (AOP) role, the Miles M 38 failed to achieve series production in substantial quantities simply because its creator, George Miles, had failed to obtain government authority before constructing his aircraft! The Messenger embodied all the criterion deemed desirable by the operators in the frontline, namely an ability to carry at least two people, a radio and other military equipment and be fitted with a modicum of armour plating. The design exhibited its ability to operate from small fields bordered by trees in any weather, whilst being flown by pilots with limited experience and having been subjected to the minimum of servicing. The prototype had displayed all these attributes by the beginning of 1943, but the only order received by Miles from the Ministry of Aircraft Production was for 21 machines to fill the VIP communications role in 1944. Amongst those deemed senior enough to receive their own personal Messengers were Field Marshal Sir Bernard Montgomery and Marshal of the RAF Lord Tedder. Postwar, 19 of the 21 Messengers were passed on to private owners, whilst Miles constructed a further 71 for civilian use. Today, four Messengers remain in airworthy condition in the UK.

Specification:

Dimensions:
Length: 24 ft 0 in (7.32 m)
Wingspan: 36 ft 2 in (11.02 m)
Height: 9 ft 6 in (2.90 m)

Weights:
Empty: 1518 lb (689 kg)
Max T/O: 1900 lb (862 kg)

Performance:
Max Speed: 116 mph (187 kmh)
Range: 260 miles (418 km)
Powerplant: de Havilland Gipsy Major (Mk 1/4A) or Blackburn Cirrus Major III (Mk 2A)
Output: 140 hp (104.3 kW) and 155 hp (114.4 kW) respectively

First Flight Date:
12 September 1942

Surviving Airworthy Variant(s):
Mk 2A and Mk 4B

Right: Bristol-based Messenger Mk 2A G-AIEK has flown for many years in the markings worn by Field Marshal Sir Bernard Montgomery's personal Mk 4, RG333 of the 2nd Tactical Air Force's Communications Squadron. The latter machine held the distinction of being the first RAF aircraft to land in France following the D-Day invasion of 6 June 1944 – RG333 was later written off in Germany on 22 August 1945.

Mitsubishi A6M Zero-Sen

Japan

Type: single-engined fighter **Accommodation:** pilot

Aside from the initial surprise of the early-morning raid on Pearl Harbor on 7 December 1941, perhaps the biggest shock for American forces in the Pacific was the outstanding performance of the Imperial Japanese Navy's main carrier fighter, the beautifully proportioned Mitsubishi A6M2 Zero-Sen. It was both fast and manoeuvrable, armed with two 20 mm cannon and two 7.7 mm machine guns, and possessed the incredible range of 1930 miles using a centreline drop tank. Totally dismissed by British and American intelligence in the months leading up to the Pearl Harbor attack, the Zero traced its origins back to an Imperial Navy Staff requirement issued in 1937 for an aircraft to replace the Mitsubishi A5M, then the main fleet fighter. Work progressed smoothly, and the first prototype flew on 1 April 1939, with the first fighters entering service the following year. Some 10,500 Zeros were built by Mitsubishi in no fewer than eight different sub-types, and although outclassed by more powerful US fighters from late 1943 onwards, the Zero retained a modicum of 'combatability' due to its weight. By late 1944 most Japanese squadrons were being forced to fly from land bases as the once proud carrier force had been all but sunk. Finally, in a last-ditch act, many Zeros were hastily converted into 'aerial bombs' and flung at the vast invasion fleets in *kamikaze* attacks off the Philippines, Iwo Jima and Okinawa. Tw examples are maintained in airworthy condition in the USA today, whilst several more are being restored to fly.

Specification:

Dimensions:
Length: 29 ft 9 in (9.07 m)
Wingspan: 36 ft 1 in (11.00 m)
Height: 11 ft 5.75 in (3.50 m)

Weights:
Empty: 4175 lb (1894 kg)
Max T/O: 6504 lb (2950 kg)

Performance:
Max Speed: 346 mph (557 kmh)
Range: 1118 miles (1800 km)
Powerplant: Nakajima NK1C Sakae 12 (A6M2), Sakai 21 (A6M5) and Pratt & Whitney R-1830 Twin Wasp (Museum of Flying A6M2)
Output: 925 hp (690 kW), 1130 hp (843 kW) and 1200 hp (894 kW) respectively

First Flight Date:
1 April 1939

Surviving Airworthy Variant(s):
A6M2 and A6M5

Right: This A6M2 was recovered from the jungles of Papua New Guinea in 1968 and restored to flying condition in Canada. It was then flown by the Confederate Air Force for a decade from 1985 to 1995, until sold to the Museum of Flying at Santa Monica in California.

Noorduyn UC-64 Norseman

Canada

Type: single-engined high-wing utility transport **Accommodation:** pilot and up to seven passengers

An unglamorous utility hack that was based on a pre-war design from Canadian manufacturer Noorduyn, the Norseman saw widespread use with the USAAF and the RCAF during the later years of World War 2. Rugged in the extreme, the Norseman was built to withstand the rigours of a Canadian winter, and to this end it was cleared to operate on skis, as well as wheels and floats. Although the initial prototype and production variants came fitted with a Wright R-975-E3 radial engine of 420 hp (313 kW), operators quickly realised that this unit was underpowered and substituted a 550 hp (410 kW) Pratt & Whitney Wasp in its pla The Norseman initially enjoyed success only in the civil market, but in 1942 both the RCAF and USAAF acquired Mk VIs (the Americans designated their aircraft UC-64As) in substantial quantities – 749 were built for the USAAF alone. These machines found employment across the globe, where their sound construction, ease of maintenance and useful load carrying capacity made them popular with both frontline and secondary units alike. Perhaps the most (in)famous wartime incident involving a UC-64A was the disappearance of legendary USAAF 'Big Band' leader Major Glenn Miller in a Norseman during a flight from southern England to Paris in December 1944. A handful of ex-military and civilian Norseman can still be found flying in North America today, although few remain in commercial use.

Specification:

Dimensions:
Length: 32 ft 0 in (9.75 m)
Wingspan: 51 ft 6 in (15.70 m)
Height: 10 ft 3 in (3.12 m)

Weights:
Empty: 4690 lb (2123 kg)
Max T/O: 7400 lb (3357 kg)

Performance:
Max Speed: 155 mph (249 kmh)
Range: 1150 miles (1851 km)
Powerplant: Pratt & Whitney R-1340-AN-1 Wasp
Output: 550 hp (410 kW)

First Flight Date:
14 November 1935

Surviving Airworthy Variant(s):
UC-64A and Norseman VI

Right: This ex-USAAF UC-64A has been restored in ETO D-Day markings from mid-1944.

35314

North American T-6 Texan/SNJ/Harvard USA

Type: single-engined advanced trainer **Accommodation:** two pilots in tandem

For decades known simply as the 'pilot maker', the T-6/SNJ/Harvard has gone from being *the* global trainer, to the world's most populous 'warbird'. Derived from the NA-16 (see inter-war entry) and initially designated the BC-1, the advanced trainer soon became the AT-6 in USAAC service. The refinement of the Texan coincided with a rapid expansion of the US armed forces, and orders flowed in ranging in size from 94 basic AT-6s requested in 1939, to an accumulated total of 3404 AT-6Ds less than five years later. In total, more than 17,000 airframes were built to train all manner of combat pilots across the continental USA. Foreign customers also appreciated the merits of this robust trainer, the RAF showing interest in the aircraft as early as June 1938 when the British Purchasing Commission placed an order for 200 BC-1s, dubbed 'Harvard Is'. These were quickly issued to training units both in the UK and Southern Rhodesia, and over the next seven years 5000+ Harvards in five distinct marks were procured principally through Lend-Lease, and issued to the RCAF and RNZAF, as well as the RAF. Although the T-6's (as it was designated postwar) career in the US forces ceased at the end of the 1950s, it continued to be the staple basic trainer for many nations across the globe well into the 1970s. In excess of 350 T-6s remain airworthy, the bulk of which are based in North America.

Specification:

Dimensions:
Length: 29 ft 6 in (8.99 m)
Wingspan: 42 ft 0.25 in (12.80 m)
Height: 11 ft 9 in (3.58 m)

Weights:
Empty: 4158 lb (1886 kg)
Max T/O: 5300 lb (2404 kg)

Performance:
Max Speed: 205 mph (330 kmh)
Range: 1118 miles (1800 km)
Powerplant: Pratt & Whitney R-1340-AN-1 Wasp
Output: 550 hp (410 kW)

First Flight Date:
April 1936 (NA-26)

Surviving Airworthy Variant(s):
AT-16, AT-6/A/B/C/D/F/G, SNJ-2/-3/-4/-5/-5B/-6/-7/-7C, T-6D/G/H/J and Harvard Mk II/IIB/III and 4

Right: These ex-RCAF Harvard Mk 4s are based at Woodstock, Ontario, with Norm Beckham of the Canadian Harvard Aircraft Association. Both had been originally taken on charge with the RCAF in 1952.

53
3222
C-FMKA
RCAF
242
20242

North American B-25 Mitchell

USA

Type: twin-engined medium bomber **Accommodation:** four/six-man crew

Built in response to a pre-war USAAC proposal for a twin-engined attack bomber by a company with no previous experience of multi-engined aircraft, bombers or high performance machinery, the B-25 Mitchell proved to be one of the most versatile combat aircraft to see action in World War 2. Tailored to fit USAAC Circular Proposal 38-385, the prototype carried out successful flight trials, but North American was encouraged to further improve their design by the army, who now stated that any future medium bomber would have to carry a payload of 2400 lbs – twice that originally stipulated in 38-385. Re-engineered, and considerably enlarged, the definitive production airframe was designated the NA-62. So impressed with what they saw on the drawing board, the USAAC ordered 184 aircraft (to be designated the B-25) before metal had even been cut on the revised design. Christened the Mitchell after maverick army bomber proponent William 'Billy' Mitchell, the bomber duly fought not only with the USAAF in the Pacific and ETO/MTO, but also with US Navy/Marine Corps, British, Dutch and Australian units. By war's end, the veteran Mitchell was still in production, having outlasted its rivals from Douglas and Martin to become the most prolific American medium bomber of the conflict – built to the tune of 9889 airframes. Its use by various air arms well into the 1950s has secured the survival of a number of B-25s, and today some 34 remain airworthy across the globe.

Specification:

Dimensions:
Length: 52 ft 11 in (16.13 m)
Wingspan: 67 ft 7 in (20.60 m)
Height: 16 ft 4 in (4.98 m)

Weights:
Empty: 19 480 lb (8836 kg)
Max T/O: 35 000 lb (15 876 kg)

Performance:
Max Speed: 272 mph (438 kmh)
Range: 1350 miles (2173 km)
Powerplant: two Wright R-2600-9 Cyclones (B-25), R-2600-13 (B-25C/D) or R-2600-29 (B-25H/J and TB-25N)
Output: 3400 hp (2536 kW) for the R-2600-9/-13 and 3700 hp (2760.20 kW) for the -29

First Flight Date:
January 1939

Surviving Airworthy Variant(s):
RB-25, B-25C/D/H/J, TB/VB-25N and Mitchell Mk II/III

***Right:* TB-25N 44-86785 *Georgia Mae* and TB-25J 44-86797 *"OL GRAY MARE"* are both owned by Wiley Sanders of Troy, Alabama.**

"Georgia Mae"
S
486 785
W S
486797

North American A-36/P-51A Mustang USA

Type: single-engined fighter **Accommodation:** pilot

The Mustang has its origins in a British Purchasing Commission deal struck with North American in April 1940 for an advanced fighter to supplant the Spitfire. With the RAF facing an impending Luftwaffe onslaught, the agreement stipulated that the American company had to have a completed prototype – tailored to the British specifications – ready for flight within 120 days of the original submission. Fortunately, North American had already made a start independently of the British deal, their NA-73X design incorporating some of the lessons gleaned from aerial combat in Europe. Three days short of the required date the airframe was completed, and testing soon bore out the 'rightness' of the design, the aircraft (christened the 'Mustang I' by the British) handling beautifully thanks to its revolutionary semi-laminar flow airfoil wing. However, it was soon realised that the fighter's Allison V-1710 'ran out of steam' above 17,000 ft due to its lack of a supercharger. By that stage in the war, fighter combat was taking place at ceilings well in excess of 20,000 ft where the 'thin' air starved a conventionally aspirated engine, so the RAF Mustang Is were fitted with cameras and relegated to the low-level tactical reconnaissance and army co-operation roles. The USAAF, too, realising that the Mustang was no good as a fighter above medium altitude, ordered a small number of A-36As and P-51As for ground attack tasks instead. One A-36A and three P-51As are still flown in the USA today.

Specification:

Dimensions:
Length: 32 ft 9.5 in (9.81 m)
Wingspan: 37 ft 0.5 in (11.29 m)
Height: 12 ft 2 in (3.72 m)

Weights:
Empty: 6300 lb (2858 kg)
Max T/O: 8600 lb (3901 kg)

Performance:
Max Speed: 390 mph (628 kmh)
Range: 450 miles (724 km)
Powerplant: Allison V-1710-81
Output: 1200 hp (1014 kW)

First Flight Date:
26 October 1940

Surviving Airworthy Variant(s):
A-36A and P-51A

Right: A former pylon racer, P-51A 43-6274 was restored by The Yanks Air Museum at Chino between 1978 and 1993. Although fully airworthy, the fighter has never been flown.

36274
H
XA

North American P-51C/D Mustang USA

Type: single-engined fighter **Accommodation:** pilot

As detailed in the previous entry, the Mustang I's performance had let it down in the high-altitude dogfights that characterised air combat in Europe. However, the airframe itself was more than sound, so the RAF quickly searched for a replacement powerplant and came up with the Merlin 61. Once mated with this battle-proven powerplant, the aircraft's performance was startling – a communiqué of the findings was immediately sent to North American, and the rest is history. Car builder Packard was granted a licence to build the Merlin as the Packard V-1650, and North American followed the British lead in mating surplus P-51A airframes with the 'new' powerplant. The Merlin-powered P-51B made its combat debut over Europe in December 1943, just when the USAAF's much-vaunted daylight bomber campaign had begun to falter due to incredible losses. Here was their 'knight in shinning armour', capable of escorting B-17s and B-24s throughout their hazardous missions. Over the next 19 months of war in Europe, the Mustang steadily became the dominant USAAF fighter. The RAF, too, got their hands on well over 1000 Merlin-powered aircraft through Lend-Lease arrangements. In total over 14,819 P-51s were built by North American, plus a further 200 under-licence in Australia. The fighter continued to serve in a frontline capacity with the USAF into the early 1950s, and further afield in Central and South America until the 1970s. Today, over 160 Mustangs remain airworthy, the majority of these being based in the USA.

Specification:

Dimensions:
Length: 32 ft 9.5 in (9.81 m)
Wingspan: 37 ft 0.5 in (11.29 m)
Height: 13 ft 8 in (4.10 m)

Weights:
Empty: 7125 lb (3230 kg)
Max T/O: 11 600 lb (5260 kg)

Performance:
Max Speed: 437 mph (703 kmh)
Range: 1300 miles (2092 km)
Powerplant: Packard V-1650-3 (Rolls-Royce Merlin 61) or V-1650-7 (P-51D), and V-1650-9 (P-51H)
Output: 1520 hp (1133.92 kW), 1590 hp (1186.14 kW) and 2218 hp (1654.62 kW) respectively

First Flight Date:
13 October 1942

Surviving Airworthy Variant(s):
P-51C/D/K, TF-51D, ETF-51D, RB-51, F-6K, Cavalier, CA-17/-18 (Australian-built)

Right: P-51D 44-74404 was issued to the RCAF as 9276 on 11 January 1951, and remained in their employ until 27 December 1957. Damaged in a crash-landing in 1960, the Mustang's remains changed hands four times until acquired by present owner, Robert J Odegaard of Kindred, North Dakota. He duly set about restoring the veteran fighter between 1990 and 1995. At least 20 other Mustangs supplied parts to 44-74404 during the rebuild.

Dazzling Donna
474404
BC
H

Percival Proctor

UK

Type: single-engined radio trainer and communications aircraft

Accommodation: pilot and up to three passengers

Based on Percival's highly successful pre-war Vega Gull (of which the RAF acquired 15 just prior to the outbreak of war), the Proctor was tailored to an Air Ministry Specification for a communications and radio training aircraft. With the first prototype having duly completed its service trials with little fuss, production Proctor Is started reaching the RAF in mid-1940. Following the building of 247 Mk Is (all of which were configured as communications aircraft with dual flying controls), Percival commenced construction of 175 Mk IIs and 437 Mk IIIs, all of which were built as radio trainers. The final variant to enter RAF service was the Mk IV (258 delivered), which boasted a longer and deeper fuselage to accommodate four crew/passengers. Although built as radio trainers, some Mk IVs were later stripped of their electronic equipment and re-configured as communications hacks. After the war more than 200 Proctors were sold to civilian buyers, although some Mk IVs were retained by communications squadrons until 1955. Percival also produced 150 'civilianised' Proctors in the shape of the Mk 5, four of which were also acquired by the RAF for use by air attachés. Due to its all-wooden construction, the Proctor has not worn the harsh British winters well, and today just three examples remain flyable.

Specification:

Dimensions:
Length: 28 ft 2 in (8.59 m)
Wingspan: 39 ft 6 in (12.04 m)
Height: 7 ft 3 in (2.21 m)

Weights:
Empty: 2370 lb (1075 kg)
Max T/O: 3500 lb (1588 kg)

Performance:
Max Speed: 160 mph (257 kmh)
Range: 500 miles (805 km)
Powerplant: de Havilland Gipsy Queen II
Output: 210 hp (157 kW)

First Flight Date:
8 October 1939

Surviving Airworthy Variant(s):
Proctor I, II and IV

Right: The sole Proctor I in airworthy condition, R7524 was originally issued to the RAF's No 1 Elementary Flying Training School in 1941. This aircraft underwent a comprehensive rebuild in the mid-1970s.

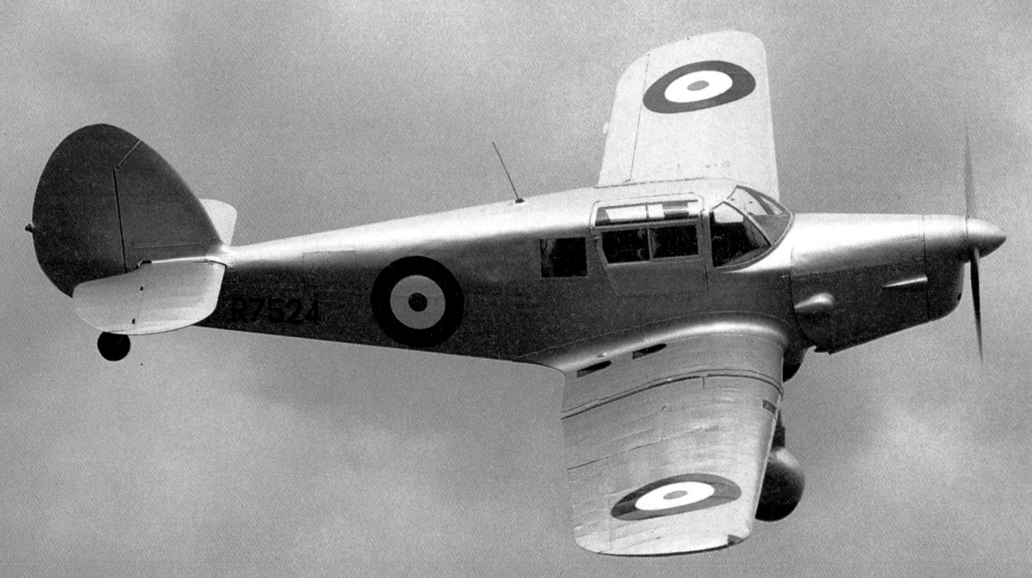
R7524

Piper O-59/L-4/L-18 Grasshopper USA

Type: single-engined high-wing liaison/observation aircraft **Accommodation:** pilot and observer/passenger in tandem

As with the Aeronca L-3 and Taylorcraft L-2 described elsewhere in this chapter, Piper's L-4 Grasshopper was also heavily used by the USAAC in the artillery spotting and frontline liaison roles. Like its contemporaries, the L-4 was essentially a militarised version of a successful civilian design of the previous decade – in this case the exceptional Taylor Aircraft Company (later Piper) J-3 Cub of the mid-1930s. The army air corps first came to realise the usefulness of the design during large-scale military manoeuvres held in August 1941, which saw 44 hastily camouflaged Cubs employed in the field. In the aftermath of the exercise the USAAC ordered 948 O-59s (redesignated L-4s by the time they entered service), which boasted certain changes over the civilian J-3, including an improved tandem cockpit arrangement. Following the Pearl Harbor raid, hundreds of ex-civilian Cubs were also impressed into military service, and by 1943 the combined total of civil and military Cubs/Grasshoppers built was nearing the 10,000 mark. In a rather odd move, Piper also received a request by the USAAC to produce a training glider utilising the Grasshopper's airframe minus its engine and undercarriage. This it duly did, and the army subsequently purchased 250 examples with the designation TG-8. The L-4 remained in service postwar, with the improved L-18 variant seeing further action with the USAF in Korea in the early 1950s. Dozens of authentic Grasshoppers and 'retro-militarised' J-3s remain airworthy today, scattered across the globe.

Specification:

Dimensions:
Length: 22 ft 0 in (6.71 m)
Wingspan: 35 ft 3 in (10.74 m)
Height: 6 ft 8 in (2.03 m)

Weights:
Empty: 730 lb (331 kg)
Max T/O: 1220 lb (533 kg)

Performance:
Max Speed: 85 mph (137 kmh)
Range: 190 miles (306 km)
Powerplant: Continental O-170-3
Output: 65 hp (48 kW)

First Flight Date:
1937 (Cub trainer) and 1941 (YO-59 military derivative)

Surviving Airworthy Variant(s):
J-3 Cub, O-59, L-4A/B/H/J and L-18B/C

Right: Grasshopper 45-55214 was one of 1680 L-4Js delivered to the USAAF, this model boasting a variable-pitch propeller.

NC
51992

Polikarpov Po-2

USSR

Type: single-engined biplane trainer/utility aircraft

Accommodation: pilot and observer/passenger in tandem

Believed by many aviation historians to be the most produced military aircraft bar none, Polikarpov's humble Po-2 can trace its lineage back to a VVS (air force) request for a simple and reliable elementary trainer built around the then new M-11 radial engine. Originally designated the U-2, production aircraft were much praised for their positive longitudinal stability and reluctance to spin. Aside from its instructional role, the new biplane design proved to be a veritable 'maid of all work' as it undertook agricultural flying, air ambulance tasks and civilian pilot training for Aeroflot. In excess of 13,500 aircraft had been built up to mid-1941, and a further 6500 were completed before production ended in the USSR in 1944. That same year the aircraft was redesignated the Po-2 in honour of N N Polikarpov, who had died on 30 July 1944. Aside from its more peaceful employment, the Po-2 was also adapted for night intruder sorties over the Russian Front, aircraft conducting nuisance sorties against German targets – the Po-2LNB could carry 441 lb (200 kg) of ordnance. Postwar, the aircraft was returned to production in Poland in 1948, with the CSS-13 being built for agricultural work and the CSS-S-13 for the air ambulance role. A large number of Po-2s remain airworthy in the former Eastern Bloc today, and a handful have also been exported into the West.

Specification:

Dimensions:
Length: 26 ft 9.33 in (8.17 m)
Wingspan: 37 ft 4.75 in (11.40 m)
Height: 9 ft 1 in (2.25 m)

Weights:
Empty: 1631 lb (740 kg)
Max T/O: 2756 lb (1250 kg)

Performance:
Max Speed: 87 mph (140 kmh)
Range: 448 miles (720 km)

Powerplant: Shvetsov M-11/G/D/K or Okromechko-developed M-11F/FM/M/FR/FR-1/FN
Output: ranging from 100 hp (48 kW) through to 200 hp (96 kW)

First Flight Date:
7 January 1928 (U-2)

Surviving Airworthy Variant(s):
U-2, Po-2A/VS/S/L and CSS-13

Right: This camouflaged Po-2 is one of a small number of Polikarpov biplane trainers currently flown in Western Europe.

045

Republic P-47 Thunderbolt

USA

Type: single-engined fighter **Accommodation:** pilot

The original P-47 design was produced to meet a 1940 USAAC requirement for a lightweight interceptor similar in size and stature to the Spitfire and Bf 109. Powered by Allison's ubiquitous V-1710-39 1150 hp inline engine, the XP-47A was to boast just two 0.50-in machine guns as armament and lacked any protective armour or self-sealing tanks. However, combat reports filtering in from Europe proved the folly of a lightweight fighter, and the USAAC modified its design requirements to include an eight-gun fitment, heavy armour plating and a self-sealing fuel system. Republic responded with an all-new design, powered, crucially, by a turbocharged R-2800 Double Wasp radial engine. Despite initial reliability problems with its powerplant, production of the Republic design forged ahead. The first P-47Bs joined the Eighth Air Force in Britain in late 1942 to undertake the much needed escort role for the latter's growing heavy bomber force. Built to absorb much damage, and rock steady as a gun platform, the Thunderbolt was soon holding its own over German skies. The arrival of the definitive P-47D in late 1943 was followed by the advent of the 'bubble top' Thunderbolt, which duly became the favoured mount over the 'razorback' 'Jug'. Some 15,677 Thunderbolts were eventually built, and a number of P-47Ns soldiered on with the Air National Guard, and a handful of other air arms, into the early 1950s. Today, twelve P-47s remain airworthy – eleven in the USA and one in the UK.

Specification:

Dimensions:
Length: 36 ft 1.25 in (11.03 m)
Wingspan: 40 ft 9.25 in (12.40 m)
Height: 14 ft 7 in (4.44 m)

Weights:
Empty: 10 700 lb (4853 kg)
Max T/O: 19 400 lb (8800 kg)

Performance:
Max Speed: 428 mph (690 kmh)
Range: 1000 miles (1600 km)
Powerplant: Pratt & Whitney R-2800-59 Double Wasp (D) or R-2800-57/-77 (M/N)
Output: 2300 hp (1715.80 kW) and 2800 hp (2088 kW) respectively

First Flight Date:
6 May 1941

Surviving Airworthy Variant(s):
P-47D/TP-47D, P-47G/TP-47G, YP-47M and P-47N

Right: P-47D 44-90447 served with the Yugoslavian Air Force during the 1950s/60s, before being put on display in a children's playground in Belgrade. Purchased in extremely poor condition by the Santa Monica-based Museum of Flying, the 'Jug' was put through a full rebuild to flying condition between 1989-93, and today flies in the colours of the 353rd FG.

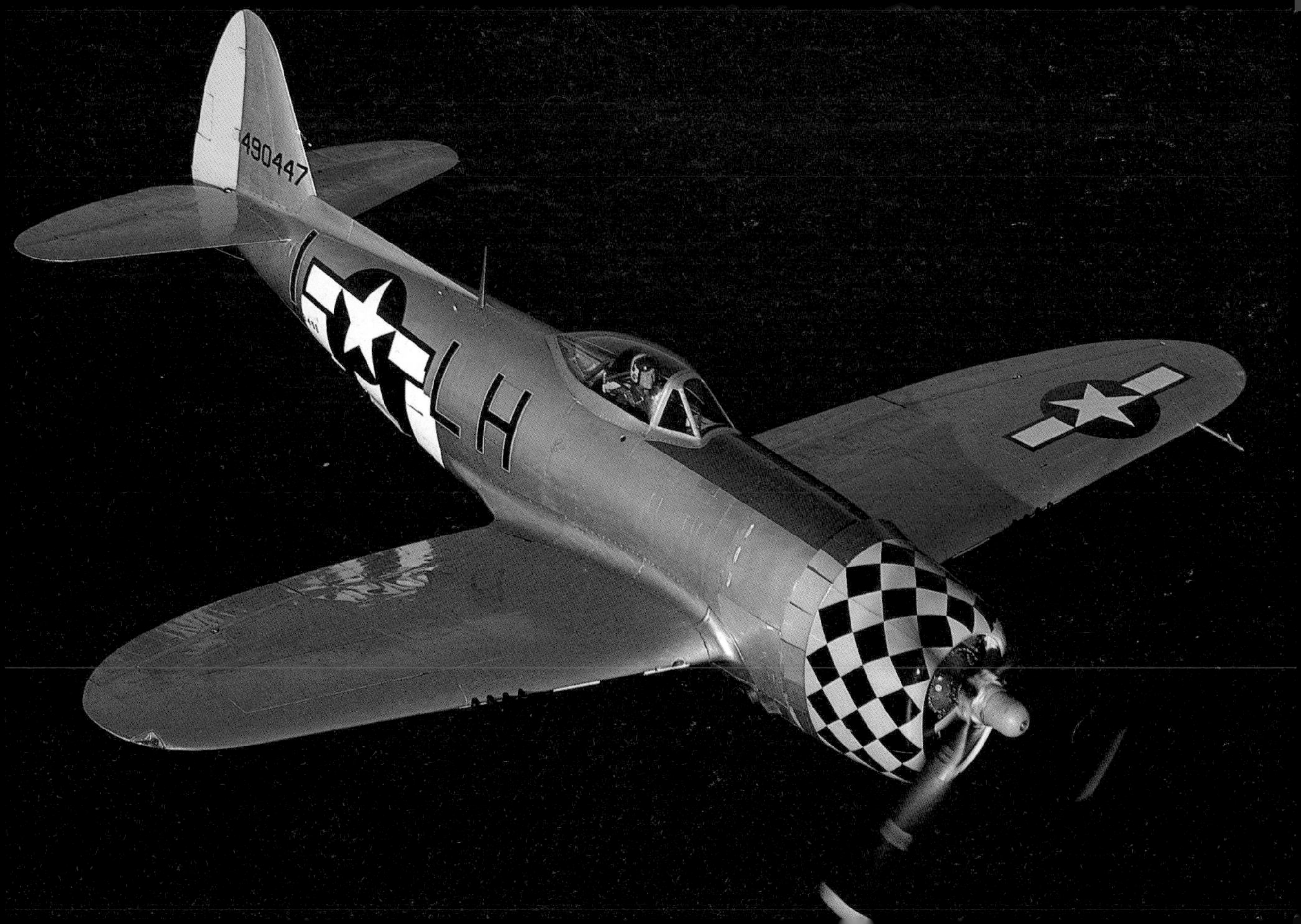
490447
LH

Saab B17A

Sweden

Type: single-engined light bomber/reconnaissance aircraft **Accommodation:** two-man crew in tandem

The first indigenous aircraft designed and built by Swedish manufacturer Svenska Aeroplan AB (Saab), the B17 started life in 1937 as the L10 two-seat reconnaissance monoplane. Adhering to strict neutrality, Sweden found itself in a difficult position when it came to procuring new aircraft for its air force in the lead up to World War 2 as traditional suppliers from Germany, the USA and Britain could not fulfil outstanding orders. Saab was therefore formed with the dual purpose of licence-building foreign aircraft, and working on new designs of Swedish origin. Powered by licence-built powerplants, the B17 was a conventional design capable of carrying ordnance both internally and externally. Its rugged construction allowed it to perform as a dive-bomber too, whilst Saab also offered variants equipped with floats or skis. The first version to enter service in late 1941 was the B17B (powered by the Bristol Mercury XXIV), followed by the B17C (fitted with a Piaggio P XIbis RC 40) and finally the Twin Wasp-powered B17A. A total of 322 production aircraft were built between 1 December 1941 and 16 September 1944, with B17s equipping six light bomber and reconnaissance wings within the Swedish Air Force. The type was finally retired from a combat role in 1948, although 20 served on into the 1960s as civilian-operated target tugs for the air force in Sweden. Ethiopia became the only foreign buyer of the B17 in 1947 when it acquired 46 ex-Swedish Air Force A-models, these remaining in service until the 1970s.

Specification:

Dimensions:
Length: 32 ft 2 in (9.8 m)
Wingspan: 45 ft 1 in (13.7 m)
Height: 13 ft 1 in (4.0 m)

Weights:
Empty: 5732 lb (2600 kg)
Max T/O: 8752 lb (3970 kg)

Performance:
Max Speed: 270 mph (435 kmh)
Range: 1120 miles (1800 km)
Powerplant: Pratt & Whitney R-1830 Twin Wasp
Output: 1200 hp (895 kW)

First Flight Date:
18 May 1940

Surviving Airworthy Variant(s):
B17A

Right: B17A Fv17239 is the sole airworthy example of its type today, this machine being one of two owned by the Swedish Air Force museum. Operated as a target tug between 1955-68, the aircraft was restored to flying condition by Saab and air force staff in 1997. It presently wears the colours of an F7 Wing aircraft in the 1940s.

7

Stinson AT-19 Reliant

USA

Type: single-engined high-wing navigation/radio trainer and communications aircraft

Accommodation: pilot and three passengers

Derived from the successful high-wing cabin monoplane of the 1930s, the first militarised Reliants were indeed ex-civilian aircraft impressed into USAAC service at the outbreak of war – these aircraft were designated UC-81s. A handful of Reliants had actually been acquired prior to the outbreak of hostilities by the US Navy and Coast Guard, these machines being designated XR3Q-1s and RQ-1s respectively. Maintaining the nautical flavour, the largest customer for the Reliant was in fact the Royal Navy, who purchased 500 Reliant Is (the USAAF designated them AT-19s) under Lend-Lease agreements for its Fleet Air Arm (FAA). The first examples arrived in Britain in the summer of 1943, and the aircraft subsequently served in the radio, navigational and photographic training roles, as well as performing general utility flights. No less than 12 FAA units operated Reliant Is until war's end, when around 350 were returned to the USA, reconditioned by Stinson and sold to civilian buyers. A healthy number of ex-military Stinsons remain airworthy today, particularly in North America.

Specification:

Dimensions:

Length: 30 ft 0 in (9.14 m)
Wingspan: 41 ft 10.5 in (12.76 m)
Height: 8 ft 7 in (2.62 m)

Weights:

Empty: 2810 lb (1275 kg)
Max T/O: 4000 lb (1814 kg)

Performance:

Max Speed: 141 mph (227 kmh)
Range: 810 miles (1303 km)
Powerplant: Lycoming R-680
Output: 290 hp (216 kW)

First Flight Date:

1933 (SR/SR-2 civilian variant)

Surviving Airworthy Variant(s):

Reliant (civilian), UC-81 and AT-19

Right: This US-based Reliant wears a glossy rendition of FAA drab grey. Unlike wartime naval aircraft, this machine has wheel spats, which tends to suggest a civilian origin.

24

Stinson O-49/L-1 Vigilant

USA

Type: single-engined high-wing liaison/observation aircraft **Accommodation:** pilot and one passenger in tandem

One of three manufacturers to submit designs in response to a requirement issued by the USAAC in 1940 for a new light observation aircraft, Stinson beat off rivals Bellanca (YO-50) and Ryan (YO-51) to be duly awarded a contract for 142 examples of its O-49. To achieve the low-speed and high-lift performance stipulated by the army air corps, Stinson had fitted the entire leading edge of the aircraft's wing with automatically-operating slats, whilst the trailing edge boasted wide-span slotted flaps and large slotted ailerons. By the time production of the Vigilant (as it was dubbed in RAF service) had begun, Stinson had been acquired by Vultee, although the new owners did not alter the aircraft's design. A follow-on contract for a further 182 Vigilants saw the aircraft modified with a slightly lengthened fuselage and minor detail and equipment changes, resulting in a designation change to O-49A. As previously mentioned, the RAF received around 100 Vigilants in 1941-42, the British using the type for both light liaison and artillery spotting predominantly in Tunisia, Sicily and Italy. All O-49/O-49As became L-1/L-1As in 1942, whilst aircraft modified into air ambulances (L-1B/C), glider pick-up trainers (L-1D) and floatplanes (L-1E/Fs) also received designation changes. Only two batches of L-1s were acquired, as the lightweight Grasshopper family was to prove far more effective in the observation role. A handful of Vigilants have survived into the 1990s in North America.

Specification:

Dimensions:
Length: 34 ft 3 in (10.44 m)
Wingspan: 50 ft 11 in (15.52 m)
Height: 10 ft 2 in (3.10 m)

Weights:
Empty: 2670 lb (1211 kg)
Max T/O: 3400 lb (1542 kg)

Performance:
Max Speed: 122 mph (196 kmh)
Range: 280 miles (451 km)
Powerplant: Lycoming R-680-9
Output: 295 hp (220 kW)

First Flight Date:
Summer 1940

Surviving Airworthy Variant(s):
O-49/A and L-1/A

Right: This O-49 has been restored as an air ambulance, although it seems to lack the dorsal door specially fitted to wartime examples.

Stinson O-62/L-5 Sentinel

USA

Type: single-engined high-wing light liaison aircraft **Accommodation:** pilot and one passenger in tandem

Like the Aeronca, Piper and Taylorcraft designs detailed in this chapter, the Stinson L-5 was derived from a successful civilian design evaluated by the USAAC in 1941, although it was not part of the US Army trial of August that year. Six 105 Voyagers were initially acquired (designated YO-54s), and after minor modifications had been carried out to 'militarise' them (changing the cabin layout from three to two seats, improving visibility out of the cockpit and generally strengthening the fuselage and undercarriage), an initial order for 275 O-62s (as they were redesignated) was placed with Stinson. A follow-on purchase of 1456 machines was received by the manufacturer in early 1942, and by the time the first of these aircraft reached the USAAC, all O-62s had been redesignated L-5s. During the type's long service career, a number of modifications were carried out which made the aircraft more suited to specific missions – an upward-hinged door was fitted to allow the L-5B to carry a stretcher, a K-20 reconnaissance camera was installed in the L-5C, and the G-model introduced the more powerful O-435-11 190 hp (142 kW) engine. Aside from USAAF use of the aircraft, the RAF utilised 100 (christened Sentinels) mainly in Burma, whilst the Marine Corps acquired 306 as OY-1s – the Y denoted that these aircraft were Consolidated-built, following the latter company's merger with Vultee in 1943. Postwar, the L-5 also saw further action with the USAF in Korea.

Specification:

Dimensions:
Length: 24 ft 1 in (7.34 m)
Wingspan: 34 ft 0 in (10.36 m)
Height: 7 ft 11 in (2.41 m)

Weights:
Empty: 1550 lb (703 kg)
Max T/O: 2020 lb (916 kg)

Performance:
Max Speed: 130 mph (209 kmh)
Range: 420 miles (676 km)
Powerplant: Lycoming O-435-1 or O-435-11 (L-5G)
Output: 185 hp (138 kW) and 190 hp (142 kW)

First Flight Date:
1940

Surviving Airworthy Variant(s):
O-62, L-5/A/B/C/E/G and OY-1

Right: More than 30 Sentinels are presently flying in North America, with the vast majority of these aircraft having only been restored to airworthiness in the past decade.

N9795F
08
08

Taylorcraft O-57/L-2 Grasshopper

USA

Type: single-engined high-wing light liaison aircraft **Accommodation:** pilot and one passenger in tandem

The third design in the triumvirate of civilian two-seaters trialled by the US Army in August 1941, the original Taylorcraft YO-57 was essentially a standard Model D hastily camouflaged in drab olive paint. All three aircraft were universally dubbed Grasshoppers, and similarly modified to improve crew visibility and airframe durability – to achieve the former, more cockpit glazing was fitted and trailing edge cut outs added at the wing root. An initial order for 336 O-57As was duly received by Taylorcraft in the wake of these design changes, followed by a further 140 in 1942. By the time delivery of the second batch had commenced, the reclassification of aircraft of this type from observation to liaison had taken place, resulting in all O-57/-57As becoming L-2/-2As. The two remaining batches of aircraft ordered from Taylorcraft comprised 490 L-2Bs optimised for field artillery spotting, and 900 L-2Ms, which had fully cowled engines and wing spoilers. As with Aeronca and Piper, Taylorcraft was also involved in producing a small number (253) of engineless gliders based on the L-2 design. Designated ST-100s, these machines were extensively used in the training of future frontline glider pilots. Many ex-military L-2s ended up on the US civilian register after the war, whilst other surplus Grasshoppers were supplied to friendly air arms across the globe. As with other observation types from World War 2, the Taylorcraft design has become a highly desirable, and relatively cheap, warbird (or 'warbug') over the past decade.

Specification:

Dimensions:
Length: 22 ft 9 in (6.93 m)
Wingspan: 35 ft 5 in (10.79 m)
Height: 8 ft 0 in (2.44 m)

Weights:
Empty: 875 lb (397 kg)
Max T/O: 1300 lb (590 kg)

Performance:
Max Speed: 88 mph (142 kmh)
Range: 230 miles (370 km)
Powerplant: Continental O-170-3
Output: 65 hp (48 kW)

First Flight Date:
1937

Surviving Airworthy Variant(s):
O-57/A and L-2/A/B/M

Right: This ex-USAAF L-2M, with its cowled engine and wing spoilers, has been a part of the Confederate Air Force collection for a number of years.

047731
N47731
CONFEDERATE AIR FORCE

Vickers-Supermarine Spitfire (Merlin) UK

Type: single-engined fighter **Accommodation:** pilot

The only British fighter to remain in production throughout World War 2 – over 22,500 were produced in mark numbers ranging from I through to 24 – the exploits of the Vickers-Supermarine Spitfire are legendary. Designed by Reginald J Mitchell following his experiences with the RAF's Schneider Trophy winning Supermarine floatplanes of the 1920s and 30s, prototype Spitfire K5054 first took to the skies on 5 March 1936, powered by the equally famous Rolls-Royce Merlin I engine. However, due to production problems encountered with the revolutionary stressed-skin construction of the fighter, it was to be another two-and-a-half years before the first Spitfire Is entered service. During its nine-year production life, the Spitfire's basic shape was to alter very little, but under the skin the story was vastly different. The power output of the Merlin was steadily increased to allow the fighter to compete on level terms with new German types, resulting in firstly the 'workhorse' Mk V and then the superlative Mk IX - the latter proving to be a match for the Bf 109F/G and Fw 190 at virtually all altitudes. The Spitfire performed sterling service in the photo-reconnaissance and fighter-bomber roles – indeed, in the last year of the war it proved to be more usefully employed as a dedicated ground attack aircraft than in its proven fighter role. Today, the Spitfire is an icon for the wartime exploits of the RAF, and the growing population of airworthy examples the world over will ensure that its fame lasts well into the next century.

Specification:

Dimensions: (all data for a Mk IX)
Length: 31 ft 1 in (9.47 m)
Wingspan: 36 ft 10 in (11.23 m)
Height: 12 ft 7.75 in (3.86 m)

Weights:
Empty: 5634 lb (2556 kg)
Max T/O: 9500 lb (4309 kg)

Performance:
Max Speed: 408 mph (657 kmh)
Range: 980 miles (1577 km) with external fuel
Powerplant: Rolls-Royce Merlin II/III (Mk IA), Merlin XII (Mk IIA), Merlin 45/46/50/50A/55/56 (Mk VB/VC) and Merlin 61/63/66/70 (Mk VIII, Mk IX, PR XI and Mk XVI)
Output: ranging from 1000 hp (746 kW) Merlin II to 1710 hp (1275.66 kW) Merlin 63

First Flight Date:
5 March 1936

Surviving Airworthy Variant(s):
Mk IA, Mk IIA, Mk VB/C, Mk VIII, Mk IX, PR XI and Mk XVI

Right: Nearly 50 Spitfires are currently maintained in airworthy condition across the globe, with the vast majority of these aircraft being Merlin-powered. Most are based in the UK, although examples can be found in North America, Australasia and South Africa. This ex-USAAF and South African Air Force HF Mk IXE (MA793, although it is painted as EN398) has been owned by the Santa Monica-based Museum of Flying since 1986.

EN398

Vickers-Supermarine Spitfire (Griffon) UK

Type: single-engined fighter **Accommodation:** pilot

The Mk XIV was without a doubt *the* wartime Spitfire that commanded the most respect! The reason for this was simple – its Rolls-Royce Griffon engine produced almost too much torque for the essentially pre-war airframe to handle, particularly when gathering speed for take-off. Indeed, a number of early Mk XIV pilots reported that the aircraft felt as if it wanted to 'rotate around the propeller', rather the other way round! Longitudinal problems aside, the Spitfire Mk XIV was an awesome fighter to fly thanks to the generous levels of horsepower cranked out by its Griffon engine, which more than offset the mark's increased weight due to the strengthening of the fuselage in preparation for the fitment of the new powerplant. Only 957 production Mk XIVs were built, with perhaps the type's finest hour coming in mid-1944 when its straight-line speed was used to great effect to counter the German V1 flying bombs – the Spitfire XIV could outpace all other frontline types, including the Tempest V. A considerable number of Griffon Spitfires were also sent to units in the Far East in the last year of the war, although in the most part they arrived too late to see action against the Japanese. The photo-reconnaissance variant of the Mk XIV was the PR XIX, which saw limited action in the final weeks of the war as the first of 225 examples arrived in the frontline.

Specification:

Dimensions:
(all data for a Mk XIV)
Length: 32 ft 8 in (9.96 m)
Wingspan: 36 ft 10 in (11.23 m)
Height: 12 ft 7.75 in (3.86 m)

Weights:
Empty: 6600 lb (2994 kg)
Max T/O: 8500 lb (3856 kg)

Performance:
Max Speed: 448 mph (721 kmh)
Range: 850 miles (1368 km) with external fuel
Powerplant: Rolls-Royce Griffon 61 (PR XIX) and Griffon 65/66 (Mk XIV)
Output: both 2035 hp (1518.11 kW)

First Flight Date:
Summer 1943

Surviving Airworthy Variant(s):
FR XIVC/E and PR XIX

Right: Four Mk XIVs and three PR XIX are presently operated as 'flyers', with two of the former variant being based in the USA and single examples in the UK and France – all three recce aircraft reside in England. One of the American 'Spits' is FR Mk XIVE NH749 of the Museum of Flying, seen here in company with the collection's HF Mk IXE MA793.

WR
H749

Vought F4U and Goodyear FG-1 Corsair USA

Type: single-engined fighter **Accommodation:** pilot

Designed as a lightweight fighter tailored around the most powerful piston engine then available, Vought's prototype XF4U-1 was ordered by the US Navy in June 1938 following a study of their V-166 proposal. In order to harness the immense power of the Pratt & Whitney XR-2800 Double Wasp engine, the largest diameter propeller ever fitted to a fighter up to that point in aeronautical history had to be bolted onto the front of the prototype – sufficient ground clearance for the prop was achieved through the use of a distinctive inverted gull wing. The future looked rosy for the aircraft, but modifications incorporated into the design as a result of lessons learned in combat over Europe detrimentally affected the Corsair. As a result of these problems it was left to land-based Marine Corps units to debut the aircraft in combat in early 1943 – the Fleet Air Arm also commenced operations with the Corsair that same year, but crucially from the decks of carriers. By mid-1944 Vought had rectified the handling problems, and the Corsair became suitable for deck operations with the US Navy. Unlike other navy fighters, the Corsair enjoyed a prosperous postwar career, with both Vought- and Goodyear-built aircraft remaining in service until after the Korean War. Indeed, the final F4U-7 (built for the French *Aéronavale*) did not roll off the Vought production line until 31 January 1952, this aircraft being the 12,571st, and last, Corsair built. Today, around 35 Corsairs remain airworthy, the majority of which are based in the USA.

Specification:

Dimensions:
Length: 33 ft 8 in (10.26 m)
Wingspan: 40 ft 11 in (12.47 m)
Height: 14 ft 9 in (4.50 m)

Weights:
Empty: 9205 lb (4175 kg)
Max T/O: 14 670 lb (6654 kg)

Performance:
Max Speed: 446 mph (718 kmh)
Range: 1560 miles (2511 km)
Powerplant: Pratt & Whitney R-2800-8W (F4U-1A/FG-1), R-2800-18W (F4U-4/-7) and R-2800-32E (F4U-5)
Output: 2000 hp (1492 kW), 2450 hp (1827.70 kW) and 2850 hp (2126.10 kW) respectively

First Flight Date:
29 May 1940

Surviving Airworthy Variant(s):
F4U-1A/-4/-4B/-5N/-5NL/-7 and FG-1D

Right: FG-1D BuNo 67087 is an ex-Salvadoran Air Force machine brought back to the USA in the 1980s. It made its first flight for almost three decades in 1996 following a long rebuild by Chuck Wentworth's Antique Aero at Rialto, California.

8

Westland Lysander

UK

Type: single-engined high-wing army co-operation aircraft **Accommodation:** pilot and observer

The first purpose-built army co-operation aircraft to enter service with the RAF, the Lysander filled a role previously performed by modified bomber types. Constructed to Air Ministry Specification A39/34, the first prototype, designated P.8 by Westland, made its maiden flight on 15 June 1936. Within three months an order had been placed for 144 aircraft, and the first unit duly re-equipped with the Lysander in June 1938. By 1939 production had got into full swing, and the RAF took delivery of 66 airframes. The type first saw action in France with the British Expeditionary Force (BEF) in May 1940 following the ending of the 'Phoney War', and once hostilities started, the true vulnerability of the type came to the fore. The Lysander was quickly relegated to second-line duties, and it was whilst performing tasks that had never previously been thought of for the aircraft that the type really came into its own. Its role with the clandestine Special Duties squadrons is the stuff of legend, the aircraft proving ideal for performing supply drops and transporting agents into and out of occupied Europe under the cover of darkness. The aircraft also proved useful in the air-sea rescue role over the Channel, and as a target tug. Some 1650 Lysanders were eventually built, a total which includes 225 constructed under licence in Canada. Of the 20 surviving Lysanders still in existence today (all Mk IIIs/TT IIIs), all bar one served with the RCAF.

Specification:

Dimensions:

Length: 30 ft 6 in (9.30 m)
Wingspan: 50 ft 0 in (15.24 m)
Height: 14 ft 6 in (4.42 m)

Weights:

Empty: 4365 lb (1980 kg)
Max T/O: 6318 lb (2866 kg)

Performance:

Max Speed: 212 mph (341 kmh)
Range: 600 miles (966 km)
Powerplant: Bristol Mercury XX or XXX
Output: 870 hp (649 kW)

First Flight Date:

15 June 1936

Surviving Airworthy Variant(s):

Mk IIIA and TT IIIA

Right: Lysander Mk IIIA G-BCWL is operated by The Aircraft Restoration Company at Duxford on behalf of Wessex Aviation. It currently wears the markings of a No 277 Sqn Mk III serving in the air-sea rescue role in 1942.

V9545
244

Yakovlev Yak-3UA

USSR

Type: single-engined fighter **Accommodation:** pilot

The second Yakovlev aircraft to be designated the Yak-3 (the first was abandoned in the autumn of 1941 due to poor engine reliability and a shortage of suitable building materials), this machine was built to fulfil a VVS requirement for an agile fighter capable of achieving its maximum performance at low altitude. By meeting these criterion, the fighter bestowed upon the Soviet Air Force the ability to maintain air superiority immediately over the battlefield – something that the Luftwaffe had enjoyed for much of the war on the Eastern Front. Utilising a modified Yak-1M fitted with a smaller wing, the prototypes completed their service trials in October 1943, by which time a small pre-series run of aircraft had been put into production at GAZ 286 at Kamensk Ural'ski. The Yak-3 was not officially cleared for full-scale production until June 1944, and the small number of regiments which rapidly re-equipped with the fighter soon proved its superiority over its Luftwaffe counterparts in a number of aerial engagements. The Yak-3 remained in production until early 1946, by which time 4848 had been built. In 1991, a deal was struck between OKB Yakovlev and the Museum of Flying, in Santa Monica, which has seen a handful of new-build Yak-3UAs built at Orenburg, in Russia, using original wartime drawings, fixtures, dies and tools, but powered by American Allison engines – hence the UA designation. A small number of radial-engined Yak-11 two-seaters (see postwar chapter) have also been converted into 'Allison Yak-3UAs'.

Specification:

Dimensions:

Length: 27 ft 10.25 in (8.49 m)
Wingspan: 30 ft 2.25 in (9.20 m)
Height: 7 ft 11.25 in (2.42 m)

Weights:

Empty: 4641 lb (2105 kg)
Max T/O: 5622 lb (2550 kg)

Performance:

Max Speed: 407 mph (655 kmh)
Range: 560 miles (900 km)
Powerplant: Allison 2L
Output: 1240 hp (925.04 kW)

First Flight Date:

28 February 1943 (original) and July 1993 (Yak-3UA)

Surviving Airworthy Variant(s):

Yak-3UA (OKB Yakovlev new-builds) and 'Yak-3UA' (Yak-11 re-engined with Allison 2L)

Right: The first two new-build Yak-3UAs to arrive in the USA formate for the camera near Mojave, California, in September 1994. The aircraft in the foreground (NX494DJ) is owned by Bruce Lockwood, whilst the second fighter (formerly NX915LP, but now ZK-YAK) resides with the Alpine Fighter Collection in New Zealand.

Yakovlev Yak-9UM

USSR

Type: single-engined fighter **Accommodation:** pilot

The original Yak-9 appeared in frontline service in late 1942, the aircraft being a lightweight version of the Yak-7, which had been the VVS's staple fighter since the end of 1941. By mid-1944, the Yak-9 outnumbered all other fighters in service on the Eastern Front, with a handful of variants fulfilling the long-range interception role, fighter-bomber tasks, nightfighting and close-support missions. The second generation Yak-9U/P version of the venerable fighter started development in late 1942 when a standard airframe had its Klimov M-105 engine replaced by the appreciably more powerful M-107 powerplant sourced from the same manufacturer. Aerodynamic improvements were also made to the overall fuselage, and plywood skinning replaced with light alloy. Designated the Yak-9U, the new fighter eventually reached VVS units in the final months of the war, its service entry having been drastically delayed due to engine problems. Indeed the first aircraft delivered by Yakovlev had to rely on the M-105 for motive power. Further development of the Yak-9 continued immediately postwar, with an enhanced version – cannon-armed Yak-9P – seeing use not only with the VVS, but also a number of other communist-bloc air forces, including North Korea. Production finally ceased in 1947 after 3900 Yak-9U/Ps (out of an overall total of 16,769 Yak-9s built) had been delivered. At least four static Yak-9U/Ps are still in existence, and in 1996 Russian-based constructor Strela built a flying Yak-9UM 'replica' for a US customer.

Specification:

Dimensions:
Length: 28 ft 0.25 in (8.55 m)
Wingspan: 32 ft 0.25 in (9.77 m)
Height: 9 ft 8.50 in (2.96 m)

Weights:
Empty: 5988 lb (2716 kg)
Max T/O: 7485 lb (3395 kg)

Performance:
Max Speed: 418 mph (673 kmh)
Range: 746 miles (1200 km)
Powerplant: Allison V-1710
Output: 1360 hp (1015 kW)

First Flight Date:
Late December 1942 (original) and late 1996 (Yak-9UM)

Surviving Airworthy Variant(s):
Yak-9UM (Strela new-build)

Right: Designated a Yak-9UM (M is the Russian designation for new production), this machine is flown by Eddie Andreini out of Half Moon Bay in California. The fighter is powered by an Allison V-1710, which drives a Hamilton Standard propeller.

Kaufman Broad
N900EA
9
YAK 9U
Barbarossa

Postwar Aircraft

Aermacchi MB-326

Italy

Type: single-engined jet basic/advanced trainer, ground attack aircraft

Accommodation: two pilots in tandem, or one pilot (ground attack variant)

Designed by Dr Ing. Ermanno Bazzochi in 1954, the straight-winged MB-326 proved to be the most successful creation of the Italian Aermacchi company, continuing in production until the early 1980s. The first of two prototypes flew in December 1957, the aircraft relying on the reliable, if underpowered, Rolls-Royce Viper turbojet. Fifteen pre-production aircraft were swiftly ordered by the *Aeronautica Militaire Italiana* (AMI) following initial flight trials, and a further 85 production standard aircraft were procured soon after. The first of these entered service in February 1962. Suitable for all stages of military jet flying training, the MB-326 soon found a ready market as air forces all over the world made the transition from World War 2 piston-engined trainers to dedicated jet aircraft boasting performances comparable to frontline aircraft. Aside from those aircraft supplied by Aermacchi to customers in Africa and South America, 97 licence-built MB-326s were also produced in Australia, 251 in South Africa and 182 in Brazil. Total production reached 761 aircraft, with the final MB-326 being built by EMBRAER in February 1983. A number of single- and two-seat variants were also produced, able to carry external weapons on six underwing hardpoints. Today, many MB-326s have been replaced in service by other jet and turboprop trainers, resulting in a small number of 'Macchis' being sold to civilian operators, mainly in the USA.

Specification:

Dimensions:
Length: 34 ft 11 in (10.64 m)
Wingspan: 35 ft 7.25 in (10.85 m)
Height: 12 ft 2.50 in (3.72 m)

Weights:
Empty: 5640 lb (2558 kg)
Max T/O: 11 500 lb (5216 kg)

Performance:
Max Speed: 539 mph (867 kmh)
Range: 1150 miles (1850 km)
Powerplant: Rolls-Royce Viper 20 Mk 540
Output: 3410 lb st (15.17 kN)

First Flight Date:
10 December 1957

Surviving Airworthy Variant(s) in civilian hands:
MB-326B/E/F/H/K/L/M, MB-326GB, Atlas Impala and EMBRAER T-26/AT-26 Xavante

***Right:* Still wearing its faded South African Air Force brown and green camouflage scheme (to which a US civil registration has been hastily applied), this Impala Mk I was one of several based at Mojave airport, in California, in the mid-1990s.**

N156

Aero L-29 Delfin

Czech Republic

Type: single-engined jet basic trainer **Accommodation:** two pilots in tandem

The L-29 was designed to replace piston-engined trainers in service with the Czechoslovakian air force. Of conventional straight wing design, the prototype XL-29 flew for the first time in April 1959 and was duly ordered into pre-production in late 1960 following the flight of a second prototype. A competition held in the following year saw the L-29 chosen over the PZL Mielec TS-11 Iskra and Yakovlev Yak-30 as the standard trainer for all Warsaw Pact air forces, the aircraft's simple, robust design and docile handling characteristics were cited as significant factors in its favour. The same attributes have made the L-29 very appealing to private owners three decades later. The first production L-29s entered service in 1963, and by the time Aero built its last aircraft 11 years later, no less than 3,600 had been constructed. Over 2,000 of these were supplied to the Soviet Union, whilst hundreds of others were employed by air forces both in eastern Europe and in Africa and south-east Asia. At least eight countries still operate the venerable trainer in the tuitional role. More than 70 L-29s are now in civilian hands, surplus L-29s having been sourced from Soviet, Czech and Indonesian stocks in the early 1990s. All but a handful of these jets are operated in the USA, the exceptions appearing on the Italian and South African civil registers.

Specification:

Dimensions:
Length: 35 ft 5.50 in (10.81 m)
Wingspan: 33 ft 9 in (10.29 m)
Height: 10 ft 3 in (3.13 m)

Weights:
Empty: 5027 lb (2280 kg)
Max T/O: 7231 lb (3280 kg)

Performance:
Max Speed: 382 mph (615 kmh)
Range: 397 miles (640 km)
Powerplant: Motorlet M 701c
Output: 1962 lb st (8.73 kN)

First Flight Date:
5 April 1959

Surviving Airworthy Variant(s) in civilian hands:
L-29

Right: A civil registered L-29 seen in the UK

TOP GUN SCHOOL - SLOVAKIA

Aero L-39 Albatros

Czech Republic

Type: single-engined jet basic/advanced trainer, ground attack aircraft **Accommodation:** two pilots in tandem

Still a frontline type with over 20 air forces, the L-39 was built as the natural successor to the L-29. Design work started on the Albatros in 1966, the team led by Dipl Ing. Jan Vlcek working closely with representatives from the Soviet air force, who would duly become the type's biggest customer. The key to the aircraft's superiority over the Delfin was the adoption of the AI-25 Turbofan engine, which boasted virtually double the power output of the L-29's Motorlet turbojet. When married to an airframe of similar dimensions to the earlier Czech trainer, it soon became obvious that the Albatros would enjoy a significantly improved maximum speed, a better rate of climb and the ability to carry offensive stores. Although the first prototype flew as early as November 1968, approval for production delivery was not given until late 1972, when the Soviet, Czech and East German air forces confirmed that they had chosen the L-39 to replace the L-29. Service trials were conducted the following year, and production aircraft began to reach the *Ceskoslovenské Letectvo* in early 1974. Since then, over 2,800 have entered service, the training variants (C, TC and V) being joined by weapons capable L-39s (ZA and ZO). The Albatros is still being built in the Czech Republic in modernised L-59 form, boasting an uprated powerplant and Western avionics. Over 30 L-39s are presently in civilian hands, the majority registered in the USA.

Specification:

Dimensions:
Length: 39 ft 9 in (12.11 m)
Wingspan: 29 ft 10.75 in (9.11 m)
Height: 14 ft 4.25 in (4.38 m)

Weights:
Empty: 6283 lb (2850 kg)
Max T/O: 9480 lb (4300 kg)

Performance:
Max Speed: 528 mph (844.80 kmh)
Range: 930 miles (1500 km) with full tip tanks
Powerplant: ZMDB Progress (Ivchenyenko) AI-25TL
Output: 3792 lb st (16.87 kN)

First Flight Date:
4 November 1968

Surviving Airworthy Variant(s) in civilian hands:
L-39C/MS/TC/ZA and ZO

Right: The L-39s currently in civilian hands have come from Estonia, Libya, Kyrghyzstan, Iraq, Czechoslovakia, Germany and the former Soviet Union. This particular L-39CT was imported into the USA from Russia in November 1992 by Dan McCue of Warbirds East, based at Somersworth, New Hampshire. It was later sold to Lou Edmondson of Lou Air in Tierra Verda, Florida. L-39s currently appear on the US, French and British civil registers.

Aero

Aerospace CT-4 Airtrainer

New Zealand

Type: single-engined primary trainer **Accommodation:** two pilots seated side-by-side

The Airtrainer can trace its lineage back to 1953 when a compact two-seat design by Henry Millicer (then chief aerodynamicist of the Australian Government Aircraft Factory) won the Light Aircraft Design Competition organised by the British Royal Aero Club. Put into production in Australia by Victa in 1960, 170 Airtourers were built before Aero Engine Services Ltd (AESL) of New Zealand acquired the company in 1968. Originally constructed in wood, the design was re-engineered in metal and developed into the four-seat Aircruiser, which went on to form the basis of the military-optimised Airtrainer. Stressed to +6/-3 G, the Airtrainer was ordered by the RAAF which took 37 airframes under the designation CT-4A. These were later joined by 14 machines built for Rhodesia, but blocked from delivery by a UN embargo in 1972. Thirty have been purchased by the Thai air force and the RNZAF ordered 19 CT-4Bs, the latter variant boasting a higher gross weight – all were built by New Zealand Aerospace Industries (NZAI), following the merger of AESL with Air Parts in 1973. Nicknamed the 'Plastic Parrot' in Australian service, the CT-4 gave sterling service in the primary training role at No 1 Flying Training School at Point Cook until retired in mid-1992 – 36 ex-RAAF CT-4s were sold to civilian operators in Australia (33) and the USA (3) in May 1993. The civil Airtourer is scheduled for production once again from 1999 by Millicer Aircraft of Victoria, Australia.

Specification:

Dimensions:
Length: 23 ft 5.50 in (7.15 m)
Wingspan: 26 ft 0 in (7.92 m)
Height: 8 ft 6 in (2.59 m)

Weights:
Empty: 1460 lb (662 kg)
Max T/O: 2400 lb (1089 kg)

Performance:
Max Speed: 265 mph (426 kmh)
Range: 808 miles (1300 km)
Powerplant: Rolls-Royce (Continental) IO-360-H
Output: 210 hp (157 kW)

First Flight Date:
23 February 1972 (CT-4)

Surviving Airworthy Variant(s) in civilian hands:
CT-4A and B

Right: The RNZAF continues to operate 18 CT-4s in the primary training role, whilst the RAAF still employs the aircraft for initial flight screening, although it relies on civilian contractor BAe-Ansett Flying College to perform this role with civil-registered/new-build CT-4Bs.

30
NZ1930

Antonov An-2

USSR/Poland

Type: single-engined biplane utility aircraft **Accommodation:** one/two pilots and up to ten passengers

As one of the last biplanes still in production, the An-2 is still in service with almost 30 air forces. An astounding production run has seen in excess of 18,000 'Colts' (the NATO reporting name) built since 1947, with 12,000 originating from the PZL Mielec factory in Poland following a licence deal struck in 1960. Indeed, the Antonov plant in Kiev built a 'mere' 5,000 before production ceased in 1965. Licence production also saw 1,500 completed as Harbin Y-5s in China between 1957 and the early 1970s. The aircraft's distinctively dated appearance was treated with some derision in the West when the first production An-2s were reported. However, the Antonov OKB design team wanted an aircraft that created significant drag so as to allow it to boast excellent short take-off and landing (STOL) characteristics. Its simple construction techniques also meant that the Colt was both easy to maintain 'in the field' and capable of operating from rugged terrain. Although initially ordered to fulfil a Ministry of Agriculture and Forestry specification, the An-2 soon found employment in the Soviet air force as a paratroop transport, glider tug and navigation trainer, whilst numerous other air arms have also used it as a light bomber. A small number of An-2s have recently appeared on European and US civil registers following the collapse of communism in the East.

Specification:

Dimensions:
Length: 42 ft 6 in (12.95 m)
Wingspan: 59 ft 8.50 in (18.18 m)
Height: 13 ft 9.25 in (4.20 m)

Weights:
Empty: 7605 lb (3450 kg)
Max T/O: 12 125 lb (5500 kg)

Performance:
Max Speed: 157 mph (253 kmh)
Range: 562 miles (905 km)

Powerplant: Shvetsov ASh-62M or PZL Kalisz ASz-621R (Polish licence-built ASh-62)
Output: 1000 hp (746 kW)

First Flight Date:
31 August 1947 (Antonov version) and 23 October 1960 (PZL Mielec variant)

Surviving Airworthy Variant(s) in civilian hands:
An-2M/P/R/S/T/TD and TP

Right: Wearing spurious Soviet markings, this An-2T has operated as a general utility 'hack' with The Planes of Fame Museum at Chino since early 1988. It was one of the first Antonovs to appear on the US civil register.

05

Armstrong Whitworth Argosy UK

Type: four-engined cargo aircraft **Accommodation:** two crew and up to 89 passengers

The final product of Armstrong Whitworth prior to the company 'disappearing' within the Hawker Siddeley Aviation 'empire', the Argosy was developed primarily for airline cargo services, but enjoyed more success in a military role with the RAF. Indeed, just 17 Argosies were sold to civilian operators in the early 1960s, the distinctive looking aircraft seeing service in Europe, North America and Australasia. Military interest in the aircraft resulted in 56 Argosy C Mk 1s being ordered by RAF Transport Command, whose crews dubbed them 'Whistling Wheelbarrows'. The reduction in Britain's military presence overseas, and swingeing budget cuts, saw the premature demise of the Argosy barely a decade after it had entered service. Its role passed to the ubiquitous Lockheed Hercules. A small number of surplus aircraft saw further use with civilian operators after their demilitarisation, but the bulk of the Argosy fleet was summarily scrapped. The sole remaining airworthy Argosy is former RAF T 2 XP447, which was sold to US operator Duncan Aviation and delivered in March 1976. The aircraft was employed on contract to the Bureau of Land Management in Alaska until retired in 1991, after which it was donated to the California-based Museum of Flying. Rarely flown, the aircraft was eventually passed on to a small museum at Fox Field in Lancaster, California, in 1994, where its engines were removed. Its current status is uncertain.

Specification:

Dimensions:
Length: 86 ft 9 in (26.44 m)
Wingspan: 115 ft 0 in (35.05 m)
Height: 29 ft 3 in (8.91 m)

Weights:
Empty: 50 000 lb (22 680 kg)
Max T/O: 88 000 lb (39 915 kg)

Performance:
Max Speed: 282 mph (455 kmh)
Range: 1780 miles (2865 km)
Powerplant: four Rolls-Royce Dart 526 turboprops
Output: 8920 shp (6654.32 kW)

First Flight Date:
4 March 1961 (Argosy C Mk 1)

Surviving Airworthy Variant(s) in civilian hands:
Argosy C Mk 1

Right: Argosy T 2 XP447 formates with the Museum of Flying's P-51D and Spitfire IX at the end of its delivery flight from Lincoln, Nebraska, to Santa Monica, California, on 23 December 1991.

GOP
EOJ
N1430Z

Auster AOP 6/9/11

UK

Type: single-engined high-wing liaison/observation aircraft **Accommodation:** pilot and observer/passenger in tandem

Derived from the highly successful observation/liaison family of light aircraft built by British Taylorcraft during the latter half of World War 2, the AOP 6/9 and 11 were improved variants of the basic wartime design. The AOP (Air Observation Post) Mk 6 differed from its predecessors in having a Gipsy Major engine fitted in place of the American Lycoming, a bigger fuel capacity and longer undercarriage legs. Its short field performance was even better than earlier Austers thanks to the adoption of auxiliary aerofoil flaps on the trailing edge of the wing in place of the split flaps employed with the Auster V. Production of the AOP 6 commenced in 1946, and a total of 312 were built for the RAF up to 26 March 1953 – some 77 dual-trainer configured T 7s were also constructed for the air force. The AOP 6 saw action in Korea and Malaya during the 1950s. Twelve months after the last AOP 6 entered RAF service, Auster completed the first flight of the type's replacement, the AOP 9. This variant was the only member of the Auster/AOP family built specifically for military use, rather than having been a development of a civil design. Fitted with a more powerful engine, and utilising a bigger wing, the first AOP 9 was delivered to the RAF in 1955, and the aircraft remained in service well into the late 1960s. A considerable number of ex-military Austers remain airworthy across the globe, the aircraft proving popular as a glider tug.

Specification:

Dimensions:
Length: 23 ft 8.5 in (7.26 m)
Wingspan: 36 ft 5 in (11.12 m)
Height: 8 ft 5 in (2.59 m)

Weights:
Empty: 1461 lb (662 kg)
Max T/O: 2130 lb (966 kg)

Performance:
Max Speed: 127 mph (203 kmh)
Range: 246 miles (393 km)

Powerplant: de Havilland Gipsy Major VII (AOP 6), Blackburn Cirrus Bombardier 203 (AOP 9) and Lycoming O-360-A1D
Output: 145 hp (108.17 kW), 180 hp (134.28 kW) and 160 hp (119.36 kW) respectively

First Flight Date:
1 May 1945 (AOP 6) and 19 March 1954 (AOP 9)

Surviving Airworthy Variant(s) in civilian hands:
AOP 6/9 and 11

Right: Seen at its former home of Middle Wallop in 1990, AOP 9 XR241 was flown in the London-Sydney Air Race of December 1969 by legendary Army Air Corps pilot Capt M Somerton-Rayner. Although the aircraft was presented to the Shuttleworth Collection upon its return to the UK in January 1970, it can now be found on display at Duxford.

ARMY AIR CORPS OFFICIAL ENTRY
BP ENGLAND — AUSTRALIA
AIR RACE
ARMY XR241
G-AXRR
25

Avro Shackleton

UK

Type: four-engined long-range maritime patrol/airborne early warning aircraft

Accommodation: flight crew of three and eight tactical operators

The final expression of Avro's classic four-engined heavy bomber design which had produced the Lancaster and Lincoln, the Shackleton was built as the RAF's first dedicated maritime patrol aircraft. It entered service with Coastal Command in February 1951, the MR 1 utilising the Lincoln bomber's mainplane and undercarriage married to an all-new fuselage. A total of 77 MR 1s was delivered to the RAF, followed by 62 MR 2s from 1952, the latter variant boasting a longer nose and a retractable 'dustbin' radar. The final new-build variant was the MR 3 of 1955, which had a tricycle undercarriage and wingtip tanks, of which 34 were constructed for the RAF and eight for the South African Air Force. Just as the maritime patrol Shackletons were nearing the end of their career in the late 1960s, the RAF hastily converted 12 surplus MR 2s into AEW 2 configuration by adding the APS-20F(I) radar into the aircraft's capacious fuselage. The radar set was an updated version of a 1944-vintage air intercept radar system, stripped out of retired Fleet Air Arm aircraft and bolted into the venerable Shackleton as a stop-gap measure. However, the final AEW 2 was not 'pensioned off' until 1991! Converted between 1971-74, all 12 AEW 2s served exclusively with No 8 Sqn at RAF Lossiemouth, flying missions over the North Sea, Arctic Ocean and western Atlantic that could last up to 15 hours.

Specification:

Dimensions:
Length: 87 ft 4 in (26.62 m)
Wingspan: 120 ft 0 in (36.58 m)
Height: 16 ft 9 in (5.10 m)

Weights:
Empty: 57 000 lb (25 855 kg)
Max T/O: 98 000 lb (44 452 kg)

Performance:
Max Speed: 273 mph (439 kmh)
Range: 3050 miles (4908 km)
Powerplant: four Rolls-Royce Griffon 57A engines
Output: 9820 hp (7324 kW)

First Flight Date:
9 March 1949 (MR 1) and 30 September 1971 (AEW 2)

Surviving Airworthy Variant(s) in civilian hands: Shackleton AEW 2

Right: Replaced in RAF service by the Boeing E-3D Sentry in 1991, five AEW 2s have survived, although only this machine –WL790/N790WL Mr MacHenery – remains airworthy. Operated from Anoka, Minnesota, by the Polar Aviation Museum and Air Atlantique, the aircraft has resided in the USA since September 1994.

90
ROYAL AIR FORCE
8

BAC Jet Provost

UK

Type: single-engined jet basic trainer **Accommodation:** two pilots seated side-by-side

Originally developed by Percival (later Hunting Percival) as a cheap, jet-powered derivative of its successful piston-engined Provost, the Jet Provost wound up being a virtually new aircraft. Built as a private venture trainer at a time when the RAF used converted frontline jet types for pilot conversion, the design soon garnered support from the air force, which appreciated the Jet Provost's purpose-built side-by-side layout and viceless handling. An initial batch of nine T 1s was purchased in 1955, and put to work on a new training syllabus with No 2 Flying Training School. Due to the success enjoyed with these aircraft, the RAF duly adopted the Jet Provost in June 1959, ordering 201 in T 3 form – these machines differed from the T 1s in having Martin-Baker ejection seats, tip tanks, updated avionics and a clear-view canopy. A follow on order for the re-engined T 4 was placed in November 1961, and 198 were built by BAC up to 1964. The final variant to enter RAF service was the T 5, which had cockpit pressurisation, a redesigned windscreen, sliding canopy and a longer nose, of which 110 were built from 1967. Export orders for the Jet Provost were received from Sri Lanka, Kuwait, Sudan, Iraq, South Yemen and Venezuela, and like the RAF fleet, these aircraft have now all been retired. Following the Jet Provost's phasing out in 1993, over 70 'JPs' have appeared on civil registers in the UK, the Netherlands, the USA, Australia and New Zealand.

Specification:

Dimensions:

Length: 33 ft 7.5 in (10.25 m)
Wingspan: 35 ft 4 in (10.77 m)
Height: 10 ft 2 in (3.10 m)

Weights:

Empty: 4888 lb (2271 kg)
Max T/O: 9200 lb (4173 kg)

Performance:

Max Speed: 440 mph (708 kmh)
Range: 901 miles (1450 km)
Powerplant: Rolls-Royce Viper Mk 102 (T 1/3) or Mk 202 (T 4/5)
Output: 1750 lb st (7.80 kN) and 2500 lb st (11.12 kN) respectively

First Flight Date:

26 June 1954

Surviving Airworthy Variant(s) in civilian hands:

Jet Provost T 1/3/4 and 5

***Right:** Easily the most popular ex-RAF jet 'warbird', the humble 'JP' offers the thrill of fast jet flying at affordable prices. This T 5 (formerly XS230 – the prototype T 5 no less) was bought by Transair of North Weald at auction in November 1994 for £22,000.*

322

BAC Strikemaster

UK

Type: single-engined jet light strike aircraft **Accommodation:** two pilots seated side-by-side

Built as a result of the export success enjoyed by the basic Jet Provost trainer, the Strikemaster could perform both the tuitional role and light attack duties, thanks to an uprated Viper engine, increased stores hardpoints (eight) beneath the wings, strengthened airframe and comprehensive communications and navigation equipment. Based on the pressurised T 5, and designated the BAC 167 by its manufacturer, the Strikemaster also featured uprated Martin-Baker ejection seats, a revised fuel layout and short landing gear designed to be more suitable for rough field operations. Production of the Mk 80 series Strikemaster commenced in 1968, and over the next decade examples were sold to Ecuador (Mk 89), Kenya (Mk 87), Kuwait (Mk 83), New Zealand (Mk 88), Oman (Mk 82), Saudi Arabia (Mk 80), Singapore (Mk 84) and South Yemen (Mk 81), resulting in a total production run in excess of 115 aircraft – final new-build Strikemasters were constructed for the Sudan (Mk 90) as late as 1984. Examples in Oman, South Yemen and Ecuador all saw combat during their service careers, although today, few, if any, Strikemasters remain in the frontline. Over 20 aircraft have appeared in private hands during the 1990s, Strikemasters from New Zealand, South Yemen, Singapore, Botswana (ex-Kuwaiti Mk 83s) and Oman being issued with civil registrations in the UK, Australia and the USA.

Specification:

Dimensions:
Length: 34 ft 0 in (10.36 m)
Wingspan: 36 ft 10 in (11.23 m)
Height: 10 ft 2 in (3.10 m)

Weights:
Empty: 6195 lb (2810 kg)
Max T/O: 11 500 lb (5216 kg)

Performance:
Max Speed: 518 mph (834 kmh)
Range: 1382 miles (2224 km) ferry range

Powerplant: Rolls-Royce Viper 20 Mk 525
Output: 3410 lb st (15.17 kN)

First Flight Date:
26 October 1967

Surviving Airworthy Variant(s) in civilian hands:
Strikemaster Mks 81/82/83/84 and 88

Right: Built in early 1969 and delivered to South Yemen in July of that year, this Strikemaster Mk 81 remained the Middle East until 1976, when it was sold to the Singaporean air force along with the three other Strikemasters. Retired in 198 the aircraft was purchased by Australian company International Air Parts, who duly sold it to Amjet Aircraft Corporation of St Paul, Minnesota, in 1990. Restored airworthiness in 1994 by Wal Fisk, the aircraft now flies in Kenyan air force colours.

TRANSAIR
PILOT SHOP
TRANSAIR
G-VIVM

BAC Buccaneer

UK

Type: twin-engined jet strike aircraft **Accommodation:** pilot and navigator seated in tandem

Built to fulfil a 1952 Royal Navy requirement for a long range carrier-based attack aircraft, Blackburn's Buccaneer enjoyed a remarkably long service career, predominantly with the RAF. Although a physically big aircraft (its airframe was predominantly machined from forgings and plate), the Buccaneer's wings and tail unit are of modest size, thanks to the employment of boundary layer control (BLC). This system ensured remarkable lift by controlling the amount of air flowing over the wings and tail through the use of full-span slits built into the flying surfaces. The small wing allowed for great speeds to be attained at sea level, and the Buccaneer remained one of the fastest combat aircraft in this environment right up to its retirement in 1992. The first Buccaneer S 1s entered service with the Royal Navy in July 1962. These were followed into the fleet by the more powerful Spey-engined S 2s three years later. From 1969, the navy's surviving Buccaneers were passed to the RAF in the wake of a political directive that denuded the Fleet Air Arm of fixed wing carriers. RAF Buccaneers finally saw combat in the twilight of their careers (South African Air Force Mk 50s had seen much action in the 1970s and 80s), operating with the Coalition force over Iraq and Kuwait in 1991 during *Desert Storm*. Two S 2Bs have recently been flown to South Africa after acquisition by a private jet collector, these aircraft being the first of their type to appear on the civil register in that country.

Specification:

Dimensions:
Length: 63 ft 5 in (19.33 m)
Wingspan: 44 ft 0 in (13.41 m)
Height: 16 ft 3 in (4.95 m)

Weights:
Empty: 29 980 lb (13 599 kg)
Max T/O: 62 000 lb (28 123 kg)

Performance:
Max Speed: 691 mph (1112 kmh)
Range: 600 miles (966 km) tactical range
Powerplant: two Rolls-Royce Spey Mk 101 turbofan engines
Output: 22 200 lb st (98.4 kN)

First Flight Date:
30 April 1958

Surviving Airworthy Variant(s) in civilian hands:
Buccaneer S 2B

Right: Formerly XW987 with the Aircraft & Armaments Experimental Establishment (A & AEE), this S 2B was flown to South Africa in April 1997 for new owner Mike Beachyhead, who has registered the aircraft ZU-BCR. A second ex-A & AEE S 2B (XW988) was delivered to South Africa exactly 12 months before.

Beech T-34 Mentor

USA/Japan

Type: single-engined primary trainer

Accommodation: two pilots seated in tandem (pilot and three passengers seated side-by-side in LM-1)

Based on the hugely successful civilian Beech Model 35 Bonanza, the Model 45 Mentor was built in 1948 in response to an expected demand by the USAF for a new primary tuitional trainer. Five years were to pass, however, before the Beech trainer was chosen to fill the role, the USAF undertaking a fly-off that saw a wide variety of designs trialled. As part of this evaluation, three pre-production Mentors were acquired by the air force, under the designation YT-34. Once selected, Beech supplied Training Command with 350 T-34As from their Wichita plant (plus a further 100 from Canadian Car & Foundry), deliveries commencing in 1954. That same year also saw the US Navy select the Mentor as its basic trainer, 423 T-34Bs being acquired. A number of other air arms across the globe chose the Mentor on the strength of the US purchase, the Argentine firm FMA assembling 75 for its air force and Japanese manufacturer Fuji building 124 under licence for the Air Self-Defence Force – the latter firm later developed both a four-seat variant and a more powerful Mentor replacement from the basic T-34A. The Mentor was replaced in USAF service from 1960 after the adoption of an all-through jet training syllabus, whilst the US Navy continued to use its T-34Bs until the late 1970s when the T-34C Turbo Mentor entered service. Although a favourite amongst 'warbird' enthusiasts (particularly in the USA), around 100 of the 1,300+ Mentors built remain in military service.

Specification:

Dimensions:
Length: 25 ft 10 in (7.87 m)
Wingspan: 32 ft 10 in (10.01 m)
Height: 10 ft 0.25 in (3.04 m)

Weights:
Empty: 2055 lb (932 kg)
Max T/O: 2900 lb (1315 kg)

Performance:
Max Speed: 188 mph (302 kmh)
Range: 770 miles (1238 km)
Powerplant: Continental O-470-13 (T-34A) or O-470-4 (T-34B)
Output: 225 hp (168 kW)

First Flight Date:
2 December 1948

Surviving Airworthy Variant(s) in civilian hands: T-34A/B and Fuji LM-1

Right: This ex-USAF T-34A was owned for a number of years by the famous Sanders family of Chino, who replaced its 225 hp O-470 powerplant and two-bladed propeller with a 285 hp Continental engine and three-blade unit – the end result was one of the fastest Mentors ever to appear on the US civil register.

U.S. AIR FORCE
N311H

Boeing C-97 Stratofreighter/Stratotanker USA

Type: four-engined transport/air refuelling tanker **Accommodation:** crew of six/seven and up to 134 passengers

The transport derivative the B-29 bomber, the C-97 was even bigger than the Superfortress thanks to the addition of a second fuselage of greater diameter on top of the existing structure–a design feature dubbed the 'double bubble' by USAF operators. Three pre-production examples of aircraft were designated the XC-97 by the USAAF, and although they had been ordered simultaneously with the B-29 as early as January 1942, the latter type took precedence. Boeing finally commenced flight trials with the XC-97s in late 1944, and an order for 50 C-97As was duly placed. Although designed as a transporter of people and air freight, it was in the postwar role of aerial tanker in support of the newly-created Strategic Air Command (SAC) that the C-97 achieved its greatest success. Indeed, no fewer than 811 KC-97 tankers in three different variants (E-, F- and G-models) were eventually built. The combination of the aircraft's capacious cargo hold and Boeing's revolutionary Flying Boom refuelling system allowed the Stratotanker to transfer huge volumes of fuel to SAC's burgeoning fleet of bombers. Following their eventual replacement in the frontline, its capacious cargo hold and Boeing's revolutionary Flying Boom refuelling system allowed the Stratotanker to survive into the 1970s. Today, a handful are operated as civilian freighters in Central and South America and as firebombers in North America.

Specification:

Dimensions:
Length: 117 ft 5 in (35.8 m)
Wingspan: 141 ft 3 in (43.05 m)
Height: 38 ft 3 in (11.75 m)

Weights:
Empty: 85 000 lb (38 560 kg)
Max T/O: 175 000 lb (78 980 kg)

Performance:
Max Speed: 370 mph (595 kmh)
Range: 4300 miles (6920 km)
Powerplant: four Pratt & Whitney R-4360-59B Wasp Major engines
Output: 14 000 hp (10 440 kW)

First Flight Date:
15 November 1944

Surviving Airworthy Variant(s) in civilian hands:
C-97G and KC-97G

Right: Stripped of its refuelling gear but still bearing traces of its USAF titling and serial on its forward fuselage, this KC-97G has been converted into a firebomber. A Stratotanker with a rear cargo door could be bought for around US$300,000 from DMI Aviation of Tucson, Arizona, in the early 1990s.

84

CAC CA-25 Winjeel

Australia

Type: single-engined primary trainer and forward air control aircraft

Accommodation: two pilots seated side-by-side

Built in response to a 1948 RAAF specification for a Tiger Moth and Wirraway replacement, the Winjeel (aboriginal for 'young eagle') was developed as the CA-22 by the Commonwealth Aircraft Corporation (CAC). Early on in the programme, thought was also given to building a home-grown powerplant (the CAC Cicada) for the new basic trainer, but this failed to reach the flight-testing stage. Two prototypes were delivered to the RAAF in early 1951, and after exhaustive trials, the air force eventually ordered 62 production aircraft. Built between 1955 and 1958, the Winjeel that entered frontline service differed from the prototype CA-22 primarily in the tail region, where work had been carried out by CAC to improve the trainer's spinning characteristics. Redesignated the CA-25, the Winjeel was the staple basic trainer until replaced by the Macchi in 1969 when the RAAF reverted to an all-jet syllabus. Problems with the new curriculum soon appeared, however, and the Winjeel was re-introduced as an *ab initio* trainer. It saw a further six years of service until finally replaced for good by the CT-4 from 1975 onwards. Despite losing its training role in 1976, the Winjeel soldiered on in RAAF colours until 1994 as a Forward Air Control (FAC) platform, operating closely with the air force's F-111, Mirage III and F/A-18 squadrons. Following replacement in this role by PC-9s, 14 surviving Winjeels were sold off to civilian owners in Australia.

Specification:

Dimensions:
Length: 28 ft 0.5 in (8.55 m)
Wingspan: 38 ft 7.5 in (11.77 m)
Height: 9 ft 1 in (2.77 m)

Weights:
Empty: 3289 lb (1492 kg)
Max T/O: 4265 lb (1935 kg)

Performance:
Max Speed: 188 mph (303 kmh)
Range: 550 miles (883 km)
Powerplant: Pratt & Whitney R-985-AN-2 Wasp Junior
Output: 445 hp (331.97 kW)

First Flight Date:
3 February 1951

Surviving Airworthy Variant(s) in civilian hands:
CA-25 Winjeel

Right: Seen in loose line-astern formation, these Winjeels are all based on the Australian east coast. A85-401 was the very first CA-25 delivered to the RAAF in August 1955, and it is now owned by the air force museum.

316
A85-460
A85-401

Cavalier F-51D Mustang Mk 2 USA

Type: single-engined fighter **Accommodation:** pilot (dual controls optional)

The Cavalier Mustang Mk 2 (12 kW) respectively (k 2) were based on *the* classic American fighter of World War 2, the Cavalier Mustang was born out of Florida newspaper magnate, David Breed Lindsay Jr's desire to convert surplus ex-military P-51s into high-performance executive transports, capable of flying in almost any weather. The first such modified aircraft were ex-RCAF P-51Ds, which were fully converted by Lindsay's company, Trans Florida Aviation Inc, in the late 1950s and early 1960s. Each Mustang was modified into a two-seater, boasting improved cockpit sound-proofing, new instrumentation and an advanced communications and navigation fit. In 1961 Lindsay began marketing five variants of Cavalier Mustang (750, 1200, 1500, 2000 and 2500), each differing primarily in respect to its range. Having quickly sold the RCAF aircraft, he expanded his business and started buying up other surplus airframes and parts. In 1966 the US Department of Defense decided that the Cavalier Mustang would be ideal as a Counter Insurgency (COIN) platform for 'friendly' countries in South America, and duly contracted the company to refurbish an undisclosed number of Mustangs as part of *Project Peace Condor*. These aircraft boasted uprated Merlin 620 engines taken from ex-RCAF C-54GM transports, a taller fin (as per the standard civil Cavalier), strengthened wings for more weapons hardpoints and optional tip-tanks. Customers for the 'new' aircraft were Bolivia, El Salvador, the Dominican Republic, possibly Haiti and Guatemala, and Indonesia. The last of the refurbished Mustangs was finally retired (by the *Fuerza Aerea Dominicana*) in 1984.

Specification:

Dimensions:
Length: 32 ft 9.5 in (9.81 m)
Wingspan: 40 ft 1 in (12.10 m)
Height: 14 ft 8 in (4.51 m)

Weights:
Empty: 7635 lb (3466 kg) approximately
Max T/O: 10 500 lb (4762.80 kg) gross

Performance:
Max Speed: 457 mph (731.20 kmh)
Range: 2000 miles (3200 km)
Powerplant: Packard V-1650-7 (F-51D) and Merlin 620 (Cavalier Mustang Mk 2)
Output: 1590 hp (1186.14 kW) and 1725 hp (1285.12 kW) respectively

First Flight Date:
December 1967 (Cavalier Mustang Mk 2)

Surviving Airworthy Variant(s):
F-51D, TF-51D and Cavalier Mustang Mk 2

Right: At least 41 Cavalier Mustangs (in a handful of different variants) remain airworthy today, including this California-based ex-*Fuerza Aerea Boliviana *TF-51D Mk 2, complete with modified canopy and taller tail fin. Many ex-Central and South American aircraft were brought back to the USA following their retirement in the 1980s.

Cessna O-1 Bird Dog

USA

Type: single-engined high-wing observation and Forward Air Control (FAC) aircraft

Accommodation: pilot and observer/ passenger in tandem

Winner of an Army competition in June 1950 for a two-seat observation and liaison aircraft, the Cessna Model 305 (as it was designated by its manufacturer) was based on the company's highly successful civil Model 170 of the late 1940s and 1950s. Built to replace the World War 2-vintage Grasshopper family of aircraft, the Cessna L-19 (US Army designation) was powered by a 213 hp engine, as opposed to the 65 hp unit of its predecessor. This allowed the aircraft to be far more flexible in its parameters of operation, and made the Bird Dog ideally suited to the Forward Air Control (FAC) role that it subsequently made its own during the early years of the Vietnam War. Re-designated the O-1 in 1962, Cessna had delivered 3,431 examples by the time production ceased in that same year–the bulk of these had been built as O-1As (L-19As), with the later variants introducing uprated equipment and the ability to carry wing stores like target marking rockets. The exploits of the O-1E over the Vietnamese jungle are legendary, USAF and South Vietnamese pilots pin-pointing enemy troop locations through communication with 'friendlies' on the ground prior to calling in air strikes to hit targets marked with smoke rockets. Although long since retired from USAF service, a modest number of O-1s continue to thrive with a handful of air arms across the globe, whilst surplus Bird Dogs have recently enjoyed a renaissance as a cheap 'warbug' in North America and Australia.

Specification:

Dimensions:
Length: 25 ft 9 in (7.85 m)
Wingspan: 36 ft 0 in (10.97 m)
Height: 7 ft 3.5 in (2.22 m)

Weights:
Empty: 1614 lb (732 kg)
Max T/O: 2400 lb (1087 kg)

Performance:
Max Speed: 151 mph (243 kmh)
Range: 530 miles (853 km)
Powerplant: Continental O-47-11
Output: 213 hp (159 kW)

First Flight Date:
December 1949

Surviving Airworthy Variant(s):
L-19, O-1A/B/E and TO-1D

Right: This beautifully restored O-1E is painted up as a US Army L-19A, complete with underwing rockets and smoke canisters.

U.S.ARMY
14871
N201SS

Cessna O-2 Super Skymaster USA

Type: twin-engined high-wing observation and Forward Air Control (FAC) aircraft

Accommodation: pilot and observer/ passenger seated side-by-side

Although the war in Vietnam provided the humble O-1 with its 'finest hour' in US military service, it highlighted the need for a more advanced FAC aircraft, capable not only of greater speed, but also increased weapons carriage. Once again Cessna provided the answer, in the form of a specially 'militarised' version of the Model 337 Skymaster, known as the O-2 Super Skymaster. The unique 'push/pull' layout of the civil aircraft gave the O-2 twin-engined performance and reliability, and allowed the USAF to fit heavy military spec radios and four hardpoints under the wings. Further modifications for the FAC role included the addition of extra windows in the fuselage, for the observer in the right-hand seat. Sadly, these mods did not stretch to the inclusion of crew protection in the form of armour plating, which had also been lacking in the O-1. More than 350 O-2As were hastily delivered to the USAF following the placement of an order on 29 December 1966, and the type duly served as a stopgap replacement for the O-1 until the dedicated North American OV-10 Bronco was produced. Aside from its use for FAC, the O-2 was also produced in Bravo configuration for psy-war ops, which took the form of leaflet drops and pro-South Vietnamese government broadcasts using 600-watt amplifiers. Retired from the USAF in the 1980s, militarised 337s can still be found in frontline service across the globe.

Specification:

Dimensions:
Length: 29 ft 9 in (9.07 m)
Wingspan: 38 ft 0 in (11.58 m)
Height: 9 ft 4 in (2.84 m)

Weights:
Empty: 2848 lb (1292 kg)
Max T/O: 5400 lb (2449 kg)

Performance:
Max Speed: 199 mph (320 kmh)
Range: 1060 miles (1706 km)
Powerplant: two Teledyne Continental IO-360C/D engines
Output: 420 hp (314 kW)

First Flight Date:
30 March 1964 (Super Skymaster)

Surviving Airworthy Variant(s):
O-2A/B and Model 337

Right: As this suitably-marked O-2 clearly shows, a healthy number of ex-USAF O-2s have found gainful (if somewhat hazardous) employment as fire spotters with the various forestry departments across the USA. Others are flown simply as warbirds, some complete with underwing dummy rockets and Minigun packs – examples have even made it as far afield as Australia.

A14

Cessna Model 185/U-17 Skywagon USA

Type: single-engined high-wing utility and Forward Air Control (FAC) aircraft **Accommodation:** pilot and up to five passengers

Yet another military Cessna developed from a successful civil design (in this case the robust Model 180), the Model 185 Skywagon was built as a multi-purpose aircraft that was both cheap to produce and operate. Both attributes made it ideally suited to the Department of Defense's Military Assistance Program (MAP), and examples were duly supplied to Bolivia, Costa Rica, Laos and South Vietnam. Operators quickly grew to appreciate the aircraft's strengthened structure, which allowed it to be stripped out and converted into a cargo hauler that could get into and out of the most modest (and hastily prepared) of landing strips – an optional glass-fibre belly Cargo-Pack could also be bolted to the Skywagon to further boost its carrying capability. The 185 was selected by the USAF for MAP in 1963, the air force redesignating the aircraft the U-17. Some 262 A-models were initially built, followed by 205 Bravos with de-rated engines. A small number of Model 185s were also procured directly from Cessna by several non-MAP countries, including South Africa. Aside from its use in the general utility role, the Skywagon has also carried on the Cessna tradition of FAC – a tasking still occasionally undertaken today by Turkish army aviation 185s, of which number there are over 100 examples (the largest fleet in the world). At least ten other air forces also currently operate 185s/U-17s. Like the O-1 and O-2, the Skywagon has also enjoyed a renewed following in warbird circles in recent years, again primarily in North America.

Specification:

Dimensions:
Length: 25 ft 9 in (7.85 m)
Wingspan: 35 ft 10 in (10.92 m)
Height: 7 ft 9 in (2.36 m)

Weights:
Empty: 1585 lb (719 kg)
Max T/O: 3350 lb (1519 kg)

Performance:
Max Speed: 178 mph (286 kmh)
Range: 1035 miles (1665 km) ferry range
Powerplant: Teledyne Continental IO-520-D
Output: 300 hp (224 kW)

First Flight Date:
July 1960

Surviving Airworthy Variant(s):
Model 185B/C/D/E, A185E/F and U-17A/B

***Right:* This US-registered Skywagon wears spurious codes and a South Vietnamese air force paint scheme. Its true identity would most probably reveal it to be a standard civil 185.**

65-12769
CS
War Wagon

Convair C-131

USA

Type: twin-engined monoplane transport aircraft

Accommodation: four-man crew and up to twenty-three passengers

The C-131 was the USAF/US Navy transport version of Convair's highly successful 240/340/440 series of twin-engined airliners, which were produced for almost two decades from the late 1940s. The C-131 was an improved version of the T-29 (itself based on the 240), 46 of which entered service with the air force in 1950-51 as navigation, bombardier and radar operator trainers, where they replaced B-25Js. Dubbed the 'Samaritan' because of its primary role of medical evacuation, the first of 26 C-131As reached MATS (Military Air Transport Service) in December 1954. Major follow-on variants included the C-131B (with more powerful engines – 36 built), C-131D (10 built for MATS European-based units), VC-131D (16 built for staff/VIP transport), R4Y-1 (US Navy variant, redesignated C-131F in 1962 – 36 built) and the C-131E (SAC ECM trainer – 11 built). Further military-optimised Convair 'twins' were also built in small numbers for the RAAF and German and Italian air forces. In US military service, the aircraft proved to be extremely versatile, performing in all manner of roles from simple cargo hauling to specialist electronic warfare–a C-131 was even converted into the prototype USAF 'gunship'. The last Convairs left the active inventory in the late 1970s, whilst a handful lingered on with the ANG and Navy reserve units until 1990. Today, a small number of ex-military C-131 are still gainfully employed in North, Central and South America as airliners and freight haulers.

Specification:

Dimensions:
Length: 79 ft 2 in (24.14 m)
Wingspan: 105 ft 4 in (32.10 m)
Height: 28 ft 2 in (8.60 m)

Weights:
Empty: 29 486 lb (13 382 kg)
Max T/O: 52 414 lb (24 682.19 kg)

Performance:
Max Speed: 314 mph (502 kmh)
Range: 2200 miles (3520 km)
Powerplant: two Pratt & Whitney R-2800-103W engines (D-model)
Output: 5000 hp (3720 kW)

First Flight Date:
28 July 1954 (C-131D)

Surviving Airworthy Variant(s):
C-131A/B/D/F and Convair 240/440

Right: Although perhaps looking a little worse for wear, and still bearing traces of its once pristine ANG scheme, this VC-131D still appears on the US civil register as N43944. Stored in the dry heat of the Californian desert, it would not take a huge amount of effort to make this Convair 'twin' airworthy once again.

N43944

Dassault MD.311/312 Flamant

France

Type: twin-engined monoplane transport/utility aircraft

Accommodation: two-man crew and up to ten passengers

One of the first postwar products of the reformed Bloch company (renamed Dassault in 1945), the twin-engined Flamant was built to fulfil the French need for a trainer and light transport aircraft. There were plenty of surplus Allied utility aircraft available (and Axis types too: Siebel Si 204s were built in France during the occupation), but the French decided that a more modern design was required, so Dassault hastily produced the MD.303. This one-off prototype was soon replaced by the definitive MD.315, which boasted more powerful Renault/SNECMA engines. Beating off the rival SO.90 design from the nationalised manufacturer SNCASO, Dassault was awarded an initial contract for 65 MD.315s in December 1947. By the time production ceased in 1952, 136 production aircraft had been delivered, the aircraft seeing service both in France and in its colonial territories in Africa and Asia. Used as a troop transport, light freighter or air ambulance, the Flamant was also converted into a ground attack aircraft during the conflicts in Algeria and French Indochina. The trainer version of the Flamant was ordered in November 1948, some 40 MD.311s (crew trainers) and 118 MD.312s (pilot trainers) being procured – the last military Flamant built (MD.312) was delivered to the *Armée de l'Air* in January 1954. Aside from the air force aircraft, an additional 25 were also built for the *Aéronautique navale* as MD.312Ms in 1952/53. The aircraft soldiered on in its designed roles until finally retired from service in 1983.

Specification:

Dimensions:
Length: 41 ft 11 in (12.78 m)
Wingspan: 66 ft 3.50 in (20.21 m)
Height: 16 ft 1 in (4.90 m)

Weights:
Empty: 11 245 lb (5100 kg)
Max T/O: 14 110 lb (6400 kg)

Performance:
Max Speed: 276 mph (445 kmh)
Range: 930 miles (1500 km)
Powerplant: two SNECMA 12S 02 engines
Output: 1060 hp (866 kW)

First Flight Date:
10 February 1947 (MD.303)

Surviving Airworthy Variant(s):
MD.311 and .312

Right: Surplus Flamants were offered to French aero clubs in the wake of the type's retirement in 1983, but they proved to be too expensive to run and were quickly grounded. Today, roughly 17 remain airworthy in France, with this example (MD.311 282), flown by the Memorial Flight, still exhibiting the (rather faded) markings of its former operator, **Groupment école *316*.**

282
316-KY

de Havilland Vampire

UK

Type: single-engined jet fighter and trainer

Accommodation: pilot (day fighter) and pilot/navigator (nightfighter) and pilot/student (trainer) seated side-by-side

The Vampire was the second jet fighter type to enter service with the RAF. Although it missed seeing action during World War 2 (the first examples were issued to No 247 Sqn in June 1946), it went on to enjoy a long career, not only in the offensive role but also as a trainer. Initially dubbed the Spider Crab, the Vampire was designed around de Havilland's compact Goblin turbojet engine. The thrust produced by these early powerplants was modest to say the least, so the company's design team (which had started work on the aircraft in 1941) adopted a twin-boom layout to minimize the length of the engine's jet tailpipe. Evolving into a number of sub-types, the Vampire was adapted from its designed role of day fighter to perform the fighter-bomber and nightfighter (the latter boasted two seats and an Air Intercept radar in the nose) missions. Finally, a highly successful trainer variant was developed from the two-seat nightfighter, which, when it entered service with the RAF's Flying Training Command in 1952, became the first jet aircraft in the air force on which pilots actually qualified for their 'wings'. Aside from the 1,500+ Vampires built for the RAF, both fighter and training variants were flown by the Fleet Arm Arm too. Export models were also produced in great numbers.

Specification:

Dimensions: (all data for T 11 trainer)
Length: 34 ft 6.5 in (10.51 m)
Wingspan: 38 ft 0 in (11.59 m)
Height: 6 ft 2 in (1.88 m)

Weights:
Empty: 7380 lb (3347 kg)
Max T/O: 11 150 lb (5060 kg) clean

Performance:
Max Speed: 538 mph (866 kmh)
Range: 853 miles (1370 km)

Powerplant: de Havilland Goblin II (F 3), Goblin 35 (T 11) or Goblin 3 (FB 6)
Output: 3100 lb st (15 kN), 3500 lb st (15.57 kN), 3350 lb st (14.91 kN) and 4400 lb st (19.30 kN) respectively

First Flight Date:
20 September 1943 (DH 100)

Surviving Airworthy Variant(s):
F 3, FB 6/9, FB 50, T 11, T 22 Sea Vampire and T 35/55

Right: Painted in the colours of the navalised Vampire I which carried out the first jet seas trials aboard* HMS Ocean *in December 1945, this aircraft is actually an ex-Swiss Air Force FB 6. It was bought at auction by Don Woods in 1991, and is operated as part of the Source Classic Jet Flight at Bournemouth. Over 80 Vampires of various marks remain airworthy across the globe, the bulk of these being ex-Swiss FB 6s and T 11s.

ROYAL NAVY
LZ 551/G

de Havilland Venom/Sea Venom UK

Type: single-engined jet fighter-bomber and two-seat nightfighter

Accommodation: pilot (day fighter-bomber) and pilot/ navigator (nightfighter) seated side-by-side

Successor to the DH 100 Vampire, the DH 112 Venom utilised a thinner wing and more powerful Ghost turbojet engine. Most RAF Venoms were based in Germany, where their ground attack capabilities were well received. The FB 1 was replaced on the production line by the slightly modified FB 4, which had a larger flat-topped fin-and-rudder design, powered ailerons, more powerful Ghost 105 engine and provision for underwing drop tanks. Some 150 were delivered to the RAF from May 1954 onwards. Export orders for both versions were also secured, with the Swiss EFW consortium building 100 FB1s and 150 FB 4s for their air force. As with the early de Havilland fighter, a two-seat nightfighter variant was also developed as the NF 2/3, which replaced the Vampire NF 10 in service from 1953 onwards (90 NF 2s and 129 NF 3s were eventually built). Finally, the Fleet Air Arm bought the navalised Sea Venom all-weather fighter, which featured a tailhook, strengthened undercarriage and folding wings, amongst other mods. Some 217 were built (FAW 20s and 21s), and they remained in service until 1960.

Specification:

Dimensions: (all data for FB 4/FB 54)
Length: 33 ft 0 in (10.06 m)
Wingspan: 41 ft 8 in (12.70 m)
Height: 6 ft 8 in (2.03 m)

Weights:
Empty: 9202 lb (4174.02 kg)
Max T/O: 15 310 lb (6945 kg)

Performance:
Max Speed: 587 mph (961 kmh)
Range: 1075 miles (1730 km)
Powerplant: de Havilland Ghost 103 (Venom FB 1), Ghost 104 (Sea Venom FAW 53) and Ghost 105 (Venom FB 4)
Output: 4850 lb st (21.60 kN) for both 103/104 and 5150 lb st (22.30 kN) for 105

First Flight Date: 2 September 1949

Surviving Airworthy Variant(s):
FB 1/1R and 4, FB 50/54 and Sea Venom FAW 53

Right: With the retirement of the Swiss Venoms in the early 1980s, the warbird population of the classic British postwar fighter dramatically swelled as numerous examples were sold across the globe. This Swiss FB 50 was just one of seven Venoms that found its way to the USA, and is presently owned by David van Liere. Around 20 Venoms and a solitary Sea Venom are currently airworthy, with examples flying in the USA, UK, Switzerland, Australia and New Zealand.

N202DM
16

de Havilland Devon/Sea Devon UK

Type: twin-engined light executive transport **Accommodation:** two-man crew and up to eleven passengers

As the first postwar design to be produced in quantity by de Havilland, the twin-engined Dove initially encountered strong opposition in a marketplace awash with surplus British and American utility aircraft. Built as a replacement for the company's highly successful pre-war Dragon Rapide, the aircraft made little sales impact until bought in quantity by the RAF in 1948 for use as a general communication aircraft. Based on the Dove 4 and christened the Devon C 1, the first military examples were issued to No 31 (Metropolitan Communications) Sqn at Hendon. With the seal of RAF approval now secured, and the number of wartime surplus 'hacks' slowly disappearing through age or expense of operation, the Dove became a more appealing option to both civil and military buyers. With a production life that lasted from 1945 to 1968, the Dove experienced a number of improvements during its 23 years 'on the line', and 544 were built to eight separate series specifications– the power output of the engines provided the major difference between variants. Aside from use by the RAF in Devon C 1 (DH Gipsy Queen 71-powered) and C 2 (Gipsy Queen 175 engines) configuration, the Royal Navy also operated a small number of Sea Devon C 20s as 'admiral's barges' well into the 1970s. Overseas, modest numbers of Doves found military application with the air forces of Ethiopia, India, Ireland, Jordan, the Lebanon, Malaysia, Paraguay and Sri Lanka, whilst a small number of RAF-specification Devons were used by India and New Zealand.

Specification:

Dimensions:
Length: 39 ft 4 in (11.99 m)
Wingspan: 57 ft 0 in (17.37 m)
Height: 13 ft 4 in (4.06 m)

Weights:
Empty: 6580 lb (2985 kg)
Max T/O: 8950 lb (4060 kg)

Performance:
Max Speed: 210 mph (338 kmh)
Range: 880 miles (1415 km) with maximum fuel
Powerplant: two de Havilland Gipsy Queen 70-3 engines
Output: 800 hp (596 kW)

First Flight Date:
25 September 1945 (civil Dove)

Surviving Airworthy Variant(s):
Devon, Sea Devon and Dove

Right: The Royal Jordanian Air Force operated Dove 6s on general utility duties from the early 1950s through to the late 1980s. This example was returned to the UK in 1993 for an extensive overhaul at Staverton, and it is regularly flown from Bournemouth-Hurn Airport with R V Aviation Ltd as part of the Royal Jordanian Historic Flight. Other ex-military Devons/Sea Devons remain airworthy elsewhere in the UK, the USA, Australia and New Zealand.

ROYAL JORDANIAN AIR
JY-RJU

de Havilland Canada DHC-1 Chipmunk Canada/UK

Type: single-engined basic training aircraft **Accommodation:** two pilots in tandem

The first aircraft designed by de Havilland Canada, the Chipmunk was developed immediately after World War 2 to replace the venerable Tiger Moth in the primary training role. Powered by the tried and tested de Havilland Gipsy Major engine, the first DHC-1 Chipmunks were only partially aerobatic (this was soon rectified). The aircraft was ordered into series production as the T 1 for the RCAF, DHC eventually building 218 Chipmunks to this standard, including military examples for Egypt, Chile and Thailand. With the introduction of the Gipsy Major 10, the aircraft's RCAF designation changed to T 2. Following flight trials in the UK, Specification 8/48 was issued by the Air Ministry to cover the purchase of 735 Chipmunk T 10s, which were subsequently issued to virtually all primary flying training units in the RAF. The British Chipmunk differed in being fully aerobatic and having a multi-panelled sliding canopy rather than a single-piece sliding unit; the Gipsy Major 8 was also substituted for the early spec engine. Aside from those supplied to the RAF (and Army Air Corps and Fleet Air Arm), de Havilland UK also produced 217 aircraft for export, whilst a further 60 were built under-licence by OGMA in Portugal. Now all but retired as a military trainer, the RAF and Army Air Corps finally 'pensioned off' its last examples (nearly 100 T 10s) in 1996, many of these having since appeared on the civil register in the UK and abroad.

Specification:

Dimensions:
Length: 25 ft 5 in (7.75 m)
Wingspan: 34 ft 4 in (10.45 m)
Height: 7 ft 0 in (2.13 m)

Weights:
Empty: 1425 lb (646 kg)
Max T/O: 2014 lb (914 kg)

Performance:
Max Speed: 138 mph (222 kmh)
Range: 280 miles (451 km)
Powerplant: de Havilland Gipsy Major 8 or 10
Output: both 145 hp (108 kW)

First Flight Date:
22 May 1946

Surviving Airworthy Variant(s):
T 1/2 and T 10/20/21

Right: Wearing an original RAF Training Command finish of all-over silver and high visibility yellow bands, this T 10 was retired from the air force and sold into private ownership many years before the recent wholesale sell-off of Chipmunks in the UK.

WB588

de Havilland Canada DHC-2 Beaver

Canada

Type: single-engined high-wing utility light transport **Accommodation:** pilot and up to seven passengers

Having enjoyed great success with their Chipmunk, de Havilland Canada produced another winner with the DHC-2 Beaver, although the two types were vastly different. As the first of the company's 'bush' aircraft (the Otter, Caribou and Twin Otter would follow), the Beaver was a rugged, reliable, 'go anywhere' type of machine, boasting incredible STOL (Short Take-Off and Landing) characteristics and the ability to carry a useful payload. The Beaver's big break came in 1951 when it was selected to fulfil a joint US Army/Air Force requirement for a liaison aircraft. By the time production on the order ceased in 1960, 968 L-20A Beavers had been delivered to the US armed forces, three-quarters of them going to the army. The Beaver proved very popular in frontline service, and saw action in both the Korean and Vietnam Wars. Redesignated U-6As (U for utility) in 1962, the Beaver remained in army and air force service well into the 1970s. Today, only the US Navy still uses the type, operating three examples with its Test Pilot's School. Other nations to buy the Beaver in quantity included Britain, which purchased 46 AL 1s for the Army Air Corps (which were used extensively over Northern Ireland), Chile bought 15 and Colombia 18, although few remain in service; a handful are reportedly still flying in Colombia. Total Beaver production reached 1,691 airframes, and a number of ex-military aircraft are still flying today in civilian guise (mostly in North America).

Specification:

Dimensions:
Length: 30 ft 4 in (9.24 m)
Wingspan: 48 ft 0 in (14.64 m)
Height: 9 ft 0 in (2.75 m)

Weights:
Empty: 2850 lb (1293 kg)
Max T/O: 5100 lb (2313 kg)

Performance:
Max Speed: 140 mph (225 kmh)
Range: 778 miles (1252 km) with maximum fuel
Powerplant: Pratt & Whitney R-985-AN Wasp Junior
Output: 450 hp (336 kW)

First Flight Date:
August 1947

Surviving Airworthy Variant(s):
DHC-2 and U-6A

Right: This US-registered U-6A is authentically marked-up as a Delaware National Guard machine from the 1960s.

DE NG
0-37920
ARMY

de Havilland Canada DHC-4 Caribou

Canada

Type: twin-engined high-wing tactical transport **Accommodation:** two-man crew and up to thirty-two troops

The DHC-4 was built in an effort to combine the load carrying capacity of the C-47 with the STOL performance of the Beaver and Otter. Like previous de Havilland Canada products, the Caribou was both robust and incredibly agile. Its STOL performance (achieved by its high-aspect-ratio cranked wing fitted with full-span double-slotted flaps) was unmatched for an aircraft of its size. Even before the prototype aircraft had flown, the US Army had committed to five evaluation aircraft (designated YAC-1s), and following extensive trials, it ordered 159 examples. Total Caribou production numbered 304 aircraft. As the largest fixed-wing type ever flown by the US Army, the first aircraft entered service in 1961 initially as AC-1s, but this was changed the following year to CV-2. Capable of carrying 32 troops, 26 paratroops, 22 stretchers, two fully-loaded jeeps or three tons of cargo, the Caribou would operate into forward landing strips, from where the troops could complete their journey by helicopter. All of these missions were undertaken in Vietnam, where US Army aircraft operated alongside RAAF Caribou in many a hazardous mission. In 1967 the responsibility for all fixed-wing tactical transports was transferred to the USAF, and the surviving 134 Caribou were duly redesignated C-7As. Retired from air force service in the late 1970s, a handful of Caribou remain in use with the RAAF and Cameroon and Malaysian air forces.

Specification:

Dimensions:
Length: 72 ft 7 in (22.13 m)
Wingspan: 95 ft 7.5 in (29.15 m)
Height: 31 ft 9 in (9.70 m)

Weights:
Empty: 18 260 lb (8283 kg)
Max T/O: 31 300 lb (14 197 kg)

Performance:
Max Speed: 216 mph (347 kmh)
Range: 1307 miles (2103 km)
Powerplant: two Pratt & Whitney R-2000-7M2 Twin Wasp engines
Output: 2900 hp (2162 kW)

First Flight Date:
30 July 1958

Surviving Airworthy Variant(s):
DHC-4, C-7A and CC-108

Right: A small number of Caribou were manufactured specially for civilian customers who needed an aircraft with STOL performance, although the bulk of the DHC-4s that have appeared in private hands have been ex-military (primarily C-7As) machines. For example, this 'propellerless' Canadian Caribou is an ex-Canadian Armed Forces CC-108 that was 'de-mobbed' in 1979.

C-GVGW
Caribou

Douglas A-1 Skyraider

USA

Type: single-engined attack aircraft **Accommodation:** pilot or pilot and observer (seated side-by-side)

Initially dubbed the 'Dauntless II', the XBT2D-1 had the overwhelming reputation of the wartime Douglas dive-bomber to live up to. That the aircraft went on to break all records for frontline longevity for a piston-engined attack type, and served with distinction in both the Korean and Vietnamese conflicts, proves that the renamed Skyraider's reputation was equal to its initial 'Dauntless' sobriquet. Reputedly designed in 24 hours in the Statler Hotel, Washington DC, in June 1944, the success of the Skyraider was due as much to its Wright R-3350 radial engine as to its rugged aerodynamics. That very same engine delayed the Skyraider's entry into service long enough for the aircraft to miss World War 2. Indeed, for a number of years it seemed that the new Douglas attack aircraft was destined to remain unproved in action with the US Navy, just like Grumman's Bearcat of the same period. However, the Skyraider refused to become obsolete, and fought throughout the Korean War. As the 1950s progressed, the frontline prospects of the unglamorous A-1 seemed limited. However, the advent of war in Vietnam gave the Skyraider a new lease of life, so much so that both the USAF and South Vietnamese Air Force used ex-Navy A-1s (taken out of storage) from 1964 until the fall of Saigon in 1975. The US Navy, meanwhile, finally retired its Skyraiders in April 1968, following four hard years of combat over Vietnam.

Specification:

Dimensions: (for A-1E)
Length: 40 ft 1 in (12.19 m)
Wingspan: 50 ft 9 in (15.47 m)
Height: 15 ft 10 in (4.83 m)

Weights:
Empty: 12 313 lb (5585 kg)
Max T/O: 25 000 lb (11 340 kg) overload

Performance:
Max Speed: 311 mph (501 kmh)
Range: 3000 miles (4828 km) with external tanks
Powerplant: Wright R-3350-26W or R-3350-26WB
Output: 3020 hp (2252 kW) and 3050 hp (2271 kW)

First Flight Date:
18 March 1945

Surviving Airworthy Variant(s):
AD-4/-4N/-4NA/-4W/-5W/-6, A-1D/E/H and EA-1E

Right: Many ex-US Navy AD-4s saw action with the* Armée de l'Air *in North Africa, the survivors then being donated to air forces in Chad and Gabon. Most survivors later returned to the USA, via France, and were restored – this AD-4N (A-1D BuNo 126959) had also previously experienced combat in Korea. Rebuilt by Pacific Fighters at Chino in 1989 and owned by Mike Schloss since 1994, it is one of 12 airworthy Skyraiders in the USA – five 'flyers' can also be found in France, one in the UK and three in Sweden.

NAKED
FANNY
TT
959

Douglas A-4 Skyhawk

USA

Type: single-engined jet attack or two-seat trainer/FAC aircraft

Accommodation: pilot (attack variant) or pilots seated in tandem (trainer/FAC)

Bucking the early 1950s trend for ever larger combat aircraft, the Douglas A-4 was the brainchild of company chief engineer, Ed Heinemann, who had also been responsible for the A-26 and A-1 almost a decade before. Weighing less than half the 30,000 lb weight stipulated by the US Navy for its new jet attack bomber, yet still capable of undertaking all the missions required of it, the A- was quickly dubbed 'Heinemann's Hot Rod' thanks to it outstanding performance. The first A-4As (then designated A4D-1s) entered fleet service in October 1956, and by the time of the Vietnam War all carrier air wings included at least two squadrons of Skyhawks. The B-, C- and E-models had all seen the capabilities (and weight) of the A-4 increase since the first examples were built, and the aircraft formed the backbone of the Navy and Marine Corps light attack mission over the jungles of South-East Asia. Export success was also enjoyed by the Skyhawk, with substantial numbers being sold to Indonesia, Australia, Malaysia, Singapore, New Zealand, Kuwait, Israel and Argentina; aircraft of the latter three countries have also experienced combat. In 1965 Douglas produced a two-seat variant of the Skyhawk, which was designated the TA-4, and 555 were subsequently built both for the US armed forces and export markets. Of the 2,405 attack models produced between 1954 and 1979, a substantial number are still in frontline service toda

Specification:

Dimensions: (for A-4B/C)
Length: 39 ft 6 in (12.04 m)
Wingspan: 27 ft 6 in (8.38 m)
Height: 15 ft 0 in (4.57 m)

Weights:
Empty: 9284 lb (4211 kg)
Max T/O: 22 000 lb (9979 kg) shipboard

Performance:
Max Speed: 676 mph (1088 kmh) clean
Range: 920 miles (1480 km) without external tanks
Powerplant: Wright J65-16A (A-4B/C) or Pratt & Whitney J52-P-8A (TA-4J)
Output: 7700 lb st (33.8 kN) and 9300 lb st (41.4 kN)

First Flight Date: 22 June 1954

Surviving Airworthy Variant(s):
A-4B/C and TA-4J

Right: Nine Skyhawks currently appear on the US civil register (none are privately operated outside of America), mostly A-4B/Cs. However, there are at least three TA-4Js in private hands too, this example (BuNo 158128) having been first registered in 1990 – it is presently owned by Betty Welcome of Kirkland, Washington. With the imminent retirement of the TA-4J from US Navy service, more and more 'two-holers' should appear on the US civil register.

NAVY
N128TA
TA-4J
158128
DANGER
RESCUE

Douglas C-133 Cargomaster

USA

Type: four-engined heavy logistic freighter **Accommodation:** four-man crew

Developed by Douglas to meet a USAF requirement for a logistic transporter, capable of lifting strategic cargo that could not be easily 'broken down' for carriage in the C-124 or C-130, the C-133 went straight from the drawing board into production. The very first C-133A doubled as the prototype, the aircraft's large pressurised fuselage of circular section being able to accept the new Atlas and Titan ICBMs through full width rear cargo doors. The first of 35 A-models was delivered to the USAF's Military Air Transport Service in August 1957, and these were followed by 15 C-133Bs from 1959 through to 1961, the latter variant boasting a more powerful version of the T34 turboprop engine and a revised rear fuselage shape combining clamshell doors. The B-model was also specially adapted for the carriage of Thor, Jupiter, Atlas, Titan and Minuteman ballistic missiles. Astoundingly, it was estimated at the time that roughly 96 per cent of all US military equipment could be carried by the Cargomaster. This was put to the test during the build up of American forces in South Vietnam in the mid-1960s, as it was found that the three squadrons of C-133s were the only viable option for the express movement of bulk cargo across the Pacific. The advent of the C-5 Galaxy in 1969 eased the overworked C-133's burden, Lockheed transporter replacing the Cargomaster within Military Airlift Command. The last C-133s were retired in 1979, and three have since spasmodically flown with civilian operators.

Specification:

Dimensions:
Length: 157 ft 6.5 in (48.02 m)
Wingspan: 179 ft 8 in (54.75 m)
Height: 48 ft 3 in (14.7 m)

Weights:
Empty: 120 263 lb (54 550 kg)
Max T/O: 286 000 lb (129 727 kg)

Performance:
Max Speed: 359 mph (578 kmh)
Range: 4300 miles (6920 km)
Powerplant: four Pratt & Whitney T34-7 engines (C-133A) or T34-9W (C-133B)
Output: 28,000 shp (20 879 kW) and 30,000 shp (22 368 kW)

First Flight Date:
23 April 1956

Surviving Airworthy Variant(s):
C-133A/B

Right: This civil-registered C-133A is one of two that have sat baking in the California sun at Mojave since flying into the airport in 1977. Their planned conversion into 'mobile hospitals' to tour the Third World fell through soon after their arrival primarily because of the aircraft's mechanical complexity and temperamental engines. However, at least three others have performed haulage work in North America.

N136AR

Douglas A-3 Skywarrior USA

Type: twin-engined electronic warfare jet aircraft **Accommodation:** three-man flight crew and four systems operators

Yet another Ed Heinemann design developed and built at the Douglas El Segundo plant in California, the A3D (as it was originally designated) Skywarrior became the world's first carrier-based strategic bomber when it entered fleet service in December 1954. Designed around both the predicted size of future thermonuclear bombs and the strength and length of the soon to be commissioned *Forrestal* class 'supercarriers', the Skywarrior boasted a large bomb bay, blind bombing radar and an Aero-21B remote tail turret. Dominating even the larger decks of the new CVAs, the aircraft was quickly dubbed the 'Whale' by both its crews and other air wing members. Douglas was contracted to build just 280 Skywarriors, and the last of these (an A3D-2Q EW aircraft) reached the fleet in January 1961. Functioning for just over a decade as a 'heavy bomber', the Skywarrior had been replaced in its intended role by the more agile, and thus more survivable, A-6 Intruder by the mid-1960s, although its fleet service continued for another 25 years. Thanks to its size, the Skywarrior proved eminently suited to performing other tasks like aerial refuelling (KA-3B), reconnaissance (RA-3B), radar/navigation training (TA-3B) and electronic countermeasures (EA-3B). Seeing action throughout the Vietnam War, the Skywarrior finally disappeared from carrier decks in the late 1980s, although a handful of EA-3Bs survived long enough to see action in the Gulf War, flying from shore bases. Today, more than a dozen Skywarriors are owned and operated by California-based Hughes Aircraft on defence-related work.

Specification:

Dimensions:
Length: 76 ft 6 in (23.35 m)
Wingspan: 72 ft 5 in (22.10 m)
Height: 23 ft 4 in (7.13 m)

Weights:
Empty: 41 193 lb (18 685 kg)
Max T/O: 78 000 lb (35 380 kg) on land

Performance:
Max Speed: 557 mph (1032 kmh)
Range: 1110 miles (2057 km)
Powerplant: two Pratt & Whitney J57-10 engines
Output: 24 800 lb st (111.17 kN)

First Flight Date: 28 October 1952

Surviving Airworthy Variant(s): EA-3B, NRA-3B and TA-3B

Right: Seen at Mojave, these two Skywarriors are amongst the handful of A-3s still flown on defence contract work. The NRA-3B in the background (BuNo 142256) was originally accepted into the Navy in April 1958, but subsequently spent its entire career as a test bed with Douglas and then Westinghouse.

14225
N256HA
NAVY

Douglas R4D-8

USA

Type: twin-engined monoplane transport aircraft

Accommodation: three-man crew and up to thirty-eight passengers

Dubbed the Super DC-3 by manufacturer Douglas, the R4D-8 was the military version of the classic aircraft that had revolutionised both civil and military air transport. Rather than produce a new design, Douglas was convinced that the market wanted another variant of the Dakota: the company held great stock in the saying, 'the only thing that could replace the DC-3 is another DC-3!' Accordingly, the R4D-8 featured a squared off tail section and a more aerodynamic wing (slightly swept and squared-off at the tips). Further streamlining was achieved by fully enclosing the main gear legs, whilst the aircraft's performance was further improved by replacing its Twin Wasp engines with more powerful Wright Cyclones. However, despite an exhaustive sales tour of America, the Super DC-3 evoked little interest with civil operators. If it had not been for the US Navy ordering 100 examples as the R4D-8, it is unlikely that the Super DC-3 would have entered series production, for only three were sold to Capital Airlines. (And of the R4D-8s, only 17 were eventually built, the remainder being converted from standard R4Ds.) In military service, the R4D-8 (redesignated the C-117D in 1962) was employed in mundane 'cargo hauling' and VIP tasks, with perhaps the most exciting flying undertaken by the aircraft being that performed by VX-6 on the snow and ice of Antarctica, where the type operated on skis.

Specification:

Dimensions:
Length: 71 ft 1 in (21.67 m)
Wingspan: 93 ft 0 in (28.34 m)
Height: 18 ft 11 in (5.51 m)

Weights:
Empty: 21 470 lb (9738 kg)
Max T/O: 30 500 lb (13 834 kg)

Performance:
Max Speed: 270 mph (432 kmh)
Range: 2125 miles (3420 km)
Powerplant: two Wright R-1820-80 Cyclone engines
Output: 3070 hp (2290.22 kW)

First Flight Date:
1949

Surviving Airworthy Variant(s):
R4D-8 and C-117D/VC-117D

Right: Flown by both the Navy and Marine Corps squadrons, the last C-117Ds were finally retired in the early 1970s. Still wearing its VIP scheme, this ex-USMC example has been a regular participant at numerous Confederate Air Force 'spectaculars' for a number of years.

N3906J

English Electric Canberra

UK

Type: twin-engined jet bomber, photo-recce and training aircraft **Accommodation:** two-man crew

Aside from being the RAF's first jet bomber, the Canberra has also proven to be the Britain's most durable jet combat type, with a handful of reconnaissance and electronic warfare aircraft still soldiering on some 47 years after the prototype's first flight. Built to Air Ministry Spec. B.3/45, the Canberra relied heavily on Bomber Command's experience with the de Havilland Mosquito, which had proven virtually untouchable over German skies due to its impressive top speed. The Canberra was built for speed too and carried no defensive weapons. Although ordered as a 'light bomber', many B.2s went into service as Avro Lincoln replacements. Indeed, the RAF was so pleased with the aircraft that 546 were constructed, and over 30 RAF units equipped with them. The key to the Canberra's success was its distinctive low-aspect wing, which gave outstanding fuel economy at a maximum cruising altitude that far exceeded the ceilings achieved by jet fighters of the same period. This meant that for a number of years prior to the advent of the air-to-air missile, the Canberra was immune to manned interception. The aircraft also enjoyed great export success, with the USAF even putting a version into production with Martin Aircraft after failing to find a home-grown medium bomber replacement for its B-26 Invaders. Designated the B-57, the aircraft saw much combat in Vietnam, operating alongside Australian Canberra B 20s.

Specification:

Dimensions: (for B 6)
Length: 65 ft 6 in (19.96 m)
Wingspan: 63 ft 11.5 in (19.50 m)
Height: 15 ft 8 in (4.77 m)

Weights:
Empty: 27 950 lb (12 678 kg)
Max T/O: 56 250 lb (25 514 kg)

Performance:
Max Speed: 518 mph (834 kmh)
Range: 3630 miles (5842 km) ferry range
Powerplant: two Rolls-Royce Avon 109 engines
Output: 7400 lb st (32.92 kN)

First Flight Date:
13 May 1949

Surviving Airworthy Variant(s):
B 2, B 6 and B 6(Mod), B(I) 8(Mod) B 20 and TT 18

Right: Although now all but retired from military service, at least seven privately-owned Canberras have appeared on the civil register – three in the UK, five in the USA and one in South Africa. This highly visible B 2 performed aerial survey work with the Luftwaffe until very recently.

Fairchild C-119 Flying Boxcar USA

Type: twin-engined tactical transport aircraft **Accommodation:** four-man crew and up to 62 fully-equipped troops

Developed from Fairchild's wartime C-82 Packet, of which 223 were built for the USAAF between 1945-48, the C-119 maintained its predecessor's highly valued near-ground level loading/unloading attributes, but had its flightdeck moved ahead of the cargo hold rather than sat on top of it. The Flying Boxcar also had a wider fuselage, strengthened wings (which allowed it to operate to higher weights) and more powerful R-3350 engines fitted in place of the C-82's R-2800s. The first C-119Bs entered service with the USAF in December 1949, and by the time production of new aircraft ceased in 1955 a total of 946 Flying Boxcars had been accepted into the air force, the Marine Corps acquired a modest number too. A further 141 were sold overseas through various assistance programmes. The aircraft saw extensive action in both the Korean and Vietnam Wars, with heavily-armed nocturnal interdiction variants fitted with Gatling guns and all manner of night sensor giving the humble Flying Boxcar an offensive role in the latter conflict – 26 AC-119G Shadows and a similar number of jet-assisted AC-119K Stingers were converted from standard C-119s in 1966/67. Relegated to the Air National Guard (ANG) by the early 1970s many early C-119s had been upgraded to J-specs (featuring a 'beaver-tail' rear door which could be opened in flight) by this stage. Finally retired from the 'Guard in September 1975, the Flying Boxcar still remains in frontline service today with the Taiwanese air force.

Specification:

Dimensions:
Length: 86 ft 6 in (26.36 m)
Wingspan: 109 ft 3 in (33.30 m)
Height: 26 ft 4 in (8.03 m)

Weights:
Empty: 39 982 lb (18 136 kg)
Max T/O: 74 400 lb (33 748 kg)

Performance:
Max Speed: 296 mph (476 kmh) clean
Range: 2280 miles (3669 km)
Powerplant: two Wright R-3350-89W Cyclone engines
Output: 6800 hp (5070 kW)

First Flight Date:
November 1947

Surviving Airworthy Variant(s):
C-119B/G and J

Right: Surplus C-119s saw many good years hauling freight and fighting forest fires in North America following retirement from USAF and Canadian service. However, a series of fatal crashes in the mid-1980s saw the aircraft's fire-fighting clearance rescinded in 1988, and many Flying Boxcars were duly 'put out to pasture' – this tatty ex-RCAF C-119G (note its modified nose) was rendered redundant before it could be converted into a fire bomber.

N8092

Fairchild C-123 Provider

USA

Type: twin-engined transport aircraft **Accommodation:** two-man crew and up to 61 fully-equipped troops

The robust Provider can trace its lineage back to the Chase Aircraft XG-20 all-metal troop/cargo glider built in 1949. The USAF expressed interest in a powered version of the design, so the company fitted two Double Wasp engines to the second prototype glider and redesignated it the XC-123 Avitruc. In 1953 a contract for 300 examples of the C-123B was awarded to Kaiser-Frazer, although the latter company soon ran into production difficulties and Fairchild stepped in to fulfil the order. The first production aircraft began to reach the USAF by late 1954, and the aircraft's rugged build and excellent handling characteristics made it popular with tactical transport crews. The Provider went on to become the first USAF transport committed to the Vietnam War, and aside from hauling troops and cargo, UC-123B variants were used to spray pesticides ('Agent Orange') as part of Project *Ranch Hand*, and two C-123Bs were modified to 'AC' standard and operated at night against communist truck convoys using sensors, flares and bomb canisters. The C-123's performance was greatly improved with the fitment of two podded J85 turbojets during the reworking of B-models into K-spec aircraft in the early 1960s, whilst the specialist H/J version (ten converted) received a similar boost in power, but with Fairchild J44 turbojets fitted in wingtip pods instead – the latter aircraft were used with a wheel/ski arrangement by the Alaskan ANG. The C-123 was finally retired from US military service in 1979.

Specification:

Dimensions:

Length: 75 ft 3 in (23.25 m)
Wingspan: 110 ft 0 in (33.35 m)
Height: 34 ft 1 in (10.38 m)

Weights:

Empty: 35 336 lb (16 042 kg) for C-123K
Max T/O: 60 000 lb (27 240 kg) all variants

Performance:

Max Speed: 245 mph (392 kmh)
Range: 1470 miles (2365 km)
Powerplant: two Pratt & Whitney R-2800-99W Cyclone engines and two General Electric J85-GE-17 auxiliary turbojets
Output: 5000 hp (3730 kW) and 5700 lb st (25.35 kN) respectively

First Flight Date: 1 September 1954

Surviving Airworthy Variant(s):

C-123B/H and K

Right: Surplus C-123s have been a great hit with freight haulers in North, Central and South America, the aircraft's rugged construction allowing it to cope with the harshest of bush strips. Few are flown with their jet pods operable, however, and this shiny Bravo, see at Chino, is no exception: the engines' intakes and exhausts have been faired over.

Fairey Firefly AS 5/6

UK

Type: single-engined naval fighter and ASW aircraft **Accommodation:** pilot and observer seated in tandem

Enjoying one of the longest production runs of any piston-engined naval fighter, the Firefly evolved from the Fulmar fleet fighter of 1940. Although the latter was obsolescent by the time it entered service, it formed the backbone of the Fleet Air Arm's fighter force during 1941-42. Soon after the first production examples had entered fleet service, Fairey commenced work on a revised design powered by a Griffon engine, which was subsequently christened the Firefly. Reaching fleet carriers in the summer of 1943, the Firefly I equipped eight squadrons by 1945. Despite the more powerful Griffon engine, the Fairey fighter could still not better 290 mph (its US Navy equivalent, the F4U-4 Corsair, was almost 200 mph faster!), so the design was revised once again and the clipped wing, Griffon 74-powered, Mk 5 was created. Realising that the aircraft's day as a pure fighter had passed, the Navy re-rolled the 'new' Firefly 5 as a fighter-bomber, nightfighter, armed reconnaissance and anti-submarine warfare (ASW) platform, purchasing 352. Seeing much combat in Korea, the Firefly was also bought by the Dutch, Canadian and Australian navies. The final two variants, the AS 6 and 7, were dedicated ASW aircraft, of which 284 were produced. More than 400 Fireflies of various marks were rebuilt in the 1950s as training aircraft and target drones, and following the type's retirement from naval service, a number performed target tug work with civilian operators.

Specification:

Dimensions:

Length: 38 ft 0 in (11.58 m)
Wingspan: 41 ft 0 in (12.49 m)
Height: 13 ft 11 in (4.24 m)

Weights:

Empty: 9859 lb (4472 kg)
Max T/O: 15 600 lb (7076 kg)

Performance:

Max Speed: 316 mph (509 kmh)
Range: 1070 miles (1722 km)
Powerplant: Rolls-Royce Griffon 74
Output: 2245 hp (1674 kW)

First Flight Date:

22 December 1941 (Firefly I) and 12 December 1947 (first production Firefly 5)

Surviving Airworthy Variant(s):

AS 5 (TT 5) and AS 6 (TT 6)

Right: Although around 20 Fireflies have survived into the late 1990s, only three remain airworthy – AS 5/TT 5 WB271 with the Royal Navy's Historic Flight, the Royal Australian Navy (RAN) Historic Flight's AS 6/TT 6 WD 826, and this aircraft, AS 6 WH632, flown by the Canadian Warbird Heritage as VH142. All three machines previously saw service with the RAN, as did seven other static survivors.

BD G
ROYAL CANADIAN NAVY
VH142

Fairey Gannet

UK

Type: single-engined ASW, AEW and utility aircraft **Accommodation:** three-man crew seated in tandem

Designed to fulfil the challenging naval Specification GR.17/45, issued in October 1945, the Gannet successfully combined the strike and ASW roles in an aircraft built to not only operate from smaller carrier decks, but also run on the ship's diesel fuel. The Gannet's unique engine was the key to the aircraft's service success: it boasted two independent power sections driving separate propellers combined in a co-axial arrangement. This meant that after both sections had been used during the critical take-off phase, one could be shut down to improve fuel consumption and extend range/patrol time: both vital factors for a maritime strike/ASW platform. A three-man crew operated the Gannet in its designed role, and 256 AS 1/4s were eventually built, with the first examples reaching fleet service in January 1955, a full decade after GR.17/45 had been issued. T 2/T 5 dual control trainers (46 in total) followed the mission-oriented aircraft, and both ASW and training variants were sold to the Australian, West German and Indonesian navies. A number of AS 4s were later upgraded in the 1960s to AS 6/7 standards, whilst five were turned into Carrier On-board Delivery (COD) transports. Finally, in a major revision of roles, 44 new-build AEW 3 aircraft were completed for the Royal Navy from 1958-61, fitted with a huge dome beneath the fuselage to house the radome for the APS-20 surveillance radar. The AEW 3s were the last Gannets retired from military service in 1978.

Specification:

Dimensions: (for AS 1)
Length: 43 ft 0 in (13.10 m)
Wingspan: 54 ft 4 in (16.50 m)
Height: 13 ft 8 in (4.16 m)

Weights:
Empty: 14 069 lb (6382 kg)
Max T/O: 22 506 lb (10 208 kg)

Performance:
Max Speed: 311 mph (500 kmh) clean
Range: 662 miles (1066 km) fully armed
Powerplant: Armstrong Siddeley Double Mamba 100
Output: 2950 shp (2199 kW)

First Flight Date:
17 September 1949

Surviving Airworthy Variant(s):
AS 1 (T 2/T 5) and AEW 3)

Right: Only two Gannets remain technically 'airworthy' today, with recently-restored T 5 XT752 (ex-AS 1 WN365, prototype T 2 and AS-14 of the Indonesian Navy) being the only example flown regularly. Operated by the Polar Aviation Museum of Minneapolis, Minnesota, it is one of two Gannet 'flyers' in the USA, the second aircraft being rarely-flown AEW 3 XL482 of Kal Aero. Finally, AEW 3 XL502 appeared on the UK register in 1986, but was subsequently placed in storage three years later.

LM
ROYAL NAVY
RESCUE
RESCUE
RESCUE

Fiat G.46

Italy

Type: single-engined trainer aircraft **Accommodation:** two pilots seated in tandem

Designed by the same team that had produced many of Fiat's successful fighter types of the previous decade, the G.46 was built as an intermediate trainer for the postwar *Aeronautica Militaire Italiano* (AMI). The first batch of Series 1 aircraft reached AMI flying schools in 1949, where they soon proved to be the ideal 'stepping stone' for fledgling pilots recently graduated from the Stinson L-5 Sentinel (then the AMI's basic trainer) and heading for the T-6 Texan or Fiat G.55. After almost a decade in this role, the G.46 was rendered redundant after the AMI embraced the 'jet age', and restructured its syllabus – pilots now started their training on T-6s and moved directly to the T-33, leaving the AMI with a number of surplus G.46s (and L-5s). Over 150 Fiat trainers had been built for the air force, and some of these remained in AMI service with obscure units like the officer currency training flight and numerous communications units. However, the bulk of the aircraft were supplied to aero clubs across Italy following their 'demilitarisation', and it is from these aircraft that most of today's 22 surviving G.46s are drawn. Of this total, five remain airworthy: two in Italy, two in the USA and one in Belgium. Aside from AMI examples, the Syrian air force ordered 11 Fiats (powered by de Havilland Gipsy Queen 30 engines), Argentina operated 70 (again Gipsy Queen-powered) and the Austrian air force five, bringing total G.46 construction to 223 airframes.

Specification:

Dimensions:
Length: 27 ft 10 in (8.47 m)
Wingspan: 34 ft 1 in (10.30 m)
Height: 7 ft 10 in (2.37m)

Weights:
Empty: 2442 lb (1107 kg)
Max T/O: 3102 lb (1407 kg)

Performance:
Max Speed: 196 mph (315 kmh)
Range: 570 miles (917 km)
Powerplant: Alfa 115*ter*
Output: 225 hp (167 kW)

First Flight Date:
25 February 1948

Surviving Airworthy Variant(s):
G.46-3A/-3B and -4A

Right: For many years a favourite 'baddy' at UK airshows, G.46-3B MM52801 G-BBII was flown with vigour by the late Hon Patrick Lindsay. Following its importation into England from Italy in 1973, the aircraft was fully restored by Personal Plane Service at Booker. Sadly, G-BBII's Permit to Fly lapsed in July 1989, and it has remained stored at Staverton (Gloucestershire Airport) ever since – in this spurious JG 53 'Pik-As' scheme.

14

Fiat G.59

Italy

Type: single-engined fighter **Accommodation:** pilot

The last of the Fiat fighters, the G.59 was created due to a shortage of war-surplus Daimler-Benz DB 603A (Fiat RA 1050 RC 58 Tifone) engines for the company's remaining G.55A airframes. The aircraft was subsequently modified to allow it to utilise the Rolls-Royce Merlin T.24-2 inline engine, the first converted G.55B (two-seater trainer variant of the single-seat fighter) flying in early 1948 with the designation G.59BM ('M' for Merlin). Egypt initially showed interest in purchasing 20 G.55AM/BMs, but following the suspension of hostilities with Israel decided not to proceed with the sale. However, a dozen existing G.55As were rebuilt as AMs for the AMI, who redesignated the 'new' aircraft G.59-1As and used them as fighter-trainers. A further 15 G.59-1As and two-seat -1Bs were also subsequently built for Italian service in 1950, followed by 40 fully-armed G.59-2s (-1A/Bs had lacked weapons due to their training role). Twenty-six of the latter variant were delivered to the Syrian air force, whilst a solitary -2A was sent to Argentina for evaluation. The final variant to be produced in any number was the G.59-4A/B trainer again for the AMI, who purchased 20 single-seaters and 10 'two-holers'. These aircraft differed from previous models by having cut-down rear fuselage decking and bubble canopies. The G.59s were retired from AMI service with the arrival of jets in the mid-1950s.

Specification:

Dimensions:
Length: 31 ft 0.75 in (9.47 m)
Wingspan: 38 ft 10.5 in (11.85 m)
Height: 12 ft 4 in (3.76 m)

Weights:
Empty: 6041 lb (2740 kg)
Max T/O: 7496 lb (3400 kg)

Performance:
Max Speed: 368 mph (593 kmh)
Range: 882 miles (1420 km)
Powerplant: Rolls-Royce Merlin T.24-2 and Merlin 500 (G.59-4A/4B)
Output: 1610 hp (1200 kW) and 1490 hp (1111 kW) respectively

First Flight Date:
early 1948

Surviving Airworthy Variant(s):
G.59-4B

Right: Of the five genuine G.59 that have survived into the late 1990s, two (both -4Bs) remain airworthy – one in Italy and one in Australia. The latter example, MM53772, is seen here being flown in the USA soon after its restoration at Chino in 1987 by Sanders Aircraft. Owned by the late Guido Zuccoli, the -4B raced at Reno prior to heading 'down under', where it has since been converted (in 1994) into a single-seater.

Ciao Bella
G59 B
FIAT G 59

Fokker S-11 Instructor

The Netherlands

Type: single-engined primary trainer **Accommodation:** two pilots seated in tandem

One of the first postwar products of the recently-defunct Dutch manufacturer Fokker, the modest S-11 was designed as a primary trainer for either military or civilian use. It was to enjoy some success in the former role, with 40 Instructors being purchased by the Royal Netherlands Air Force (deliveries began in 1949) and 41 by the Israeli Defence Force. Licence-production of the aircraft was also undertaken in Italy for the AMI by Macchi (150 built as M.416s) and in Brazil by the specially-created Fokker Industria Aeronautica SA (100 delivered). The latter company also developed the S-12 variant of the Instructor, which utilised a nosewheel undercarriage – 50 were built for the Brazilian air force. In Dutch service, the S.11s also performed the primary training role for the naval component until finally retired, along with the surviving air force examples, in late 1973. A number of ex-military S-11s subsequently made their way onto European civil registers during the 1970s, the aircraft proving particularly popular with flying clubs in both Holland and Italy. A single ex-Dutch Navy example (E-31) also appeared on the UK civil register as G-BEPV in 1977 as part of the Strathallan Collection, and although flown throughout the 1980s, its Certificate of Airworthiness was left to expire in April 1993, and it was last seen in a dismantled state at Elstree Aerodrome in Hertfordshire. A small number of Instructors also made it across to North America soon after the type's retirement, although few now remain airworthy.

Specification:

Dimensions:
Length: 26 ft 8 in (8.18 m)
Wingspan: 36 ft 1 in (11.00 m)
Height: 7 ft 10.5 in (2.70 m)

Weights:
Empty: 1785 lb (810 kg)
Max T/O: 2425 lb (1100 kg)

Performance:
Max Speed: 130 mph (209 kmh)
Range: 430 miles (695 km)
Powerplant: Lycoming O-435A
Output: 190 hp (141 kW)

First Flight Date:
18 December 1947

Surviving Airworthy Variant(s):
S-11 and S-12

Right: Wearing the appropriate US civil registration N11J, this privately-owned S-11 Instructor regularly appears at the Confederate Air Force's displays at Midland Airport, in Texas. One of the first S-11s delivered to the Dutch air force in 1949, the aircraft has been kept in the scheme it wore during its final years of military service.

E 11
N911J

Folland Gnat T 1

UK

Type: single-engined advanced jet trainer **Accommodation:** two pilots seated in tandem

Derived from the revolutionary Folland Fo 139 Midge lightweight fighter, the Gnat proved to be a success with the RAF where its single-seat predecessor had not. The Midge tipped the scales at less than half the Hawker Hunter's weight, and cost less than half the price of the air force's then new frontline fighter. Despite the RAF showing little interest in the 'cheap' fighter, all was not lost for Folland as the air force had been attracted to the two-seat advanced trainer variant, primarily because of its ability to achieve near-supersonic speeds. Following testing of six development aircraft, the air force committed to the Gnat T 1 by placing an order for 14 pre-production machines with Folland in January 1958 – this was followed by a contract for a further 91 production aircraft. Once in service the Gnat was found to be over-complex, resulting in engineering headaches for maintainers, particularly in respect to longitudinal control runs and supporting systems. The small rear cockpit provided the instructor with virtually no forward visibility, and its use as a platform for weapons instruction was spoiled by pitch control difficulties that were never solved, despite several expensive attempts. Indeed, arguably the type's greatest contribution to the RAF during its two decades of service was as a recruiting tool when used as the original mount of the now world famous Red Arrows. Retired from flying in 1979, surplus Gnats served in ground instructional roles until a number were sold to civilian owners in 1987-89.

Specification:

Dimensions:
Length: 31 ft 9 in (9.65 m)
Wingspan: 24 ft 0 in (7.32 m)
Height: 10 ft 6 in (3.20 m)

Weights:
Empty: 5613 lb (2546 kg)
Max T/O: 9350 lb (4240 kg)

Performance:
Max Speed: 636 mph (1026 kmh)
Range: 1180 miles (1900 km) with drop tanks
Powerplant: Bristol Siddeley Orpheus 101
Output: 4230 lb st (18.84 kN)

First Flight Date:
31 August 1959 (T 1)

Surviving Airworthy Variant(s):
T 1

Right: Some 15 Gnat T 1s are currently airworthy, five being operated in the UK and the balance flown in the USA. Enthusiasm for the high-performance trainer in America was dampened after two fatal crashes in a matter of months in 1990-91. This ex-Cranwell T 1 (N1CL) spent a number of years as an instructional airframe at RNAS Culdrose prior to being exported to the USA in 1989. It is currently owned by McDonnell Enterprises of California City.

EXPERIMENTAL

Fouga CM 170 Magister

France

Type: twin-engined basic jet trainer **Accommodation:** two pilots seated in tandem

The world's first jet trainer to enter series production, the distinctive butterfly-tailed (also a first) Magister was built to an *Armée de l'Air* specification. Manufacturer Fouga relied heavily on pioneering work performed by designer Pierre Mauboussin, that had seen him power light aircraft and gliders with small jet engines. Reflecting his achievements, the prototype CM 170 Magister relied on two tiny Turboméca Marboré IIA turbojet engines, and so impressed the air force that ten pre-production aircraft were swiftly followed by large orders. Some 400 Magisters were eventually delivered to the *Armée de l'Air*, with a further 32 'navalised' trainers (boasting an arrestor hook and other minor strengthening changes) being taken on charge as CM 175 Zéphyrs by the *Aéronavale*. Production of the Magister continued until 1970, with its original parent company Fouga being acquired by the Potez group in 1958, followed by Sud-Aviation in 1967 and finally Aérospatiale shortly afterwards. The Magister also enjoyed remarkable export success, and aside from those CM 170s built in France for foreign customers (190 aircraft), Flugzeug Union Sud completed 188 in Germany, Valmet of Finland 62 and Israeli Aircraft Industries 36. The Magister remained little changed throughout its production life, with the later CM 170-2 featuring uprated Marboré VICs engines and the CM 170-3 (subsequently dubbed the Super Magister) increased fuel capacity, a modified canopy and Martin-Baker ejection seats. Although all *Armée de l'Air/Aéronavale* aircraft have now been retired, others remain in active service across the globe.

Specification:

Dimensions:
Length: 33 ft 0 in (10.06 m)
Wingspan: 37 ft 5 in (11.40 m)
Height: 9 ft 2 in (2.80 m)

Weights:
Empty: 4740 lb (2150 kg)
Max T/O: 7055 lb (3200 kg)

Performance:
Max Speed: 444 mph (715 kmh)
Range: 746 miles (1200 km) ferry range
Powerplant: two Turboméca Marboré IIA (CM 170-1) or VIC (CM 170-2) engines
Output: 1764 lb st (7.84 kN) and 2116 lb st (9.42 kN)

First Flight Date: 23 July 1952

Surviving Airworthy Variant(s): CM 170-1/-2/-3 and CM 175 Zéphyr

Right: This ex-Finnish Magister was one of a number imported into the USA by Warplanes Inc in the early 1980s. In Europe, ex- Armée de l'Air/Aéronavale CM 170/175s have been slow to reach private hands because of a French ruling blocking their classification as civil aircraft due to their ongoing military use. However, following the trainer's recent retirement from service in France, the dozen that are presently flying should be joined by 22 recently sold at auction in late 1997 – a further 30 were also acquired by US buyers at the same time.

3050
C

Gloster Meteor

UK

Type: twin-engined fighter, nightfighter and advanced trainer

Accommodation: pilot (dayfighter), pilot/navigator (nightfighter) and two pilots seated in tandem (trainer)

The only Allied jet combat design to reach the frontline during World War 2, the Meteor F 1 was handicapped because its large size and generous wing area had a detrimental effect on the modest power output of its Welland engines. However, these very design features came into their own following development work undertaken by Rolls-Royce which resulted in the Meteor being matched up with the far better Derwent series of turbojet engines from the F 3 onwards. The staple dayfighter of Fighter Command and the 2nd Tactical Air Force from 1945 until the early 1950s, the Meteor's ability to perform other roles was also exploited through the development of the radar-equipped Armstrong Whitworth series of two-seat nightfighters. The first of these (the NF 11) made its service debut in 1951, and the T 7 trainer of 1949; the latter variant was the RAF's first jet trainer. The ultimate dayfighter variant was the F 8, which dominated Fighter Command ranks from 1950-55. The final Meteor versions to reach RAF service were also derived from the basic F 8, the FR 9 being produced to perform the combined tactical fighter-reconnaissance role that had previously been the domain of the Spitfire FR 18, whilst the PR 10 replaced the Spitfire PR XI and 19 in the high-altitude strategic recce mission. With the completion of the final Meteor (a T 7) in 1954, production totalled 3,947 aircraft.

Specification:

Dimensions: (for F 8)
Length: 44 ft 7 in (13.59 m)
Wingspan: 37 ft 2 in (11.30 m)
Height: 13 ft 10 in (4.22 m)

Weights:
Empty: 10 626 lb (4820 kg)
Max T/O: 19 100 lb (8664 kg)

Performance:
Max Speed: 595 mph (958 kmh)
Range: 1000 miles (1610 km)
Powerplant: two Rolls-Royce Derwent 8 turbojet engines
Output: 7200 lb st (32 kN)

First Flight Date:
5 March 1943

Surviving Airworthy Variant(s):
T 7(Mod), F 8, NF 11 and D 16

Right: Today, just five Meteors remain potentially airworthy, and they are all based in the UK. This Armstrong Whitworth-built NF 11 (which later served as a TT 20 with the Royal Navy on Malta) was acquired by Al Letcher & Associates and flown from Biggin Hill to Mojave, California, in June 1975. It was later acquired by Al Hansen and Ascher Ward and flown in this scheme until struck off the civil register in January 1994. It presently resides in the museum at Edwards AFB.

Grumman F8F Bearcat

USA

Type: carrier-based piston-engined fighter-bomber and nightfighter **Accommodation:** pilot

Last in the long line of piston-engined Grumman 'cats', the Bearcat embodied all the lessons learned by the US Navy in the first two-and-a-half years of combat in the Pacific. Bucking the unwritten law of the day that stated that a new fighter had to be larger in order to be better than its predecessor, the Bearcat was both appreciably shorter (28 ft 3 in) and lighter (12,947 lbs max take-off weight) than the F6F Hellcat (33 ft 7 in and 15,413 lbs mto) it replaced. Both types shared a similar powerplant in the Pratt & Whitney R-2800 Double Wasp engine, but due to its more compact design, the Bearcat could easily out-perform the F6F. The US Navy was so pleased with the new fighter that they ordered 2,023 F8F-1s for delivery commencing in the New Year of 1945. VF-19 was the first unit to receive Bearcats, and it was just completing work-ups prior to heading for the war zone when the A-bomb raids brought the Pacific conflict to a dramatic halt. In the aftermath of war, the contract was slashed by 1,258 aircraft, and production ceased in May 1949 following the delivery of 1,266 F8Fs. No less than 24 active and reserve units flew Bearcats with the US Navy, the last F8Fs being retired in late 1952. A number of surplus aircraft were then sold to the French and Thai air forces, and whilst serving with these countries, the Bearcat saw limited action in south-east Asia.

Specification:

Dimensions: (for F8F-1)
Length: 28 ft 3 in (8.61 m)
Wingspan: 35 ft 10 in (7.87 m)
Height: 13 ft 10 in (4.2 m)

Weights:
Empty: 7070 lb (3206 kg)
Max T/O: 12 947 lb (5873 kg)

Performance:
Max Speed: 421 mph (680 kmh)

Range: 1105 miles (1775 km) on internal fuel
Powerplant: Pratt & Whitney R-2800-34W Double Wasp
Output: 2800 hp (2087 kW)

First Flight Date:
21 August 1944

Surviving Airworthy Variant(s):
XF8F-1, F8F-1/-1B/-1D, F8F-2/-2P and G-58B

Right: Owned by the Confederate Air Force, this F8F-2P is one of at least 12 Bearcat 'flyers' in the USA. A thirteenth F8F can be found with the Fighter Collection at Duxford, whilst one of the American Bearcats is due to be sent to France following restoration in late 1998. A high performance machine popular with pylon racers, the Bearcat has suffered more than its share of fatal accidents over the years, with seven lost in crashes.

S
201
201

Grumman AF-2 Guardian

USA

Type: carrier-based piston-engined ASW search and strike aircraft **Accommodation:** three-man crew

The result of at least two earlier attempts by Grumman to produce a replacement for the venerable TBF/TBM Avenger, the AF-2 was the 'jetless' derivative of the combination-powered XTB3F-1 (designated G-70 by the manufacturer). Built specifically to counter the growing Soviet submarine threat, the AF-2 entered production in two separate variants which combined to perform the ASW mission. The AF-2W (153 built) was the 'hunter' element of the team, its four-man crew searching for submarines with the aircraft's belly-mounted APS-20 radar and other dedicated sensors, calling in the three-man AF-2S 'killer' when a contact was encountered. The latter aircraft would then 'locally acquire' the target using underwing APS-31 radar, AVQ-2 searchlight and sonobuoys, before despatching the submarine with either bombs, a torpedo or depth charges – all of which could be carried in the aircraft's cavernous weapon bay (which contained the APS-20 radar equipment on the -2W). An initial production run of 193 AF-2Ss was undertaken by Grumman, with the first examples reaching the fleet in time for the Korean War in October 1950. A follow-on batch of 40 MAD-equipped S-models completed the production run in 1953. Swiftly replaced in the fleet by a single ASW platform in the form of the S-2 Tracker, the Guardian had been consigned to the navy reserve by 1955. Following complete retirement, a small number of AF-2Ss found further employment as fire-bombers in the USA.

Specification:

Dimensions:
Length: 43 ft 4 in (13.2 m)
Wingspan: 60 ft 8 in (18.49 m)
Height: 16 ft 2 in (4.93 m)

Weights:
Empty: 14 580 lb (6613 kg)
Max T/O: 25 500 lb (11 567 kg)

Performance:
Max Speed: 317 mph (510 kmh)
Range: 1500 miles (2415 km)
Powerplant: Pratt & Whitney R-2800-48W Double Wasp
Output: 2400 hp (1789 kW)

First Flight Date:
19 December 1946

Surviving Airworthy Variant(s):
AF-2S

Right: The world's sole airworthy Guardian (BuNo 126792) is owned by Jimmy Leeward of Leeward Air Ranch/Bahia Oaks Incs of Ocala, central Florida. One of the later MAD-toting AF-2Ss, this aircraft is an ex-Aero Union Corporation fire-bomber, five of which survived this hazardous occupation to earn retirement with various warbird collectors/collections across the USA. Since this photo was taken Leeward has had his Guardian repainted in a gloss sea blue scheme, with VS-27 markings.

Grumman F9F Panther

USA

Type: carrier-based jet-engined fighter-bomber and photo-recce aircraft **Accommodation:** pilot

As Grumman's first jet fighter, the F9F was originally designed to be powered by four small axial-flow Westinghouse 19XB (J30) engines identical to those slated for fitment into the AF-2's predecessor, the XTB3F-1. However, the US Navy had been monitoring the performance of the Rolls-Royce Nene being developed in Britain, and duly had two examples shipped to the Naval Air Center Philadelphia for bench testing. The engine's performance was so revelatory that it was soon placed in licence-production by Pratt Whitney as the J42. The first prototype XF9F-1 Panther made use of one of the British 'imports' to complete its flight trials in 1947-48. A conventional design with straight wings and excellent low speed handling for carrier operations, the first of 567 F9F-2 reached the fleet in May 1949. The first carrier-based jet to see action over Korea on 6 August 1950, the Panther went onto perform almost half the attack missions flown during the conflict by US Navy/Marine Corps units. The later -5 introduced a longer fuselage, taller tail and more powerful J48 turbojet, and went some way to improving the Panther's lack of straightline speed, although this problem was not totally addressed until the advent of the swept-wing F9F-6 Cougar in late 1951. The original straight-wing Panther was also a popular photo-recce platform, with about 100 of the 761 F9F-5s built converted into -5Ps. The Panther disappeared from the fleet in the late 1950s, although the Cougar was to see another decade of service.

Specification:

Dimensions:

Length: 37 ft 3 in (11.4 m)
Wingspan: 38 ft 0 in (11.58 m) excluding tip tanks
Height: 11 ft 4 in (3.47 m)

Weights:

Empty: 11,000 lb (4990 kg)
Max T/O: 19 494 lb (8840 kg)

Performance:

Max Speed: 526 mph (849 kmh)
Range: 1353 miles (2164 km) with external fuel
Powerplant: Pratt & Whitney J42-2 or -6 turbojet engine
Output: 5000 lb st (22.26 kN)

First Flight Date:

24 November 1947

Surviving Airworthy Variant(s):

F9F-2B and F9F-3

Right: Created out of two F9F-2 hulks between 1979-83 by Jack Levine and William Pryor in Pontiac, Michigan, this F9F-2 (BuNo 123072) won the Warbird Grand Champion prize at Oshkosh in 1984. Painted up in the VF-112 scheme it wore during a Korean War tour, the aircraft was bought by present owner Arthur Wolk in October 1985 following the death of Levine in a P-51D crash. One other F9F-2B (BuNo 123078) also remains airworthy in the USA, owned by the Cavanaugh Flight Museum.

V
NAVY
123072
VF112

Grumman Albatross

USA

Type: high-winged rescue, utility and ASW amphibian **Accommodation:** five/six-man crew and up to 22 passengers

Having gained a wealth of experience in the design and production of amphibians thanks to the huge number of JRF Goose aircraft it built during World War 2, Grumman decided to embark on a study to replace its earlier products with an all-new type, three times their size. The result was the G-64 Albatross, which retained a link with previous Grumman amphibians through the employment of the trademark cantilever high wing and main gear retraction into the fuselage sides. Both the US Navy and the USAF were so impressed by the performance of the Albatross prototype that they each ordered their own variants into series production. Whilst the air force adopted the designation SA-16A (later changed to HU-16), the navy opted initially for JR2F-1 and then UF-1 (also later redesignated). Production aircraft entered service in July 1949, and the improved SA-16B/UF-2 followed in 1955 – many A-model aircraft were also upgraded. The Albatross saw action over the Gulf of Tonkin during the early years of the Vietnam War, the aircraft continuing to serve American forces (including the Coast Guard) well into the 1970s. Also operated by other 'friendly' nations, the Albatross was built to the tune of 418 airframes. In the late 1970s Grumman and US operator Resorts International converted the Albatross from a military workhorse into a civil airliner, the resulting product being designated the G-111. Although 57 ex-military aircraft were purchased for reworking, only 12 were eventually modified.

Specification:

Dimensions: (for HU-16B)
Length: 62 ft 10 in (19.18 m)
Wingspan: 96 ft 8 in (29.46 m)
Height: 25 ft 10 in (7.87 m)

Weights:
Empty: 22 883 lb (10 380 kg)
Max T/O: 37 500 lb (17 010 kg)

Performance:
Max Speed: 236 mph (379 kmh)
Range: 2850 miles (4587 km)
Powerplant: two Wright R-1820-76A/-76B or R-1820-82 radials
Output: 2850 hp (2125 kW) and 3050 hp (2274 kW) respectively

First Flight Date: 24 October 1947

Surviving Airworthy Variant(s):
SA-16A/B, HU-16C/D/E, UF-1G/-2G, UF-1L/-1T, G-111

Right: Built as an SA-16A, this ex-USAF Albatross (51-5303) was upgraded into an HU-16B in the late 1950s. Formerly on display at Lackland AFB, Texas, this aircraft was restored by Ascher Ward in late 1994 and is now flown by Robert F Carlson. The current Albatross population in the USA alone numbers well over 150 aircraft, although only a fraction of these remain airworthy.

U.S. AIR FORCE
RESCUE
15303

Grumman S-2 Tracker/C-1 Trader USA

Type: piston-engined ASW and COD transport aircraft

Accommodation: four-man crew (S-2), or two-man crew and nine passengers (C-1)

Built as a single aircraft replacement for the 'hunter/killer' Guardian, the Tracker has enjoyed a frontline service life that is now well in to its fourth decade. Developed over an incredibly short time span, the S-2's modest dimensions nevertheless proved capable of housing all the ASW radar, sensor equipment and weaponry necessary to locate and destroy enemy submarines. A combination of fuel-efficient Wright Cyclone radials and long span wings gave the aircraft a superb loitering ability and good handling characteristics 'around the boat'. With space at a premium aboard ship, all the S-2's mission equipment was installed in such a way so as to allow its retraction back into the fuselage when not in use: the APS-38 was housed in a ventral 'bin', the MAD boom retracted into the tail and eight sonobuoys were stored in each of the rear engine nacelles. The first S2F-1s (redesignated S-2As in 1962) entered fleet service in February 1954, and when production ceased with the final S-2E in 1968, Grumman had built 1,181 Trackers/Traders. Progressively upgraded and improved in the ASW role, the Tracker also formed the basis for the specialist E-1B Tracer AEW aircraft and the C-1A Trader Carrier On-board Delivery transport. Although retired from the US Navy in the mid-1970s, at least eight of the twelve countries who also acquired the ASW variant continue to use them in daily service, whilst in North America and France, both piston-engined S-2s and turboprop conversions have been used as firebombers since the 1970s.

Specification:

Dimensions:
Length: 42 ft 3 in (12.88 m)
Wingspan: 69 ft 8 in (21.23 m)
Height: 16 ft 3.5 in (4.96 m)

Weights:
Empty: 17 357 lb (7873 kg)
Max T/O: 26 300 lb (11 929 kg)

Performance:
Max Speed: 287 mph (462 kmh)
Range: 900 miles (1448 km)
Powerplant: two Wright R-1820-82WA Cyclone radials, or AlliedSignal TPE331-15 or Pratt & Whitney Canada PT6A-67CF turboprops
Output: 3050 hp (2274 kW), 3290 shp (2450 kW) 2400 shp (1790 kW) respectively

First Flight Date: 4 December 1952

Surviving Airworthy Variant(s):
S-2A/E, C-1A and Turbo-Tracker

Right: Beautifully restored in the colours it wore whilst serving as the base COD at NAF Sigonella, in Italy, this C-1A (BuNo 136719) is just one of several Trader 'warbirds' flying in the USA. Aside from the numerous Tracker firebombers still earning their keep, a single S-2G is also regularly flown by the Royal Australian Navy's Historic Flight from NAS Nowra, in New South Wales.

719
NAVY

Grumman OV-1 Mohawk

USA

Type: turboprop-engined Elint and observation aircraft

Accommodation: two-man crew seated side-by-side

Truly a one-off design, Grumman's OV-1 Mohawk was built to fulfil the US Army's perceived need for a dedicated battlefield observation platform. Boasting STOL capability, crew armour and systems redundancy in order to allow it remain operational even after having been hit by small-arms fire, the Mohawk soon proved itself to be the ideal aircraft for the task. Its twin turboprop engines combined with the aircraft's short, high lift, wings to make the OV-1 the most agile of battlefield interdictors at low level, whilst its long-stroke undercarriage allowed for rough-field operations. The first OV-1As entered Army service in February 1961, and by the time of the Vietnam War, more than 150 were in the frontline. Although originally planned as an unarmed aircraft, early action over the jungles of south-east Asia proved the folly of such an idea, and Mohawks were quickly adapted to carry grenade launchers, bombs, rocket launchers and Minigun pods. The final OV-1s were delivered in 1970, bringing production to a close after the 375th airframe had been completed. The Mohawk's passive electronic intelligence role (Elint) saw the D-model become an important weapon in the 'Cold War' arsenal particularly in Europe, where aircraft were converted to carry infrared linescan and side-looking aircraft radar. The surviving OV-1D/RV-1s were retired in 1996 when fatigue lives were reached, although a handful of surplus aircraft were duly supplied to Argentina. Prior to that, several older OV-1A/Bs had also appeared in civilian hands in the USA.

Specification:

Dimensions: (for OV-1A)
Length: 41 ft 0 in (12.5 m)
Wingspan: 42 ft 0 in (12.8 m)
Height: 12 ft 8 in (3.86 m)

Weights:
Empty: 9937 lb (4507 kg)
Max T/O: 15 031 lb (6818 kg)

Performance:
Max Speed: 310 mph (500 kmh)
Range: 1410 miles (2270 km) with external fuel
Powerplant: two Lycoming T53-701 turboprops
Output: 2800 shp (2087.96 kW)

First Flight Date: 14 April 1959

Surviving Airworthy Variant(s):
OV-1A/B/C/D and JOV-1A

Right: The Mohawk is one of the more modern 'warbirds' flown by collectors in the USA, this OV-1C (68-15936/N134AW), for example, having only retired from Army National Guard service in 1992. It is owned and flown by the American Wings Air Museum of St Paul-Anoka County, Minnesota.

Hawker Fury/Sea Fury

UK

Type: piston-engined land- or carrier-based fighter-bomber and two-seat trainer

Accommodation: pilot, or two pilots seated in tandem

The final word in single piston-engined British fighter design, the Hawker Fury can trace its origins to the capture of an airworthy Focke-Wulf Fw 190 in June 1942. Prior to the arrival of this aircraft, British designers had considered air-cooled radial engines inferior to liquid-cooled inline powerplants. However, the performance derived from the Fw 190's compact BMW 801D dispelled previous beliefs, and resulted in Specification F.6/42 being issued by the Air Ministry for a 'Light Tempest'. Using the wings of the Tempest without the centre section, which were joined under an all-new monocoque fuselage, the Sir Sydney Camm-designed fighter was christened the Fury and married to the Centaurus radial engine, which had made its debut with the Tempest II. The Fleet Air Arm (FAA) also showed great interest in the new Hawker fighter, and Boulton Paul duly developed a navalised version for carrier deployment. Hefty RAF orders were summarily cancelled in the wake of VE-Day, and only 65 Furies were completed for Iraq, Egypt and Pakistan. Fortunately, the FAA remained committed to the Sea Fury variant, and purchased 50 F 10s and 615 FB 11s. Export sales of the Sea Fury were also achieved in Australia, Canada, the Netherlands, West Germany, Burma and Cuba. The FB 11 saw much action in Korea with the British, Australian and Canadian fleets, and although most Sea Furies had been phased out of frontline service by the late 1950s, Pakistani Furies remained active until 1973.

Specification:

Dimensions:
Length: 34 ft 8 in (10.56 m)
Wingspan: 38 ft 4.75 in (11.69 m)
Height: 15 ft 10 in (4.81 m)

Weights: (for Sea Fury FB 11)
Empty: 8977 lb (4090 kg)
Max T/O: 12 500 lb (5669 kg)

Performance:
Max Speed: 460 mph (740 kmh)
Range: 760 miles (1223 km) on internal fuel
Powerplant: Bristol Centaurus 15 or 18
Output: 2470 hp (1841 kW) and 2550 hp (1901 kW)

First Flight Date:
1 September 1944

Surviving Airworthy Variant(s):
Fury FB 10, Sea Furies FB 11, FB 50, T 20S and TT 20

Right: The Fury/Sea Fury is well represented on the global stage, with at least 36 potential 'flyers' (out of 60+ survivors) currently in private hands. The bulk of these are ex-Iraqi Fury FB 50s, retrieved from the desert and returned to the USA in 1979 – the Old Flying Machine Company's aircraft heading this line-up at Duxford is one such machine. Aside from airworthy examples in the USA and UK, single Fury FB 10s also appear on the registers in Australia and New Zealand.

HOUCHIN

Hawker Sea Hawk

UK

Type: carrier-based jet fighter-bomber **Accommodation:** pilot

The first jet fighter designed by Sir Sydney Camm, the Sea Hawk was of conventional appearance but unique internally: it had a jet pipe that split to serve two propelling nozzles, one on each side of the wing trailing edge. By adopting such an arrangement, Camm not only produced one of the best looking jet fighters of the period, but also created space to house a large internal fuel tank. Although initially designed for the RAF as the P.1040, the Sea Hawk evolved following the air force's decision to wait for the Hunter. Boasting a slightly greater wingspan, folding flying surfaces and other naval equipment, the first production F 1 was issued to the Fleet Air Arm in March 1953. Orders for this variant totalled 151 aircraft, the bulk of which were built by Armstrong Whitworth. After the delivery of the 95th F 1, production reverted firstly to the F 2 (40) and then the bomb rack-equipped FB 3 (116). Further new-builds were to follow, with 90 FGA 4s and 86 FGA 6s also being delivered to the FAA. Many earlier FB 3s were also updated to FB 5 specs, whilst FGA 4s were upgraded into FGA 6s. Part of the FAA for over a decade, the Sea Hawk was see action during the Suez Crisis of 1956. Foreign usage of the aircraft saw 22 supplied to the Royal Netherlands Navy, 68 for the newly-reformed German *Marineflieger* and 74 for the Indian Navy – these latter aircraft were the last retired from service in 1977.

Specification:

Dimensions:
Length: 39 ft 8 in (12.08 m)
Wingspan: 39 ft 11 in (11.89 m)
Height: 8 ft 8 in (2.79 m)

Weights:
Empty: 9720 lb (4410 kg)
Max T/O: 16 200 lb (7355 kg)

Performance:
Max Speed: 599 mph (958 kmh)
Range: 1400 miles (2253 km) with external fuel
Powerplant: Rolls-Royce Nene 103
Output: 5400 lb st (24.05 kN)

First Flight Date:
2 September 1947

Surviving Airworthy Variant(s):
Sea Hawk FG 6

Right: The world's sole airworthy Sea Hawk, FGA 6 WV908 returned to British skies in 1997 with the Royal Navy Historic Flight (RNHF) after having being grounded since 1989. Rebuilt at British Aerospace Dunsfold, the jet had only completed 30 hours of post-restoration flying before a catastrophic crack in its jet pipe was discovered after a flight in early July 1997, resulting in it being grounded for the foreseeable future at the RNHF's Yeovilton home.

A
ROYAL NAVY
WV908
188

Hawker Hunter

UK

Type: jet fighter-bomber, fighter-reconnaissance and two-seat advanced trainer
Accommodation: pilot, and two pilots seated side-by-side in trainer variant

The most successful postwar British fighter, the Hunter was to prove as popular in the export market as it was in RAF service. Built to Specification F.4/48, the jet could attain supersonic speeds in a shallow dive and was as manoeuvrable as any other jet fighter of the period. The first of 139 production F 1s was issued to Fighter Command in mid-1953, followed by 45 improved F 2s (Armstrong Siddeley Sapphire-powered) later that same year. These early Hunters suffered engine reliability problems particularly when the Aden guns were fired, but gas ingestion difficulties were overcome with the definitive F 4 (365 built), F 5 (105) and F 6 (383). The power of the jet's Avon (and Sapphire in the F 5) engine steadily increased with every new variant, and by the time the ground-attack optimised FGA 9 appeared, the Rolls-Royce Avon 207 powerplant was good for 10,150 lb st. Aside from engine improvements, aerodynamic details had also been addressed with the advent of the extended-chord dog-tooth wing from the F 6 onwards. A more drastic modification, which used the F 4 as a basis, was the T 7 advanced trainer variant, the first of which flew in October 1957. The last new-build Hunter was completed in 1966, which brought the production total to 1,985 aircraft. Aside from the 429 Hunters exported as new aircraft, 700+ had also been refurbished and supplied to 17 air forces across the globe. In 1998, only a handful of Hunters remain in frontline service in Zimbabwe.

Specification:

Dimensions: (for FGA 9)
Length: 45 ft 10.5 in (13.98 m)
Wingspan: 33 ft 8 in (10.26 m)
Height: 13 ft 2 in (4.01 m)

Weights:
Empty: 14 400 lb (6532 kg)
Max T/O: 24 600 lb (11 158 kg)

Performance:
Max Speed: 620 mph (978 kmh) clean
Range: 1840 miles (2961 km) ferry range
Powerplant: Rolls-Royce Avon RA.28 Mk 207
Output: 10 150 lb st (45.15 kN)

First Flight Date:
20 June 1951

Surviving Airworthy Variant(s):
F 4, F 6A, FGA 9, F 58, F 58A, GA 11, T 7, T 8C, T53 and Mk 51,

Right: The Hunter is second only to the Vampire as the most popular British fighter within the jet warbird fraternity, well over 70 having been bought by civilian operators. Around 30 are maintained in an airworthy condition, the bulk of these being ex-Singaporean, Swiss, RAF and FAA aircraft. This Mk 51, however, is actually an ex-Danish Hunter, flown by the EAA Aviation Foundation and based at Oshkosh. Airworthy Hunters can be found in the USA, UK, Australia, South Africa and Sweden.

WB188

Helio AU-24 Stallion

USA

Type: high-winged armed light utility turboprop aircraft **Accommodation:** two-man crew and up to nine passengers

A military derivative of Helio's family of civil utility STOL aircraft, the Kaman-developed Stallion was built specifically for the counter-insurgency role in south-east Asia. To achieve its incredible short-field performance, it was equipped with full-span automatic leading-edge slats, an augmented lateral control system and slotted flaps. Unlike Helio's H-250 and H-295 Courier (the U-10 Super Courier version of which was used extensively by the USAF and allied air forces in Vietnam), the Stallion relied on a turboprop engine to offset its increased all up weight. It had five underwing hardpoints and carried up to 1,900 lbs of assorted weaponry (rockets, bombs, flares and other 'goodies'), plus a cabin-mounted machine-gun or M197 20 mm cannon. Designated the H-550A by Helio, 15 were ordered as the AU-24A by the USAF with 1972 funds, these aircraft being sent to South Vietnam and evaluated during Project *Credible Chase*. Fourteen unarmed Stallions were subsequently handed over to the Khmer (Cambodian) Air Force in 1973. A solitary AU-24A has survived in the USA, being restored to airworthiness by the Museum of Flying in Santa Monica in the late 1980s and then sold at auction in October 1991 for $440,000.

Specification:

Dimensions:
Length: 39 ft 7 in (12.07 m)
Wingspan: 41 ft 0 in (12.50 m)
Height: 9 ft 3 in (2.81 m)

Weights:
Empty: 2860 lb (1297 kg)
Max T/O: 6300 lb (2857 kg)

Performance:
Max Speed: 216 mph (348 kmh)
Range: 1090 miles (1755 km)
Powerplant: Pratt & Whitney (UACL) PT6A-27
Output: 680 shp (507 kW)

First Flight Date:
5 June 1964

Surviving Airworthy Variant(s):
AU-24A

Right: Helio AU-24A 72-1322 seen over Los Angeles just a month prior to being sold by the Museum of Flying at their second Warbird & Classic Aircraft Auction, held at Santa Monica, 5-6 October 1991.

Hispano HA-1112 Buchón

Spain

Type: piston-engined fighter-bomber **Accommodation:** pilot

In 1942 the Spanish government agreed a licence-production deal with Messerschmitt for the Bf 109G-2, but finished aircraft only started trickling out of the Hispano Aviación plant in 1945, delayed by a lack of complete technical drawings and appropriate jigs. The most important 'piece' missing from the Gustav 'puzzle' was the Daimler-Benz DB 605 engine, which had been withheld in Germany because of a general shortage of powerplants. The Spanish were forced to use the less powerful, French-built, Hispano Suiza HS 12Z 17 instead, and some 69 HA-1112-K1Ls were built. Production of Bf 109 airframes quickly outstripped engine availability, and with the thawing of relations between the Spanish government and the West from 1952, a more powerful engine was sourced from Britain: the Rolls-Royce Merlin 500/45. The mating of the ex-German airframe with the engine of its arch wartime opponents was a happy one, and the first prototype Buchón (pigeon) completed its flight trials with few problems. Although the advent of the jet fighter had rendered the HA-1112-M1L obsolete before it had even reached service, the Spanish air force believed that the aircraft could still be valuable in the fighter-bomber role, and 171 were completed from 1955-58. The Buchón engine remained in service until 1965, and in 1968 23 survivors were acquired by Spitfire Productions for use in the film *Battle of Britain*.

Specification:

Dimensions:
Length: 29 ft 10 in (9.10 m)
Wingspan: 32 ft 6.5 in (9.92 m)
Height: 8 ft 6.5 in (2.60 m)

Weights:
Empty: 5855 lb (2656 kg)
Max T/O: 7011 lb (3180 kg)

Performance:
Max Speed: 419 mph (674 kmh)
Range: 476 miles (766 km)
Powerplant: Rolls-Royce Merlin 500-45
Output: 1632 hp (1217 kW)

First Flight Date:
30 December 1954

Surviving Airworthy Variant(s):
HA-1112-M1L

Right: Today, a handful of ex-Spanish HA-1112-M1Ls are still flown in the UK, the USA, Germany and Belgium, with several having had their Merlin engines replaced with DB 605s. US-registered Buch171 were completed from 1955-58. The Buchl engine was sourced ned by the Cavanaugh Flight Museum of Addison, Texas. It was photographed at the USAF Golden Air Tattoo at Nellis AFB in April 1997, resplendent in its new Luftwaffe scheme inspired by the Bf 109F flown by JG 26's Adolf Galland in 1941.

S

Hispano HA-200/-220 Saetta/Super Saetta Spain

Type: jet-engined basic trainer and light attack aircraft **Accommodation:** two pilots in tandem (HA-200), or pilot only (HA-220)

Built as a basic jet trainer by Hispano for the Spanish air force, the straight-winged Saetta (Arrow) relied on the same small Turboméca Marboré turbojet engines used by Fouga's Magister. Production of the aircraft was relatively slow, with just ten pre-production HA-200s being delivered up to 1960, when work commenced on the improved A-model. The latter variant enjoyed greater success with the air force, 30 being built as T-6G Texan replacements in the early 1960s, equipped with two underwing weapons pylons and two 7.62 mm machine-guns. The more heavily-armed HA-200D was placed in production in late 1965, 55 eventually being completed. Five years earlier the Egyptian air force had received its first HA-200Bs (armed with 20 mm cannon), before going on to licence-build the aircraft in Helwan – 63 were delivered as the Al-Kahira between 1961-69. The Saetta's ground attack capabilities were further increased during 1965 when Hispano fitted the HA-200Ds with uprated Marboré VI engines and doubled the number of underwing hardpoints. The success enjoyed by the Saetta in this role prompted the manufacturer to produce a dedicated ground attack variant known as the HA-220 Super Saetta, which was flown as a single-seater (an additional fuel tank replaced the second seat). Boasting better armour protection, Browning M3 machine-guns and six hardpoints, 25 Super Saettas were built for the Spanish, and these saw action over the Sahara in 1974-75. The last HA-220s were retired from Spanish service in December 1981.

Specification:

Dimensions:
Length: 29 ft 5 in (8.97 m)
Wingspan: 34 ft 2 in (10.42 m)
Height: 9 ft 4 in (2.85 m)

Weights: (for HA-200)
Empty: 4035 lb (1830 kg)
Max T/O: 7385 lb (3350 kg)

Performance:
Max Speed: 404 mph (650 kmh)
Range: 930 miles (1500 km)
Powerplant: two Turboméca Marboré II (HA-200) or Marboré VI (HA-220) turbojet engines
Output: 1760 lb st (15.50 kN) and 2116 lb st (9.42 kN)

First Flight Date:
12 August 1955

Surviving Airworthy Variant(s):
HA-200A/D and HA-220D

Right: No fewer than 50 HA-200 and -220s have been imported into the USA from Spain since 1983, the bulk of these subsequently appearing on the US civil register. This A-model (A.10B-85) was one of eight Saettas shipped into Truckee, California, by the Sierra Warbirds Corporation in 1991-92. The aircraft was acquired by Dayn Patterson of Oroville, California, in 1995.

A.108-85
N3180T
EXPERIMENTAL

Hunting Percival Provost

UK

Type: piston-engined basic trainer **Accommodation:** two pilots seated side-by-side

As the re-equipment of the RAF's frontline force with jet aircraft got into its stride in the late 1940s, the Air Staff realised that the Prentice/Harvard sequence in its training programme was not providing tyro fast jet pilots with sufficient experience for frontline flying. The Air Ministry issued Operational Requirement OR.257, which detailed the need for a new piston-engined trainer with greater performance. Although speed was not viewed as a driving force behind the potential design, it had to be able to cruise at 110 knots and have an endurance of at least two hours. Percival's response to OR.257 was the pugnacious Provost. The company had pre-empted the RAF requirement by privately producing a mock-up trainer called the P.56, which embodied many of the Air Force's criteria. The competition for the Prentice replacement was fierce, and no less than 15 companies submitted proposals. However, the early start made by Percival paid dividends as they were the only firm who could guarantee delivery of a prototype within the time specified by the RAF, and an initial order for 200 machines was placed with Percival in May 1951. The first production-standard Provosts made their service debut with the Central Flying School's Basic Training Squadron exactly two years later. Over 330 Provosts were eventually delivered to the RAF over a three-year period, and these remained in service until progressively replaced by Hunting's follow-on trainer, the Jet Provost.

Specification:

Dimensions:
Length: 28 ft 8 in (8.74 m)
Wingspan: 35 ft 2 in (10.72 m)
Height: 12 ft 2.5 in (3.73 m)

Weights:
Empty: 3350 lb (1519.56 kg)
Max T/O: 4400 lb (1995.84 kg)

Performance:
Max Speed: 201 mph (322 kmh)
Range: 648 miles (1036 km)
Powerplant: Alvis Leonides 126
Output: 550 hp (410 kW)

First Flight Date:
23 February 1950

Surviving Airworthy Variant(s):
T 1

Right: The MoD sold off the last of the RAF's Provosts in 1969, and today, ten out of 30 aircraft in the UK remain airworthy. Other examples can also be found in Australia and the USA – the aircraft featured in this photograph (still wearing its full FTS scheme) has been resident in America for over a decade.

WV666

Lockheed C-69/C-121 USA

Type: multi-engined transport, radar warning and fighter control, sensor relay and airborne television transmitting aircraft
Accommodation: four/five-man crew and 64 (C-69) or 88 passengers (C-121), or 22-26 systems operators (EC-121)

Developed for Howard Hughes' TWA, the majestic Constellation donned drab olive rather than red and white airliner trim as the first production airliners were requisitioned as strategic transports for the USAAF, designated C-69s. Just 22 were taken on charge, but these aircraft made a huge impression, and a number of longer-range C-121s were bought postwar. With the development of the stretched Super Constellation in 1950, the full military potential of the aircraft was realised, as specialist AEW (dubbed Warning Stars) and Elint variants were procured by the USAF and the US Navy. Some 20 distinct sub-types would eventually see operational service. The aircraft's 'finest hour' came during the Vietnam War, when firstly EC-121D radar surveillance platforms were despatched to monitor electronic traffic in North Vietnam. These machines were supplemented by improved H/J/Q-models, directing MiG intercepts, steering fighters towards tankers and plotting the position of downed airmen. No less than 72 RC-121Ds were acquired by the armed forces, and many were later rebuilt as EC-121T Elint and EW aircraft. Other roles performed by the EC-121 during the war included acting as airborne relay stations (EC-121R) for the *Igloo White* electronic surveillance network, set up in Laos to detect truck traffic passing along the Ho Chi Minh Trail; airborne command and control (EC-121H) for TAC strikes; and transpac shuttle missions (EC-121C/G) with MAC. The US Navy was the final military operator of the aircraft, its EC-121K/Q surveillance aircraft finally being retired in the late 1970s.

Specification:

Dimensions: (for C-121)
Length: 116 ft 2 in (35.41 m)
Wingspan: 123 ft 0 in (37.49 m)
Height: 27 ft 0 in (8.1 m)

Weights:
Empty: 80 611 lb (36 275 kg)
Max T/O: 143 600 lb (64 620 kg)

Performance:
Max Speed: 321 mph (517 kmh)
Range: 4600 miles (7405 km)
Powerplant: four Wright R-3350-34 or -91 Turbo-Compound radials
Output: 8800 hp (6562 kW)

First Flight Date: 9 January 1943 (C-69), 1953 (RC-121)

Surviving Airworthy Variant(s):
C-121A/C and EC-121T

Right: Four C-121s are presently airworthy in the USA, with this aircraft (ex-USAF EC-121T 53-0548) being operated by the Global Aeronautical Foundation (GAF) out of Camarillo, California. A fifth C-121C is operated in Australia, having been donated by the USAF and flown 'downunder' in 1996.

U.S. AIR
548

Lockheed T-33 and Canadair CL-30 USA and Canada

Type: jet-engined trainer **Accommodation:** two pilots in tandem

The world's most widely-used jet trainer, the T-33 (of which the CL-30 is a Canadian derivative) was built to the tune of some 6,750 airframes during the 1950s. Sired by the USAAF's first operational jet fighter, the F-80 Shooting Star, the prototype T-33 was a stretched F-80C fitted with a second seat and a long canopy. First examples were designated TF-80Cs, and these entered service with the USAF in the late 1940s as replacements for the veteran T-6 Texan. Dubbed the 'T-Bird' following the type's redesignation as the T-33, the trainer proved to be so successful that production of the two-seater soon outstripped that of the F-80. A total of 1,718 examples of the pioneering fighter had been built by the time production ceased in the early 1950s. The T-33's selection as the USAF's standard jet trainer convinced the US Navy that it too would benefit from operating the type, and 700 'T-Birds' were modified for 'blue water' operations as the TO-2 (later TV-2) SeaStar. Canada secured a licence, as did Kawasaki in Japan, to build its own variant, replacing the aircraft's Allison J33-A-35 turbojet powerplant with a Rolls-Royce Nene 10. Total CL-30 production ran to 656 aircraft between 1952-59, and although the last T-33s were retired from Training Command in 1974, the CT-133 (as the survivors had by now been redesignated) has soldiered on in ever-dwindling numbers, performing electronic warfare, target tug and general utility roles.

Specification:

Dimensions:
Length: 37 ft 9 in (11.48 m)
Wingspan: 38 ft 10.5 in (11.85 m)
Height: 11 ft 8 in (3.55 m)

Weights:
Empty: 8084 lb (3667 kg)
Max T/O: 14 442 lb (6551 kg)

Performance:
Max Speed: 600 mph (960 kmh)
Range: 1345 miles (2165 km)
Powerplant: Allison J33-A-35 or Rolls-Royce Nene 10
Output: 5200 lb st (23.16 kN) and 5100 lb st (22.71 kN) respectively

First Flight Date:
22 March 1948 (TF-80C)

Surviving Airworthy Variant(s):
T-33A/B, RT-33A, TV-2, CL-30 Mk 3 and CT-133

Right: Aside from those aircraft still in frontline use in Canada and Japan, roughly 50 are presently operated by civilians – the bulk of these are US-based, although a solitary CT-133A is based at Duxford with the OFMC. The CL-30 Mk 3 (RCAF 21265) seen in the photo opposite was imported into the USA in 1974 and eventually acquired by Raymond Mabrey in 1982. Sadly, both Mabrey and the Silver Star were lost in a crash at Selfridge ANGB, in Michigan, in June 1994.

U.S.AIR FORCE

Lockheed P-2 Neptune

USA

Type: maritime patrol and ASW aircraft **Accommodation:** seven-man crew

Designed with extreme range and endurance in mind, the P2V can trace its origins to work carried out by Lockheed subsidiary Vega (and designer Mac Short in particular) into an aircraft combining a high aspect ratio wing with two then new R-3350 radial engines. With Lockheed focusing its efforts on other high-priority designs like the P-38 and Ventura, it was not until the last months of World War 2 that the prototype XP2V-1 Neptune finally flew. Aside from the previously mentioned features, the aircraft also had large Fowler for good short-field performance, a large weapons bay and two defensive turrets. As if to prove the point about its range, the third production P2V-1 set a world distance record of 11,235 miles (18,077 km) in October 1946. The first of 838 Neptunes was delivered to the US Navy in March 1947, and the aircraft went on to serve as the standard ASW platform for many Western countries well into the 1960s. Built over seven distinct sub-types, the Neptune evolved into a superb maritime patrol aircraft, which was also produced in piston-engined form by Kawasaki in Japan. Aside from its use with the navies of the world, modified OP-2E Elint and AP-2H 'gunship' versions were also employed to great effect by the USAF and Army in Vietnam. Now fully retired from military service, near on 40 SP-2E/Hs are gainfully employed as firebombers in North America.

Specification:

Dimensions: (for SP-2H)
Length: 91 ft 8 in (27.94 m)
Wingspan: 103 ft 10 in (31.65 m)
Height: 29 ft 4 in (8.94 m)

Weights:
Empty: 49 935 lb (22 650 kg)
Max T/O: 79 895 lb (36 240 kg)

Performance:
Max Speed: 356 mph (573 kmh)
Range: 2500 miles (4000 km)

Powerplant: two Wright R-3350-30W Turbo-Compounds and two Westinghouse J34-36 turbojets (SP-2E) or two R-3350-32Ws and J34-36s (SP-2H)
Output: 6500 hp (4847 kW) and 6800 lb st (30.24 kN), and 7400 hp (5518 kW) and 6800 lb st (30.24 kN) respectively

First Flight Date: 17 May 1945

Surviving Airworthy Variant(s):
SP-2E (P2V-5), SP-2H (P2V-7) and P-2H

Right: Incorporating many specialist modifications including a 'solid' nose and lower fuselage retardent tank, SP-2H BuNo 145920 was the prototype Firestar tanker conversion (hence tanker #01) completed in 1988 by Aero Union Corporation of Chico, California. At least ten other Neptunes have since being modified to this standard. Aside from firebombers, several 'warbird' Neptunes are based in the USA, with a further two operating in Australia.

01
01

Lockheed F-104 Starfighter

USA

Type: jet fighter and two-seat fighter trainer **Accommodation:** pilot, and two pilots in tandem (TF-104)

Designed by Clarence L 'Kelly' Johnson after extensive briefings by USAF pilots back from Korea in 1951, the XF-104 Starfighter subordinated every usual requirement (manoeuvrability, weapons carriage and endurance) to deliver superior flight performance. Achieving Mach 2.2 and a hugely impressive initial climb rate, the Starfighter combined the power of the afterburning GE J79 with a wing of minuscule span and razor-thin chord (which produced little performance-sapping drag). With such features, the Starfighter was right on the limits of available technology. For example, the ailerons' power units had to be just one inch in depth due to the thickness of the wing. This caused delays in the development of production-standard aircraft. When the F-104A was released for use by the USAF's Air Defense Command in 1958, just 153 were purchased. Later, the tactically-optimised C-model was also procured (77 aircraft), and this variant saw limited service over South Vietnam. The aircraft would have been deemed a commercial failure had it not been for Lockheed securing a huge sale to NATO countries in 1960 for the strengthened and totally re-equipped F-104G. Led by the Luftwaffe, who bought the Starfighter for tactical nuclear strike and photo-recce roles, seven other European air forces and Canada procured 1,466 aircraft, which remained in service until retired in the early 1980s. Italy, Turkey and Greece still operate dwindling numbers of F-104Gs today, however. Further afield, Japan and Taiwan also flew substantial quantities of Starfighters.

Specification:

Dimensions:
Length: 54 ft 9 in (16.69 m)
Wingspan: 21 ft 11 in (6.68 m)
Height: 13 ft 6 in (4.11 m)

Weights:
Empty: 14 082 lb (6387 kg)
Max T/O: 28 779 lb (13 054 kg)

Performance:
Max Speed: 1450 mph (2330 kmh)
Range: 1380 miles (2220 km) with drop tanks
Powerplant: General Electric J79-GE-11A
Output: 15 800 lb st (70.28 kN) with afterburning

First Flight Date:
7 February 1954

Surviving Airworthy Variant(s):
F-104A, CF-104G/D and TF-104G

Right: Although NASA pioneered the use of civilian-manned NF-104As as early as 1963, a small number of surplus Starfighters have also found their way into the hands of non-government affiliated operators over the years. Currently, only two privately-owned Starfighters are flown in the USA, one of which is this ex-RCAF (12633) and Norwegian air force CF-104D. Restored at Chino in 1987, N104JR was operated by the Combat Jets Flying Museum of Houston, Texas, until donated to the EAA Foundation in 1992.

Lockheed P-3 Orion

USA

Type: maritime patrol and ASW aircraft **Accommodation:** ten-man crew

Although still very much a frontline type at the end of the 1990s (production slowly continues at Lockheed's Marietta plant in Georgia) the Orion has also become a civilian-operated aircraft in recent years. Several surplus P-3As have been converted into firebombers by the Aero Union Corporation of Chico, California. Derived from the L-188 Electra passenger airliner as an 'off-the-shelf' replacement for the P-2 Neptune, the P-3 Orion has proven so successful that well over 500 have been built in a handful of different variants. The first of 157 P-3As entered US Navy service in August 1962, this variant being followed by the improved B-model (124) in 1965, which boasted uprated engines and the provision to carry the Bullpup missile. The final ASW version built was the P-3C, which made its frontline debut in 1969. Steadily upgraded, the P-3C Upgrade III is still the most effective maritime patrol and ASW platform in today's US Navy, with in excess of 20 frontline and reserve units equipped with the aircraft. Specialist Elint and Sigint versions have also been acquired by the navy, whilst 21 foreign air arms have also bought either new or second-hand P-3A/B/Cs during the aircraft's long production run.

Specification:

Dimensions:
Length: 116 ft 10 in (35.61 m)
Wingspan: 99 ft 8 in (30.37 m)
Height: 33 ft 8.5 in (10.27 m)

Weights:
Empty: 61 491 lb (27 890 kg)
Max T/O: 142 000 lb (64 410 kg)

Performance:
Max Speed: 473 mph (761 kmh)
Range: 2383 miles (3853 km)
Powerplant: four Allison T56-14 turboprops
Output: 18 040 shp (13 452 kW)

First Flight Date:
19 August 1958

Surviving Airworthy Variant(s):
P-2A/B

Right: With its MAD boom cropped and weapons bay converted into a huge belly tank for the carriage of Fire-trol, this ex-US Navy P-3A was one of the first converted at Chico by Aero Union Corporation.

25
25
N925AU

Martin JRM-3 Mars

USA

Type: long-range transport aircraft **Accommodation:** 11-man crew and up to 180 passengers

The original Martin Mars was ordered on 23 August 1938 by the US Navy as a flying boat/patrol bomber. However, progress on the prototype was slowed by war priorities, and the first XPB2M-1 did not fly until July 1942. By that time the aircraft's long-range patrol mission had been passed to navalised Liberators (PB4Ys) and the ubiquitous PBY Catalina, forcing Martin to convert the huge flying boat into a troop transport. Redesignated the JRM-1, 20 Mars were ordered by the US Navy in January 1945, but only five were built before VJ-Day, followed by a sixth JRM-2 powered by uprated R4360 Wasp Major engines, which allowed the aircraft to operate with a higher take-off weight. The earlier aircraft were also subsequently re-engined, and all six machines given the designation JRM-3. Production JRMs differed from the XPB2M prototype principally by having a longer nose and a single tailfin in place of the traditional Martin endplate-type fins and rudders. All six aircraft were issued to NAS Alameda-based VR-2 of the navy's Air Transport Service, and the four survivors (one was lost in an accident in 1945 and another in a fire five years later) were declared obsolete in 1956. All four aircraft (and a massive stock of spares) were sold to MacMillan Bloedel in 1959 for service with Forest Industries Flying Tankers (FIFT), and although two were lost in 1961-62, the two survivors continue to operate in the firebomber role from Sproat Lake, Vancouver Island, British Columbia.

Specification:

Dimensions:
Length: 120 ft 3 in (36.66 m)
Wingspan: 200 ft 0 in (60.96 m)
Height: 47 ft 11 in (14.35 m)

Weights:
Empty: 77 920 lb (35 344 kg)
Max T/O: 165 000 lb (74 844 kg)

Performance:
Max Speed: 220 mph (352 kmh)
Range: 3315 miles (5304 km)
Powerplant: four Pratt & Whitney R4360 Wasp Major engines
Output: 14 000 hp (10 439 kW)

First Flight Date:
21 July 1945 (JRM-1)

Surviving Airworthy Variant(s):
JRM-3

***Right: Converted into a firebomber in 1962, this aircraft is the older of the two surviving JRM-3s flown by. FIFT – BuNo 76820 (C-FLYK) retains its US Navy sobriquet of* Philippine Mars *behind the cockpit. Sister-ship BuNo 76823/C-FLYL bears the title* Hawaii Mars.**

Max Holste M.H.1521M Broussard

France

Type: high-wing light utility transport and AOP aircraft **Accommodation:** pilot and five passengers

Developed from the smaller and less powerful M.H.152 Air Observation Post (AOP) prototypes of the late 1940s, the M.H.1521 was built as a private-venture by small French manufacturer Max Holste. Dubbed the Broussard (Bushman), the high-wing utility aircraft was a tough machine that combined the reliability of the Wasp radial engine with a sturdy airframe of useful size. Of the initial batch of 24 built by the manufacturer, 18 were quickly sold to the French army, under the designation M.H.1521M. Further orders from both the army and air force would subsequently keep Max Holste busy for 1954-59, as 363 Broussards were completed. Aside from its military use as a general utility 'hack' and occasional artillery spotter, the Broussard was also built in very limited numbers as a civil freighter, receiving the designation M.H.1521C. Surplus French Broussards were duly supplied to many former colonies in Africa for use by their embryonic air arms, the air forces of Cameroon, Ivory Coast, Maritania, Niger, Senegal, Togo and Upper Volta being amongst those that received examples. The final French M.H.1521Ms were retired from military service in the very early 1980s, and today a number of these remain airworthy in Europe – predominantly with aeroclubs in France. A further three are flown in the UK and USA.

Specification:

Dimensions:
Length: 28 ft 2.5 in (8.60 m)
Wingspan: 45 ft 1 in (13.75 m)
Height: 9 ft 2 in (2.79 m)

Weights:
Empty: 3373 lb (1530 kg)
Max T/O: 5953 lb (2700 kg)

Performance:
Max Speed: 168 mph (270 kmh)
Range: 745 miles (1200 km)
Powerplant: Pratt & Whitney R-985-AN-1 Wasp
Output: 450 hp (335 kW)

First Flight Date:
17 November 1952

Surviving Airworthy Variant(s):
M.H.1521M

Right: Still wearing its original Armée de l'Air scheme, this UK-registered M.H.1521M has been a regular attendee of summer airshows for almost a decade.

192

McDonnell Douglas F-4 Phantom II

USA

Type: all-weather jet interceptor **Accommodation:** two-man crew seated in tandem

The most famous post-World War 2 fighter, the McDonnell Douglas F-4 Phantom II is still very much a part of today's military scene, with 910 examples flown by nine air forces across the globe. However, this number is shrinking by the year, and most of the 5,195 built during a 19-year production run have now been retired. Initially developed as a company private venture by McDonnell, the Phantom II evolved from an attack aircraft armed with four 20 mm cannon to an advanced gunless all-weather interceptor boasting state-of-the-art radar and advanced missiles. Ordered by the US Navy for deployment aboard its carriers, the first production F-4Bs were delivered in December 1960. The following year a fly-off took place between a navy Phantom II and various frontline USAF fighter types, with the results clearly showing that the F-4 was vastly superior to its air force contemporaries. The USAF immediately ordered the aircraft in slightly modified form as the F-4C, and the jet went on to equip 16 of its 23 TAC fighter wings. The advent of the Vietnam War saw the Phantom II thrust into action, and the design's true multi-role capability soon saw it delivering tons of bombs in large-scale attack formations. Improved versions of the Phantom II (F-4E and F-4J) also made their debut in combat in the late 1960s, whilst other foreign customers like Britain, Israel, Germany and Japan all purchased the F-4 in large numbers.

Specification:

Dimensions: (for F-4D)
Length: 58 ft 3 in (17.76 m)
Wingspan: 38 ft 5 in (11.7 m)
Height: 16 ft 3 in (4.96 m)

Weights:
Empty: 28 000 lb (12 700 kg)
Max T/O: 58 000 lb (26 308 kg)

Performance:
Max Speed: 1500 mph (2414 kmh)
Range: 2300 miles (3700 km) ferry range
Powerplant: two General Electric J79-15 turbojets
Output: 34 000 lb st (151 kN)

First Flight Date:
27 May 1958

Surviving Airworthy Variant(s):
F-4D/E/F/G, QF-4N and RF-4C/E

Right: The largest fleet of civilian-operated Phantom IIs belongs to Tracor Flight Systems of Mojave, who have the contract to convert surplus F-4s into QF-4 target drones for the USAF – over 50 have so far been modified. Aside from drones, Tracor also utilises a quartet of F-4Ds for general trials work with the US military, the aircraft seen opposite (64-0965/N424FS) having been acquired by the company in March 1991.

N424FS

Mikoyan MiG-15

USSR and Poland

Type: jet fighter and dual-seat jet trainer **Accommodation:** pilot, or two pilots seated in tandem

As the first successful Soviet jet fighter, the MiG-15 arrived virtually unannounced in the skies over Korea in 1950 and gave UN pilots a disagreeable surprise. With its all-swept wing and aerodynamic design, the MiG could easily out-climb, out-dive, out-manoeuvre and out-pace its US and British jet contemporaries. Only with the arrival of the F-86 Sabre in December 1950 did UN forces have a fighter capable of matching the MiG-15 in most areas. At the 'heart' of the nimble fighter from the Mikoyan-Gurevich bureau was the compact Klimov RD-45F turbojet engine, which was a direct descendent of the Rolls-Royce Nene. Examples of the latter engine had been sent to the USSR by a then-friendly British government in 1947; these proved to be the answer to the powerplant problem that had delayed Soviet jet fighter development. Soviet designers were also heavily influenced by German data captured in 1945. Following flight testing in early 1948, the MiG-15 was placed into series production, and within five years 8,000 had been built in the USSR. Further improved variants (including the two-seat UTI trainer) entered service during the 1950s, with licence production continuing in Poland (Lim-1 fighter and SBLim-2 two-seater) into the early 1960s.

Specification:

Dimensions: (for MiG-15UTI)
Length: 33 ft 2 in (10.11 m)
Wingspan: 33 ft 0.75 in (10.08 m)
Height: 12 ft 1.7 in (3.7 m)

Weights:
Empty: 8210 lb (3724 kg)
Max T/O: 11 905 lb (5400 kg)

Performance:
Max Speed: 631 mph (1015 kmh)
Range: 655 miles (1054 km) with drop tanks
Powerplant: Klimov RD-45F
Output: 5004 lb st (22.26 kN)

First Flight Date:
20 December 1947 (MiG-15) and 23 May 1949 (MiG-15UTI)

Surviving Airworthy Variant(s):
MiG-15bis, F-2, Lim-1 and SBLim-2/-2A

Right: Now all but retired from frontline service, the MiG-15/-15UTI has become a popular warbird over the past decade, with ex-Polish-built and Chinese air force/navy examples appearing on the UK, US, Australian and New Zealand registers. This SBLim-2 is one of the most recent examples to appear in American skies.

25

Mikoyan MiG-17

USSR, Poland and China

Type: jet fighter and dual-seat jet trainer **Accommodation:** pilot, or two pilots seated in tandem

Built to in order to overcome the MiG-15's snaking and pitching at high speed, which rendered the fighter near-useless as a gun platform, the MiG-17 was an all-new design despite Western reports at the time that it was little more than an enlarged version of the earlier aircraft. Although physically resembling the MiG-15, the MiG-17 had a reduced-thickness wing with no fewer than three upper surface fences hindering the span-wise flow of air over the flying surface, particularly at transonic speed. Lacking taper, and with an inboard sweep of 47 degrees, the new wing vastly improved the jet's high speed handling. Other external changes saw the angle of sweep of the vertical tail surface increased and the fuselage lengthened by three feet. Internally, systems and equipment were also drastically improved. MiG-17s began replacing MiG-15s in Soviet service in October 1952, and definitive F-models (introducing the afterburning VK-1F) made their frontline debut in February of the following year. Numerous versions of the MiG-17 were to follow, some fitted with radar for use with the first Soviet air-to-air missiles. Production in the USSR totalled 8,000+ aircraft, and as with the MiG-15, licence-built examples were churned out in Poland (1,000) as Lim-5/6s and, on this occasion, in China as J-5/F-5s (767). Now all but retired from the air forces of the world, perhaps the MiG-17 is best remembered for its role in the Vietnam war.

Specification:

Dimensions: (for MiG-17F)
Length: 38 ft 0 in (11.59 m)
Wingspan: 31 ft 7 in (9.62 m)
Height: 11 ft 0 in (3.35 m)

Weights:

Empty: 8373 lb (3798 kg)
Max T/O: 13 078 lb (5932 kg)

Performance:

Max Speed: 671 mph (1080 kmh)
Range: 1230 miles (1880 km) with drop tanks
Powerplant: Klimov VK-1F
Output: 7451 lb st (33.14 kN) with afterburning

First Flight Date:

29 September 1951

Surviving Airworthy Variant(s):

MiG-17F, Lim-6bis and J-5

Right: Restored in a glossy rendition of the camouflage scheme it wore whilst serving in the Polish air force, this Lim-6bis was shipped into the USA from Poland in July 1993 and rebuilt in Salt Lake City for Dr George Lazik of Van Nuys, California (who also owns two SB Lim-2s). A rarer 'bird' than the MiG-15, airworthy MiG-17s currently number just three in the USA and one on the verge of flying in Australia.

619

Mikoyan MiG-21

USSR

Type: jet fighter and dual-seat advanced jet trainer **Accommodation:** pilot, or two pilots seated in tandem

Like its great Vietnam War foe the F-4 Phantom II, the MiG-21 is still a frontline fighter type, in service with some 50 air forces today. With well over 10,000 examples built in multifarious variants in the former Soviet Union alone (not to mention the improved Chinese F-7 version which is still in production), the famous delta-winged design will continue to serve well into the next century. Designed in the aftermath of the Korean War as a small, daytime interceptor with the best possible performance (identical performance criteria for Lockheed's F-104), the MiG-21 was developed over a series of prototypes and no less than 40 pre-production aircraft during the mid-1950s. The end result was the definitive MiG-21F-13, which began to enter frontline Soviet service in early 1958. This variant was also built under-licence in both Czechoslovakia and China. Later models (there have been at least 14 subsequent variants identified by Western observers) saw the basic lightweight fighter interceptor develop into a multi-role combat aircraft, boasting more internal fuel, heavier armament and vastly superior avionics. To cope with the increase in all up weight associated with these additions, more powerful 'Soyuz' engines were fitted into the MiG-21. The final variant to enter service was the MiG-21bis, which was essentially the third generation of this famous fighter to reach production.

Specification:

Dimensions: (for MiG-21PFM)
Length: 51 ft 8.5 in (15.76 m)
Wingspan: 23 ft 5.7 in (7.15 m)
Height: 13 ft 6.2 in (4.12m)

Weights:
Empty: 11,795 lb (5350 kg)
Max T/O: 20 018 lb (9080 kg)

Performance:
Max Speed: 1320 mph (2125 kmh)
Range: 808 miles (1300 km) with drop tanks
Powerplant: MNPK 'Soyuz' (Tumanskii) R-11F2S-300
Output: 13 613 lb st (60.57 kN) with afterburning

First Flight Date:
16 June 1955 (Ye-4)

Surviving Airworthy Variant(s):
MiG-21PF and MiG-21UM

Right: For many years the only MiG-21s flying in the America were those operated under a veil of secrecy by the USAF's 4474th FS out at Groom Dry Lake in Nevada. However, the civil register is now 'awash' with ex-Eastern Bloc hardware, which includes this Texas-based MiG-21PF of the Cavanaugh Flight Museum. A second airworthy two-seat MiG-21UM is also flown privately in Australia.

4603

Morane-Saulnier MS.760

France

Type: jet basic trainer, photo-survey and liaison aircraft

Accommodation: two pilots seated side-by-side and two passengers

The MS.760 was a direct descendent of MS.755 Flueret, which had been of the first light aircraft to embrace jet power. Relying on the small Turboméca Marboré IICs working in tandem (as with its contemporaries, the Magister and Saetta), the Paris was bought by the *Armée de l'Air* for use in the communications role. The first aircraft entered air force service in late 1958, being designated the MS.760A Paris I. A small number of aircraft were also supplied to the *Aéronavale* to perform a similar task, whilst the Paris I and uprated II also enjoyed notable export successes in both Argentina and Brazil. Argentinean manufacturer FAMA assembled 48 Paris Is for use as both trainers and ground attack platforms, as well as liaison duties. Neighbour Brazil acquired an identical number of more powerful Paris IIs, which they too used for similar roles – Argentine aircraft were later re-engined with Marboré VIs to upgrade them Paris II specification. Total Paris production numbered 150 MS.760As and 63 MS.760Bs, and today the aircraft has been retired from French service, although roughly 20 can still be found performing various roles in Argentina. A small number of ex-*Armée de l'Air/Aéronavale* machines have appeared on the French civil register, and one or two have also made it across to the USA.

Specification:

Dimensions:
Length: 33 ft 7.1 in (10.24 m)
Wingspan: 33 ft 3.6 in (10.15 m)
Height: 8 ft 6.4 in (2.60 m)

Weights:
Empty: 4557 lb (2067 kg)
Max T/O: 8642 lb (3920 kg)

Performance:
Max Speed: 432 mph (695 kmh)
Range: 1081 miles (1740 km)
Powerplant: two Turboméca Marboré VI turbojet engines
Output: 2116 lb st (9.42 kN)

First Flight Date:
29 July 1954

Surviving Airworthy Variant(s):
MS.760A Paris I

Right: This pristine Paris II was photographed at RAF St Mawgan just prior to its retirement from the* Armée de l'Air *in 1992. The last* Aéronavale *aircraft were not finally retired until late 1997.

N° 29
4-WA

North American F-86 Sabre

USA, Canada and Australia

Type: jet fighter-bomber **Accommodation:** pilot

Aside from the Bell UH-1 Huey, no other postwar Western military aircraft has been built in as great a numbers as the F-86. Total production, including licence-built examples in Canada, Australia and Japan, amounted to 9,502 airframes, covering no less than 13 separate land- and sea-based variants. The first contracts for the fighter were placed jointly by the USAAF and the US Navy in 1944, although the initial design featured unswept wings and a fuselage of greater diameter to allow it to house the Allison J35-2 engine. Following examination of captured German jet aircraft and related documentation, North American radically altered the design's shape, although the navy still received 30 FJ-1 Furys, which featured the original wing, fuselage and powerplant. The revised XP-86, however, was a vastly superior machine, setting a new world speed record in 1949 thanks to the aerodynamic overhaul of its fuselage and incorporation of the all new GE J47 turbojet. F-86A Sabres were thrust into battle over Korea in December 1950, where the aircraft soon achieved the status of 'ace maker' in pitched battles against the MiG-15. Combat ushered in further improvements to the aircraft, whilst the radar-equipped F-86D also enjoyed widespread use with Air Defense Command as its first all-weather interceptor. A dynasty of navy fighters in the form of the FJ-2/3 and -4 also served the fleet well into the late 1950s. Examples of the F-86 remained in the active inventory of a number of air forces into the early 1990s.

Specification:

Dimensions: (for F-86F)
Length: 37 ft 6 in (11.43 m)
Wingspan: 39 ft 1 in (11.9 m)
Height: 14 ft 8.75 in (4.47 m)

Weights:
Empty: 11 125 lb (5045 kg)
Max T/O: 20 611 lb (9350 kg)

Performance:
Max Speed: 678 mph (1091 kmh)
Range: 850 miles (1368 km) with external tanks
Powerplant: General Electric J47-GE-1 (F-86A), J47-GE-27 (F-86F), Avro Orenda 10 (CL-13A Mk 5), Orenda 14 (CL-13B Mk 6) and Rolls-Royce Avon 26 (CA-27 Mk 32)
Output: 4850 lb st (21.59 kN), 5970 lb st (26.56 kN), 6355 lb st (28.2 kN), 7275 lb st (31.7 kN) and 7500 lb st (33.4 kN) respectively

First Flight Date: 27 November 1946

Surviving Airworthy Variant(s):
F-86A/F, QF-86E, CL-13A Mk 5, CL-13B Mk 6 and CA-27 Mk 32

Right: This Canadair CL-13A Mk 5 has been recently restored to airworthiness in the USA in the colours of an early Korean War F-86A. Around a dozen Sabres are flown by enthusiasts in the USA, with a further five maintained as trials aircraft by Tracor (the majority of these are ex-Canadair aircraft). A solitary F-86A is also flown in the UK, and the RAAF Museum has maintained a CA-27 Mk 32 in airworthy condition since 1981.

U.S. AIR FORCE
FU-067

North American F-100D/F Super Sabre USA

Type: jet-powered two seat operational trainer **Accommodation:** two pilots seated in tandem

The natural successor to the F-86, the F-100 Super Sabre was both larger and more powerful than its famous forebear. It was also capable of breaking the sound barrier in level flight, which was a first for any combat aircraft. Development on the F-100 commenced at North American in the form of the NAA-180 as early as February 1949, and the overall size and shape of the fighter was barely influenced by the results of air combat over Korea. The F-100 made rapid progress through flight testing to the point where the 479th TFW declared itself operational with the Super Sabre in early 1954. However, a series of crashes saw the F-100A grounded in November of that same year, North American tracing the problem to the inertia coupling between the roll and yaw axes, which made the aircraft uncontrollable in certain flight regimes. This was rectified by lengthening both the wings and the vertical fin, and the manufacturer went on to construct 2,294 F-100s over five different variants. The C/D- and specialised two-seat F-100F 'Wild Weasel I' went on to see much service as fighter-bombers and anti-SAM missile platforms respectively, flying more missions than over 15,000 Mustangs during World War 2. Aside from its use by the frontline USAF and ANG and AFRes, F-100s also saw service with the French, Turkish, Danish and Taiwanese air forces, with the last examples being retired in the late 1980s.

Specification:

Dimensions:
Length: 52 ft 6 in (16 m)
Wingspan: 38 ft 9.5 in (11.81 m)
Height: 16 ft 2.75 in (4.96 m)

Weights:
Empty: 22 300 lb (10 115 kg)
Max T/O: 30 700 lb (13 925 kg)

Performance:
Max Speed: 864 mph (1390 kmh)
Range: 1500 miles (2415 km) with external tanks
Powerplant: Pratt & Whitney J57-PW-21A
Output: 16 950 lb st (75.18 kN) with afterburning

First Flight Date:
25 May 1953 (YF-100)

Surviving Airworthy Variant(s):
F-100F

Right: Six F-100Fs currently appear on the US civil register, five of which are operated by Tracor as target tugs or photo-chase platforms. These aircraft are the survivors of six ex-Danish air force machines acquired in January 1983, and they have seen service across the globe. The sixth F-100F 'flyer' is also an ex-Tracor machine, bought from the Turkish air force in 1989 and now operated by Texas-based Thomas Hickman of Sierra Hotel Inc.

N415FS

North American T-28 Trojan/Fennec USA and France

Type: piston-engined trainer and COIN aircraft **Accommodation:** two pilots seated in tandem

The T-28 was built by North American to fulfil an Army Air Force request for a training aircraft to replace the T-6 Texan, which had been used in the tuitional role for almost a decade. The resulting design featured a tricycle undercarriage, large frameless canopy and a powerful Wright R-1300 radial engine, which gave the Trojan (as it was named) a top speed in excess of 280 mph. Some 1194 T-28As were duly procured, and the type was also adopted by the US Navy/Marine Corps. The latter services re-engined their Trojans with more powerful 1425 hp R-1820-86 Cyclones, which drove a three-bladed propeller as opposed the T-28A's 'two-blader'. Designated the T-28B, 489 were acquired, followed by 299 carrier-capable C-models. Foreign sales were also achieved in substantial numbers, with the French purchasing over 250 aircraft. In 1960 the USAF expressed an interest in acquiring an armed counter-insurgency (COIN) variant of the T-28 for use in the close-support role, and several hundred surplus T-28As were so modified by North American and Fairchild in to AT-28D Nomads. These aircraft featured the R-1820 engine and three-bladed propeller, armour protection for the crew and six underwing hardpoints. Sud Aviation in France carried out a similar conversion on *Armée de l'Air* T-28As, the resulting aircraft being renamed the Fennec. Both types would see much action in South-East Asia and North Africa respectively, and today only a handful remain in service.

Specification:

Dimensions:
Length: 32 ft 10 in (10 m)
Wingspan: 40 ft 0 in (12.19 m)
Height: 12 ft 8 in (8.36 m)

Weights:
Empty: 7750 lb (3515 kg)
Max T/O: 15 600 lb (7075 kg)

Performance:
Max Speed: 360 mph (580 kmh)
Range: 2760 miles (4440 km) ferry range
Powerplant: Wright R-1300-1 (T-28A) or R-1820-86 Cyclone (T-28D)
Output: 800 hp (596 kW) and 1425 hp (1062 kW) respectively

First Flight Date: 26 September 1949

Surviving Airworthy Variant(s):
T-28A, GT-28A, T-28A Fennec, T-28B, T-28C, AT-28D and T-28R-2 Nomair

Right: One of the most popular warbirds in the USA, the T-28 has dominated airshows across North America for over a decade, whilst other examples can be found in Australia, New Zealand, the UK and France. These two California-based T-28Ds (ex-T-28A Fennec 51-3626 in the foreground and T-28A 49-1742 behind) are owned by the Museum of Flying and Wayne Brooks respectively.

42
WD
21
WD
USS LEXINGTON
NAVY
742
USS LEXINGTON
NAVY
VT-5
121

North American (Rockwell) OV-10 Bronco USA

Type: turboprop FAC and COIN aircraft

Accommodation: pilot and observer seated in tandem, and room for up to five troops in the rear cargo compartment

Unlike previous COIN aircraft used by the USAF and Marine Corps, the OV-10 Bronco was a purpose-built machine derived from Department of Defense studies carried out between 1959-65. North American's NA-300 had been one of several aircraft put forward by US manufacturers to meet the Marine Corps' LARA (Light Armed Recon Aircraft) specification, the Bronco emerging as the winner in August 1965. Aspects which gained it favour with the USMC included its superb all-round vision cockpit, STOL rough-field operability and rear cargo compartment. An initial batch of 271 OV-10As was delivered in 1967-68, of which 157 were supplied to the USAF for use in the FAC role in place of O-1s and -2. Unlike the previous types, the Bronco had four machine-guns with which to return enemy ground-fire. Surviving OV-10Cs soldiered on with both the USAF and Marine Corps into the early 1990s, with the later service developing a specialised night FAC variant that drew on experience gained by the USAF with 11 hastily-modified OV-10As in Vietnam. Designated the OV-10D, and featuring a modified nose housing sensor equipment, a 20 mm cannon turret and uprated engines, 17 former OV-10As were converted in 1979-80. These aircraft subsequently saw action during the 1991 Gulf War, although all American Broncos had been retired by 1994. A small number remain in frontline service with the air forces of Thailand, Venezuela, Morocco, the Philippines and Indonesia.

Specification:

Dimensions: (for OV-10A)
Length: 41 ft 7 in (12.67 m)
Wingspan: 40 ft 0 in (12.19 m)
Height: 15 ft 2 in (4.62 m)

Weights:
Empty: 6893 lb (3127 kg)
Max T/O: 14 444 lb (6552 kg)

Performance:
Max Speed: 281 mph (452 kmh)
Range: 1428 miles (2298 km) ferry range
Powerplant: two Garrett T76-G-416/417 turboprops
Output: 1430 shp (1066 kW)

First Flight Date: 16 July 1965

Surviving Airworthy Variant(s): YOV-10A, OV-10A and D

Right: Although now retired from military service in the USA, at least 22 ex-USAF and Marine Corps Broncos have been found work flying as fire-spotters with federal and state agencies – this ex-USAF YOV-10A is operated by the Department of the Interior in Boise, Idaho. Further Broncos are flown by NASA and American Warbirds Inc.

BLM
N646

North American (Rockwell) T-2 Buckeye USA

Type: basic jet trainer **Accommodation:** two pilots seated in tandem

The T-2A Buckeye was built as a result of a US Navy study into pilot training, which identified the need for an aircraft capable of taking a student that had graduated from the *ab initio* phase through to the point of initial carrier qualification. It incorporated many features seen on previous North American designs: the T-28C's flight control system and the wing of the FJ-1 Fury. Carrier landings are the most challenging phase of flight training for prospective naval aviators, and in order to make the T-2 as forgiving in the pattern 'over the boat', on approach to recovery and during the arrestor phase, the Buckeye featured robust landing gear, powered flight controls, large trailing edge flaps and airbrakes on either side of the rear fuselage. The single-engined T-2A entered service in July 1959, and some 201 were eventually delivered. The original Buckeye was underpowered, particularly when the aircraft's all up weight was taken into consideration, so the North American engineers commenced work on a twin-engined version soon after the first T2J-1s (redesignated T-2As in 1962) had been delivered. The B-model of which 97 were built from 1965-67 was powered by a pair of J60-P-6s. Yet another engine change saw the less powerful J85-GE-4 fitted in pairs into the T-2C, of which 231 were procured by the navy between 1969-75. The C-model is the only variant still in service today, and is slowly being replaced by the T-45 Goshawk.

Specification:

Dimensions:
Length: 38 ft 3.5 in (11.67 m)
Wingspan: 38 ft 1.5 in (11.62 m)
Height: 14 ft 9.5 in (4.51 m)

Weights:
Empty: 8115 lb (3680 kg)
Max T/O: 13 179 lb (5977 kg)

Performance:
Max Speed: 540 mph (840 kmh)
Range: 1047 miles (1685 km)

Powerplant: one Westinghouse J34-WE-36/-48 (T-2A) turbojet, or two Pratt & Whitney J60-P-6 (T-2B) or General Electric J85-GE-4 (T-2C) turbojets
Output: 3400 lb st (15.4 kN), 6000 lb st (26.68 kN) and 5900 lb st (26.2 kN) respectively

First Flight Date:31 January 1958

Surviving Airworthy Variant(s):
T-2B and C

Right: Two ex-navy Buckeyes have so far appeared on the US civil register, although this number will no doubt change as aircraft like VT-26 T-2C BuNo 158317 are retired over the next few years. Both civilian aircraft have been restored to airworthiness by Vancouver Island-based firm Victoria Air Maintenance.

54
C
158317
NAVY
VT-26
654
JET
DANGER
INTAKE

North American L-17A Navion

USA

Type: liaison and light utility aircraft **Accommodation:** pilot and three passengers

With massive military contracts for performance aircraft like the P-51 and B-25 cancelled just days after VJ-Day, North American was forced to break into the civilian market. Its first attempt was the NA-145 Navion four-seater monoplane, which enjoyed great success in 1946-47: over 1,100 were built, mostly for the domestic US market. The USAAF also showed an interest in procuring the Navion, and a prototype was duly flown in April 1946. Later that year the first of 83 L-17As (as the type was designated in army air force service) was delivered. The aircraft were employed as liaison 'hacks', personnel/cargo carriers and *ab initio* trainers within the USAF university Reserve Officers' Training Corps programme. In the summer of 1947 Ryan Aeronautical Company acquired the design and manufacturing rights for the Navion, selling a further 158 improved L-17Bs to the newly-created USAF. The first of these was delivered in November 1948, and a further order for five was placed in 1949. However, by February of that same year regular production of the L-17 had ceased, although 35 A-models were later upgraded into L-17Cs through the fitting of improved brakes and increased fuel capacity. Surviving L-17s became U-18s following the 1962 overhaul of all US military aircraft designations, although the Navion's service life ended soon afterwards. A handful of ex-military L-17s/U-18s can still be found on the US register today, although very few wear USAF colours.

Specification:

Dimensions:
Length: 27 ft 6 in (8.38 m)
Wingspan: 33 ft 5 in (10.19 m)
Height: 8 ft 7 in (2.65 m)

Weights:
Empty: 1945 lb (882 kg)
Max T/O: 2950 lb (1338 kg)

Performance:
Max Speed: 163 mph (260 kmh)
Range: 700 miles (1120 km)
Powerplant: Continental O-470-7
Output: 185 hp (140 kW)

First Flight Date:
April 1946

Surviving Airworthy Variant(s):
L-17A/B and C (U-18A/B and C)

Right: A veritable rarity in its USAF markings, this Navion has been fully restored to factory-fresh condition.

N8527P
G113
1650
N8068E
U.S. AIR FORCE

Northrop T-38 Talon and F-5 Freedom Fighter USA

Type: advanced jet trainer (T-38) and fighter-bomber (F-5) **Accommodation:** two pilots in tandem (T-38) and one pilot (F-5)

As the first supersonic aircraft designed from scratch as a trainer, the T-38 has enjoyed a remarkably successful, and long, career primarily with the USAF. Developed by Northrop as the N-156T, the Talon was a spin-off product from the company's lightweight fighter programme (N-156C), which eventually saw the F-5 Freedom Fighter produced in large numbers for export. As with its forebear, work on the N-156T proceeded for two years as a private venture before the USAF finally draughted a requirement for just such a supersonic advanced trainer. The first contract issued in May 1956 was for six YT-38 pre-production aircraft, whilst the premier production example completed its first flight in May 1960. By the time the final Talon had been delivered in January 1972, 1,187 had been constructed. The first trainer able to reproduce the flying characteristics of operational supersonic aircraft, the T-38 has been flown by every USAF pilot since its arrival in Air Training (and Education) Command in 1961. With no replacement even in the testing phase, it should remain in this role until at least 2015. The F-5A/B family of fighter-bombers was the result of a 1954 US government initiative to produce a simple lightweight fighter that could be supplied to friendly nations through the Military Assistance Program (MAP). The Northrop N-156C was officially chosen as the 'FX' fighter in 1962, and over 1,000 were subsequently produced and duly supplied to over a dozen air forces across the globe. Many are still in service today.

Specification:

Dimensions: (for T-38)
Length: 46 ft 4.5 in (14.14 m)
Wingspan: 25 ft 3 in (7.70 m)
Height: 12 ft 10.5 in (3.92 m)

Weights:
Empty: 7174 lb (3254 kg)
Max T/O: 12 050 lb (5465 kg)

Performance:
Max Speed: 858 mph (1381 kmh)
Range: 1094 miles (1761 km) ferry range
Powerplant: two General Electric J85-GE-5 turbojets
Output: 5360 lb st (23.84 kN)

First Flight Date:
10 April 1959

Surviving Airworthy Variant(s):
T-38A, F-5A/B and CF-5A/B

Right: The first Talon appeared on the civil register in private hands (excluding the 30+ that have been operated ostensibly as civil aircraft by NASA since the 1960s) as long ago as 1984. Indeed, this T-38A was that Talon, rebuilt from several damaged airframes by Chuck Thornton at Unlimited Aircraft Ltd at Chino in the early 1980s. It has since been followed onto the US register by a handful of surplus T-38s and F-5A/Bs.

N638TC

Percival Prentice

UK

Type: piston-engined basic trainer **Accommodation:** two pilots seated side-by-side plus one passenger

Built in the immediate postwar years as a replacement for the Tiger Moth in the basic flying training role, the Prentice was designed to meet Air Ministry Specification T.23/43 issued in late 1943. It incorporated many features deemed necessary following several years of wartime pilot training: a variable-pitch propeller, radios, flaps and considerably more powerful engine than that fitted to either the Tiger Moth or Magister. With pilot and instructor seated side-by-side, this aircraft was also the first of its type to feature such an arrangement in RAF service. Air force trials were carried out at the Central Flying School (CFS) with 30 aircraft commencing in November 1947, and following several modifications to the design in order to improve its general handling qualities, the first of 370 production T 1s was delivered to the FTSs in 1948. Well liked by students and instructors alike, the Prentice was used by the Basic Training Squadron of the CFS, numerous FTSs and as a communications 'hack' in the Middle East. Replaced by another Percival product in the form of the Provost from 1953 onwards, all bar one of the 253 ex-RAF aircraft sold off was bought by Aviation Traders, who had plans to convert the aircraft for civilian use. However, rendering the aircraft suitable for private use proved a more complex, and therefore costly, exercise than had at first been thought. Only a small number of Prentices made it onto the civil register in the UK. The rest were unceremoniously scrapped.

Specification:

Dimensions:
Length: 31 ft 6.5 in (9.60 m)
Wingspan: 46 ft 0 in (14.02 m)
Height: 12 ft 10 in (3.68 m)

Weights:
Empty: 3140 lb (1424 kg)
Max T/O: 4100 lb (1859 kg)

Performance:
Max Speed: 143 mph (230 kmh)
Range: 466 miles (745 km)
Powerplant: de Havilland Gipsy Queen 32
Output: 251 hp (187 kW)

First Flight Date:
31 March 1946

Surviving Airworthy Variant(s):
T 1

Right: Aside from four flyable Prentices (out of 16 known survivors) in the UK, a solitary T 1 is also flown in the USA. Bought by the American Aeronautical Foundation at the 1991 Museum of Flying Auction, this aircraft wears the colours of the original Prentice prototype.

N1041P

Percival Pembroke/Sea Prince

UK

Type: piston-engined light utility/transport aircraft **Accommodation:** two-man crew and up to eight passengers

Derived from the civilian Percival Prince feeder-liner and executive transport of the late 1940s, the RAF Pembroke entered service as an Anson replacement with a number of Communications Flights in 1953. Slightly larger, it had an increased wing span and the interior passenger seating facing aft, in accordance with standard RAF practice. Some 45 Pembroke C 1s were issued to the air force, serving until 1988 in a variety of roles ranging from air freight work to photo-recce and aerial survey taskings. Preceding the RAF's use of the Pembroke by at least three years, the Royal Navy's Fleet Air Arm (FAA) acquired its first (of three) Sea Prince C 1s in late 1950. Unlike the later Pembroke, these first FAA aircraft were near-identical to the civilian Prince Series II, and were used for special communications duties, including serving as an 'Admiral's Barge'. The follow-on Sea Prince T 1 greatly resembled the RAF's Pembroke C 1, being used as a 'flying classroom' to train observers navigation techniques and anti-submarine warfare. A lengthened nose was fitted, housing a radar dish, and the interior of the fuselage fitted out with a comprehensive suite of associated systems and wireless equipment arranged so as to accommodate three students. A total of 41 T 1s were delivered to the FAA from 1953 onwards, and the last examples were finally replaced by Jetstream T 2s at RNAS Culdrose in 1979.

Specification:

Dimensions:

Length: 46 ft 0 in (14.02 m)
Wingspan: 64 ft 6 in (19.66 m)
Height: 16 ft 0 in (4.87 m)

Weights:

Empty: 9589 lb (4349 kg)
Max T/O: 13 500 lb (6125 kg)

Performance:

Max Speed: 224 mph (360 kmh)
Range: 1150 miles (1850 km)
Powerplant: two Alvis Leonides 127 radial engines
Output: 1120 hp (835 kW)

First Flight Date:

13 May 1948 (civilian Prince)

Surviving Airworthy Variant(s):

Pembroke C 1 and Sea Prince T 1

Right: A number of surplus Pembrokes and Sea Princes were sold to private buyers following the respective types' gradual retirement, but today only a single example of each remain airworthy in the UK, with at least a second Pembroke C 1 also flying in the USA. This Pembroke C 1 was retired from No 60 Sqn service in the early 1980s, and flew for a brief while in the UK as G-BFKK before being exported to the USA.

ROYAL AIR FORCE
DINGHY RELEASE AND
EMERGENCY EXIT
EMERGENCY EXIT

Piaggio P.149D

Italy

Type: piston-engined basic trainer and communications aircraft

Accommodation: two pilots seated side-by-side and room for two/three passengers

Piaggio originally developed this aircraft as a civil four-seater, using many structural components from its 'tail-dragging' P.148 in use with the Italian air force. Small number were initially built in the mid-1950s, although production only really increased to profitable levels after an order for 72 received from the Luftwaffe in 1956. A licence deal was then struck between Piaggio and Focke-Wulf which saw 190 aircraft constructed by the famous German manufacturer. Designated the P.149D in Luftwaffe service, the aircraft was used for training and liaison tasks and was eventually used by three 'C' schools teaching future piston-engined pilots; the aircraft supplanted the venerable T-6 Texan in this role. Surplus P.149Ds were subsequently transferred to the air forces of Nigeria, Tanzania and Uganda as part of the German military assistance programmes in the late 1960s and early 1970s. The last German examples were retired in the early 1980s, while those in Africa had been declared unserviceable some years prior to this. A small number of ex-Luftwaffe P.149Ds have appeared on the civil registers of several European countries.

Specification:

Dimensions:
Length: 28 ft 9.5 in (8.80 m)
Wingspan: 36 ft 6 in (11.12 m)
Height: 9 ft 6 in (2.90 m)

Weights:
Empty: 2557 lb (1160 kg)
Max T/O: 3704 lb (1680 kg)

Performance:
Max Speed: 192 mph (304 kmh)
Range: 680 miles (1090 km)
Powerplant: Lycoming GO-480-B1A6
Output: 270 hp (201 kW)

First Flight Date:
19 June 1953

Surviving Airworthy Variant(s):
P.149D

Right: This German-registered P.149D (92+03) still bears the markings of its previous Luftwaffe owner, F/TF-104G-equipped **Waffenschule 10** ***at Jever. Here, the aircraft made more sense as a liaison and utility hack than a Starfighter! The unit was disbanded in 1983 as part of the phasing out of the Luftwaffe's F-104 force.***

92 03

Pilatus P-2

Switzerland

Type: piston-engined basic trainer **Accommodation:** two pilots seated in tandem

Designed specifically to operate from the high altitude airfields found in Switzerland, the Pilatus P-2 relied heavily on German engineering technology obtained through a licence to build Bf 109Es in the late 1930s. Serving exclusively with the Swiss air force as a basic trainer, the P-2 prepared pilots for eventual postings to Bf 109E and Morane-Saulnier MS.406 units well into the 1960s. The first 27 aircraft delivered to the Swiss from 1946 were dedicated pilot trainers, boasting full night flying equipment, oxygen equipment and comprehensive radios, whilst the second batch of 26 were completed weapons and observer trainers. To this end, the latter P-2s were fitted with a single 7.9 mm machine-gun and underwing racks for practice bombs and unguided rockets. Despite the advent of the more advanced P-3 in Swiss air force service from the late 1950s, P-2s were retained as aerobatics trainers (a role in which they excelled) until 1981. As with other Swiss aircraft sold off in the 1980s and 1990s, the P-2s were disposed of at auction, resulting in a number appearing on various European registers. Around half a dozen made it to the UK, where they were marked up in Swiss and German air force colours and used as adversaries for the growing number of Spitfires and Mustangs appearing at British airshows. Today, only one or two remain airworthy in the UK, as engine maladies with the aircraft's As 410A-2 have taken their toll.

Specification:

Dimensions:
Length: 29 ft 9 in (9.07 m)
Wingspan: 36 ft 1 in (11 m)
Height: 13 ft 4 in (4.08 m)

Weights:
Empty: 3040 lb (1378 kg)
Max T/O: 4335 lb (1966 kg)

Performance:
Max Speed: 211 mph (340 kmh)
Range: 535 miles (860 km)
Powerplant: Argus As 410
Output: 465 hp (346 kW)

First Flight Date:
1945

Surviving Airworthy Variant(s):
P-2.05

Right: Still retaining its original Swiss air force natural metal finish, P-2 U-110 (G-PTWO) has been present on the civil register for a number of years.

U-110
G-PTWO

PZL-104 Wilga

Poland

Type: piston-engined high-winged light utility aircraft **Accommodation:** pilot and up to three passengers

A purpose-built utility aircraft designed by PZL to replace the Polish-built Yak-12, the Wilga boasted a STOL performance similar to its Russian predecessor. The aircraft has proven to be very popular with flying clubs across the former Eastern Bloc, particularly as a glider tug thanks to its short take-off roll and the excellent 'pulling power' of its radial or inline engine. It has also been used for parachuting and air ambulance duties. The advent of the Wilga 3 in 1967 saw PZL redesign the fuselage to increase the cabin accommodation for up to three passengers, and modify the aircraft's undercarriage. Engine power was also increased to 260 hp thanks to the fitting of the licence-built Ivchyenko AI-14RA radial. The PZL-104 has enjoyed limited success in military ranks over the years, with a version known as the *Lipnur Gelatik* (Rice Bird) 32 being built under-licence in Indonesia in the early 1970s. The first aircraft manufactured under such an arrangement in this country, around 56 were constructed and 24 supplied to the Indonesian army. A further 15 are also operated by the Polish air force, and others have seen military service in Mongolia and Egypt. Continually updated and re-engined during its 35 years in production, over 900 Wilgas have been built by PZL. A handful have appeared in military markings primarily in the USA.

Specification:

Dimensions:
Length: 26 ft 6.75 in (8.10 m)
Wingspan: 36 ft 5.75 in (11.12 m)
Height: 9 ft 8.5 in (2.75 m)

Weights:
Empty: 1918 lb (870 kg)
Max T/O: 2866 lb (1300 kg)

Performance:
Max Speed: 173 mph (279 kmh)
Range: 317 miles (510 km)
Powerplant: PZL (Ivchyenko) AI-14RA or M-14P
Output: 260 hp (194 kW) and 360 hp (261 kW) respectively

First Flight Date:
24 April 1962

Surviving Airworthy Variant(s):
Wilga 3 and 80

Right: An unusual sight in Californian skies, this privately-owned Wilga has been repainted in a spurious Polish air force scheme. Note the matching seat covers and glider tow attachment on the tailwheel.

162

PZL TS-11 Iskra

Poland

Type: jet-engined basic trainer **Accommodation:** two pilots seated in tandem

Runner up in the early 1960s competition to provide the Warsaw Pact air forces with a jet basic trainer, the Iskra (Spark) was nevertheless selected by the Polish Air Force (PAF) instead of the winner (the Czech L-29) in an effort to keep the country's aircraft industry in business. The type entered service in 1964, where its viceless design and rugged construction soon made it very popular with students and instructors alike. Indeed, the aircraft has been used since its service introduction to provide an all through jet training syllabus at the PAF's two Officers' Flying Schools. There are a number of sub-variants, with the differences centring around the number of hardpoints available for weapons, or the fitment of photo-recce training equipment. TS-11 production was halted in 1978 following the delivery of around 500 aircraft, including 50 Iskra-Bis Ds to India, which became the only country to use the TS-11 aside from Poland. However, a small number of Iskra-Bis DF photo-recce trainers was built after 1982. PAF aircraft (around 150 are still in service) are being steadily retired as new PZL Iryda and Orlik trainers are delivered, whilst the Indian aircraft (38 survivors) are also due for retirement in the near future. A small number of surplus early-build Iskras have appeared on the US civil register in the past six years, where the type has proven to be an ideal fast VIP transport as well as affordable jet warbird.

Specification:

Dimensions: (for Iskra-bis B)
Length: 36 ft 7.75 in (11.17 m)
Wingspan: 33 ft 0 in (10.06 m)
Height: 11 ft 5.5 in (3.50 m)

Weights:
Empty: 5644 lb (2560 kg)
Max T/O: 8465 lb (3840 kg)

Performance:
Max Speed: 466 mph (750 kmh)
Range: 776 miles (1250 km)
Powerplant: IL SO-3
Output: 2205 lb st (9.81 kN)

First Flight Date:
5 February 1960

Surviving Airworthy Variant(s):
TS-11 Iskra-Bis A/B

Right: Few of the US-based TS-11s have been left in PAF colours, most owners preferring to repaint their aircraft in their own personal schemes. Iskras have also appeared on the Australian civil register in recent years too.

N21HW

Saab J 29

Sweden

Type: jet-engined fighter-bomber **Accommodation:** pilot

Western Europe's first swept-wing fighter to reach series production, the portly J 29 Tunnan (barrel) was designed by Lars Brising as a replacement for the Saab 21A/R and the P-51 Mustang. Combining a solid swept wing with the power of the licence-built de Havilland Ghost (produced as the Svenska Flygmotor RM2), the J 29 encountered very few development problems during its pre-production phase. First issued to a frontline unit (F 13) in May 1951, the J 29A immediately impressed its service pilots with its excellent turn radius and impressive rate of roll. Some 224 A-models were produced by Saab before production switched to the improved J 29B (capable of carrying external stores and drop tanks) of which 360 were delivered. Further improvements to the Tunnan saw the aircraft fitted with a 'dog tooth' wing and eventually an afterburning version of the RM2. The combination of the two resulted in the definitive J 29F, the 308 aircraft so designated being reworked J 29B/Es. The last new aircraft was delivered by Saab in March 1956. The Tunnan saw action briefly during UN peace-keeping operations in the Congo in 1961-63, but the only export customer for the jet was Austria, which acquired 30 surplus Swedish air force J-29Fs in 1961-62. The Tunnan remained in Swedish service until August 1976; the Austrian ones were retired in 1972. Today, a solitary J 29F is kept airworthy on the Swedish register by the air force museum.

Specification:

Dimensions: (for J 29F)
Length: 33 ft 2.5 in (10.12 m)
Wingspan: 36 ft 1 in (11 m)
Height: 12 ft 3.5 in (3.75 m)

Weights:
Empty: 10 141 lb (4600 kg)
Max T/O: 17 637 lb (8000 kg)

Performance:
Max Speed: 659 mph (1060 kmh)
Range: 1678 miles (2700 km) ferry range
Powerplant: Svenska Flygmotor RM2B
Output: 6170 lb st (27.4 kN) with afterburning

First Flight Date: 1 September 1948

Surviving Airworthy Variant(s):
J 29F

Right: The world's sole airworthy Tunnan is marked up in the colours it wore whilst flying with F 10 at Angelholm as part of the South air defence sector wing during the 1950s and 1960s.

R
SE-DXB
29670
R

Saab A/J 32 Lansen

Sweden

Type: jet-engined fighter-bomber **Accommodation:** pilot and navigator in tandem

Built as a jet replacement for the Saab 18 twin piston-engined medium bomber, the Type 32 Lansen was a swept wing design produced well in advance of other similar aircraft in western Europe. Work on the aircraft commenced in 1946, with permission to begin construction following two years later. Seating two crewmen in tandem, the Lansen was a deceptively large aircraft, and Saab utilised every inch of its airframe size to produce three variants capable of performing vastly different roles. The dedicated A 32A bomber was the first to enter squadron service (with F 17) in 1956; the Swedes taking delivery of 287 A-models between December 1955 and June 1957. The next version to be built was the S 32C reconnaissance aircraft; fitted with a battery of different cameras and radar equipment in place of the integral cannon, 44 were delivered during 1959-60. Finally, 120 J 32B night and all-weather fighters were constructed between July 1958 and May 1960, and shared between three fighter wings. In the early 1970s 24 surplus Lansens were modified into target tugs (redesignated J 32Ds) and ECCM trainers (J 32E); these aircraft were only retired from air force service in October 1997. Prior to these conversions, three J 32Bs had found their way onto the Swedish civil register in the early 1960s and flown as target tugs with the Svensk Flygtjänst. Following the Lansen's retirement from the frontline, a quantity of airframes were also sold to US operators for target tug and general high-speed flight calibration work.

Specification:

Dimensions: (for A 32A)
Length: 49 ft 0.75 in (14.94 m)
Wingspan: 42 ft 7.75 in (13 m)
Height: 15 ft 3 in (4.65 m)

Weights:
Empty: 16 398 lb (7438 kg)
Max T/O: 28 660 lb (13 600 kg)

Performance:
Max Speed: 692 mph (1114 kmh)
Range: 2000 miles (3220 km) with external tanks
Powerplant: Svenska Flygmotor RM5A2
Output: 10 362 lb st (42.1 kN) with afterburning

First Flight Date:
3 November 1952

Surviving Airworthy Variant(s):
J 32B and J 32D/E

Right: Parked in a quiet corner of a Swedish airfield, this J 32B was one of a trio sold to Svensk Flygtjänst (later Swedair) for target tug duties. Further aircraft were sold to US operators in California in the 1980s for similar work, although virtually all of these are now grounded at Chino or Mojave.

Saab J 35 Draken

Sweden

Type: jet-engined fighter-bomber **Accommodation:** pilot

Continuing Saab's tradition of producing advanced combat aircraft well ahead of western European rivals, the radically-styled Draken was designed in 1949-51 as a supersonic all-weather fighter, capable of operating from small airfields. Designer Erik Bratt chose the aircraft's unique 'double delta' shape because it offered the best aerodynamic package for arranging fuel and equipment in sequence behind each other. Although the resulting J 35 was quite long for a combat aircraft of its type, the fighter possessed a very small frontal area, making it extremely difficult to acquire visually. The first production contract was signed in August 1956 and 90 J 35As were completed between 1959-62. The improved J 35B, of which 73 were built, had improved radar and carried more weapons. The re-engined and appreciably heavier D-model was the next version bought by the air force, 120 being issued to five fighter wings in 1962-63. An unarmed reconnaissance variant, the S 35E, was developed at around this time too, and 32 new-build and a number of converted D-models were acquired for frontline use. The final variant to be built was the Falcon missile-equipped J 35F, of which no less than 230 were produced between 1965-72. Denmark, Finland and Austria also bought new or refurbished Drakens for use by their respective air forces. Only Sweden, Finland and Austrian still fly Drakens, with the former country being due to replace the 'double delta' with Grippens in 1999.

Specification:

Dimensions:
Length: 50 ft 4 in (15.4 m)
Wingspan: 30 ft 10 in (9.40 m)
Height: 12 ft 9 in (3.9 m)

Weights:
Empty: 25 132 lb (11 400 kg)
Max T/O: 35 275 lb (16 000 kg)

Performance:
Max Speed: 924 mph (1487 kmh)
Range: 2020 miles (3250 km) ferry range
Powerplant: Volvo Flygmotor RM6B (J 35A/B and SK 35C) or RM6C (J 35D/E/F)
Output: 15 000 lb st (66.78 kN) and 17 650 lb st (78.51 kN) with afterburning respectively

First Flight Date: 25 October 1955

Surviving Airworthy Variant(s):
J 35A, F 35 and RF 35

Right: A number of surplus Danish RF 35s were sold to American civilian operators soon after the type was retired in 1993, and these have found employment in high speed trials work with government agencies such as NASA and the Department of Defense. Three ex-Swedish F 35Fs had earlier been brought into the USA in the late 1980s by jet importers Dean Martin and Bill Marizan, whilst a solitary Draken is operated in Europe by the Scandinavian Historic Flight.

AR-117
N217FR
NASA
NASA

Saab 91 Safir

Sweden

Type: piston-engined basic trainer and communications aircraft **Accommodation:** two pilots seated in tandem with two passengers

Built as a basic trainer/tourer for both civil and military use, the Safir was developed in 1944-45 as one of three Saab products aimed specifically at the civil market – the Saab 90 Scandia airliner and the Saab 92 motorcar were the remaining two. Quantity production of the Saab 91 commenced in the spring of 1946 but sales were slow, and only 46 de Havilland Gipsy Major X A-models were produced. Most of these were sold to the Ethiopian Air Force as part of the large package of Swedish military equipment sold there in 1947. In 1949 the more powerful 91B was put into production, its flat six Lycoming O-435A significantly improving the Safir's performance. Two years later the Swedish air force ordered the aircraft for use as its new basic trainer after evaluating several different types, Saab building 74. Most of these were actually constructed under-licence by De Schelde in The Netherlands because of capacity problems at Saab's Linköping plant. Total Dutch production numbered 120 Safirs between 1951-55, as other civil and military buyers were also found for the 91B. Production returned to Sweden in 1956, and Saab had built 323 Safirs in all variants by the time the last aircraft was delivered to Ethiopia in 1966. Other military users of the Safir were Finland, Tunisia and Austria. Today, more than 50 Safirs remain in airworthy condition primarily in Europe, with two appearing on the UK civil register.

Specification:

Dimensions: (for Saab 91D)
Length: 26 ft 4 in (8.03 m)
Wingspan: 34 ft 9 in (10.60 m)
Height: 7 ft 2.66 in (2.20 m)

Weights:
Empty: 1570 lb (710 kg)
Max T/O: 2660 lb (1205 kg)

Performance:
Max Speed: 165 mph (265 kmh)
Range: 660 miles (1062 km)
Powerplant: Lycoming O-360-AIA
Output: 180 hp (134 kW)

First Flight Date:
20 November 1945

Surviving Airworthy Variant(s):
Saab 91B/D/D Mod/D2 and C

Right: This Saab 91D Mod has been owned by Shropshire-based pilot Dave Williams for over a decade. It was a regular participant in the DEC Schneider races of the 1980s and early 1990s.

117
FINA
G-BCFW
117

Scottish Aviation Twin Pioneer

UK

Type: twin piston-engined utility transport aircraft **Accommodation:** two pilots and sixteen passengers

Designed by specialist STOL manufacturers Scottish Aviation in the early 1950s as a successor to the single-engined high-wing Pioneer, the much larger 'Twin Pin' looked assured of a healthy production run when first unveiled in 1955. However, just 87 examples were built between 1956-64, the bulk of these being supplied as CC 1s and 2s to the RAF. The air force's initial order was for 20 aircraft, which were supplied to No 78 Sqn in Aden in 1958. A further 19 were subsequently acquired, and these saw extensive use with the overseas commands in Bahrain, Singapore and, of course, Aden. Used for a variety of general utility roles including paratrooping (11 fully equipped paratroops could be carried) and medical evacuation (six stretchers and five sitting casualties/medical attendants). Budget cuts saw the shrinking of the overseas force, and the 'Twin Pin' was subsequently deemed surplus to requirements and withdrawn from service in 1968. Several UK companies had operated brand new aircraft in civilian guise, and a number of ex-RAF CC 1 and 2s also made it onto the civil register. Today, only one aircraft remains in flying condition in the UK, ex-CC 2 XT610/G-APRS being operated by Air Atlantique. Other potentially airworthy examples can be found in Australia.

Specification:

Dimensions:
Length: 45 ft 3 in (13.80 m)
Wingspan: 76 ft 6 in (23.33 m)
Height: 12 ft 3 in (3.74 m)

Weights:
Empty: 10 200 lb (4630 kg)
Max T/O: 14 600 lb (6628 kg)

Performance:
Max Speed: 165 mph (266 kmh)
Range: 791 miles (1287 km)
Powerplant: two Alvis Leonides 531 radial engines
Output: 1280 hp (950 kW)

First Flight Date:
25 June 1955

Surviving Airworthy Variant(s):
Twin Pioneer 3 (CC 2)

Right: Seen operating in Air Atlantique's 'house colours' in 1996, the UK's sole airworthy 'Twin Pin' has recently been painted in an A&AEE-inspired 'raspberry ripple' scheme of red, white and blue.

ATLANTIC
G-APRS

Shorts Skyvan 3M

UK

Type: twin piston-engined utility transport aircraft

Accommodation: two pilots and seating for up to twenty-two troops

Shorts' Skyvan stemmed from a decision made in 1959 to make a small utility transport with a square-sided fuselage in order to accommodate oversized loads. The aircraft would also boast good STOL performance thanks to the incorporation of Miles' research into high aspect ratio wings – the flying surface on the Skyvan was based closely on that utilised by the Miles Aerovan. The first Series 1 Skyvans entered production powered by Continental GTSIO-520 piston engines, but these were swiftly replaced with the advent of the Series 2 by Astazou XII turboprop engines. Finally, Shorts settled on the Garrett TPE331-2-201As in the mid-1960s, the re-engined aircraft being designated the Skyvan 3M – a number of Series II were upgraded to this standard. Military sales were achieved at an early stage in the aircraft's production life, with the Royal Air Force of Oman being amongst the first customers with an order for 16 3Ms, which made it the operator of the largest fleet by some margin. A further 11 countries across the globe also acquired Skyvans. Most military aircraft have been used in the utility transport role, although the six acquired by Singapore had radar fitted in a thimble nose blister and were employed in the SAR/coastal patrol role. Production of the Skyvan ended in 1987, with Shorts having built 150 examples of which around 60 were supplied to military customers. The aircraft is still in use today with both military and civilian operators.

Specification:

Dimensions:
Length: 40 ft 1 in (12.21 m)
Wingspan: 64 ft 11 in (19.79 m)
Height: 15 ft 1 in (4.60 m)

Weights:
Empty: 7400 lb (3355 kg)
Max T/O: 14 500 lb (6577 kg)

Performance:
Max Speed: 203 mph (327 kmh)
Range: 694 miles (1115 km)
Powerplant: two Garrett TPE 331-2-201A turboprops
Output: 1430 shp (1070 kW)

First Flight Date:
17 January 1963 (civil prototype)

Surviving Airworthy Variant(s):
Skyvan 3M-300

Right: The Singaporeans were one of the first military users to retire their Skyvans, selling three of their fleet of six aircraft to Australian company Aerodata for conversion into aerial survey platforms for work with the World Geoscience Corporation. This shot shows ex-Royal Singaporean Air Force Skyvan 3M-300 serial 701 prior to the conversion at Jandakot Airport, in Western Australia, in 1995. These aircraft are the only civil-registered Skyvans in Australia.

VH-WGL
VH-WGL
DANGER
PROP
DANGER

Soko G-2A Galeb

Yugoslavia

Type: jet-engined basic trainer **Accommodation:** two pilots seated in tandem

The Galeb (Seagull) was the first indigenous Yugoslav jet design to enter series production. Built as a two-seat trainer initially, it was developed into a single-seat light strike aircraft. Similar in both powerplant and configuration to the MB-326 Macchi, the Galeb entered service with the Yugoslav air force in 1965, which eventually procured over 120 examples for use by the Air Academy and fighter and ground-attack schools. Export orders were also received from Zambia (six aircraft, plus 20 single-seat J-1s), and Libya, the later buying 120 G-2As in two batches. Production ended in 1985 with the delivery of the last Libyan aircraft. With the break up of Yugoslavia during the bloody civil war of the early 1990s, surviving G-2As were pressed into offensive action with the newly-created Serbian air force, equipping the 105th Fighter-Bomber Regiment. These aircraft saw much action between 1991-95, attacking Muslim forces in Bosnia-Herzegovina. Other Galebs remain in service in their designed role with the 'new' Yugoslavian air force and its Croatian counterpart. Prior to the civil war, a small number of surplus G-2As were acquired by jet warbird traders in the USA and imported into America to help satisfy the burgeoning demand for such aircraft in the late 1980s and early 1990s. Most of these remain on the civil register today.

Specification:

Dimensions:

Length: 33 ft 11 in (10.34 m)
Wingspan: 34 ft 4.5 in (10.47 m) without tip tanks
Height: 10 ft 9 in (3.28 m)

Weights:

Empty: 5775 lb (2620 kg)
Max T/O: 7690 lb (3488 kg)

Performance:

Max Speed: 470 mph (756 kmh)
Range: 770 miles (1240 km)
Powerplant: Rolls-Royce Viper II Mk 22-6
Output: 2500 lb st (11.12 kN)

First Flight Date:

May 1961

Surviving Airworthy Variant(s):

G-2A Galeb

Right: Only the addition of its US serial number and the word EXPERIMENTAL below the canopy denote that this G-2A is no longer in the employ of the Yugoslavian air force. Even the 12.7 mm machine-gun muzzles have been retained in the nose.

101
EXPERIMENTAL

Vickers-Supermarine Spitfire Mks XVIII and IX UK

Type: piston-engined fighter, fighter-reconnaissance and reconnaissance aircraft **Accommodation:** pilot

Representing the final Griffon-engined development of the original Spitfire airframe, the Mk XVIII and dedicated photo-recce PR XIX looked remarkably similar to the interim Mk XIV, which had been rushed into service with the RAF in early 1944 whilst design work continued on the definitive Griffon Spitfires. The delay in service entry of these marks meant that only the PR XIX would actually see action during World War 2. Unlike the 'temporary' Mk XIV (of which, rather ironically, there were many more built), the Mk XVIII/XIX had specially strengthened wings in place of the universal flying surfaces used by the earlier variant, a more robust undercarriage and a rear-view 'bubble' hood. The new aircraft also had increased internal fuel tankage, which went a some way to improving the Spitfire's notoriously poor range. Produced as either a standard fighter (F XVIII – 100 built) or fighter-recce (FR XVIII - 200 built) platform, the aircraft became available for frontline use in mid-1945 and was issued primarily to units in the Far East. The last RAF Spitfire variant to fire its guns in anger, the FR XVIII was retired in 1952. Turning to the unarmed PR XIX, this aircraft did see limited use in the strategic recce role prior to VE-Day, and remained in service as the PR 19 well into the 1950s. Some 225 PR XIXs were eventually constructed, the aircraft boasting the longest range of any Spitfire variant. Retired from frontline service in April 1954, three PR XIXs and two Mk VXIIIs remain airworthy today.

Specification:

Dimensions: (for Mk XIX)
Length: 32 ft 8 in (9.99 m)
Wingspan: 36 ft 10 in (11 m)
Height: 12 ft 8 in (3.9 m)

Weights:
Empty: 6550 lb (3016 kg)
Max T/O: 10 450 lb (4740 kg)

Performance:
Max Speed: 460 mph (736 kmh)
Range: 1550 miles (800 km)
Powerplant: Rolls-Royce Griffon 65/66
Output: 2050 hp (1528 kW)

First Flight Date:
Spring 1945

Surviving Airworthy Variant(s):
F XVIIIE, FR XVIIIE and PR XIX

Right: The rarely seen Warbirds of Great Britain Spitfire F XVIIIE SM969 is the only one of its type potentially airworthy in the UK. A second FR XVIIIE is flown by Rudy Frasca in the USA, whilst three PR XIXs remain resident in the UK, two being operated by the Battle of Britain Memorial Flight and the third by Rolls-Royce.

SM969
D A

Yakovlev Yak-11

USSR and Czechoslovakia

Type: piston-engined intermediate training aircraft **Accommodation:** two pilots seated in tandem

Designed as an advanced fighter/trainer variant of the Yak-3 for use with the VVS (air force), the concept of the Yak-11 was first discussed officially in mid-1944. Given a low production priority, a converted Yak-3 prototype, designated Yak-3UTI, finally flew in 1945. A definitive Yak-11 made its first flight 12 months later, the aircraft utilising many slightly modified Yak-3 fighter parts. Powered by a Shvetsov ASh-21 radial engine, the aircraft passed all facets of its flight testing and was put into series production in early 1947, with the first completed aircraft being delivered by the middle of that year. Unlike its fighter predecessor, the Yak-11 was only noted for being exceptionally agile whilst performing rolls. Yakovlev produced 3,859 basic Yak-11s before progressing to the U-model which featured a nosewheel for the training of jet fighter pilots. This variant replaced many standard Yak-11s during 1958. With production of the latter aircraft having ceased in the USSR in 1954, LET of Czechoslovakia commenced building the aircraft under licence with the designation C.11 that same year. Some 707 were constructed, and aside from use by Warsaw Pact nations, the aircraft was also exported to numerous communist countries. All but retired from frontline service today, the Yak-11 is now a highly-prized warbird due to its World War 2 fighter lineage. Over 100 survive in airworthy condition across the globe, the bulk of these being C.11s. 'Flyers' can be found in Belgium, UK, USA, France, Sweden and the Czech Republic.

Specification:

Dimensions:
Length: 27 ft 10.7 in (8.50 m)
Wingspan: 30 ft 10 in (9.40 m)
Height: 10 ft 9 in (3.28 m)

Weights:
Empty: 4189 lb (1900 kg)
Max T/O: 5379 lb (2440 kg)

Performance:
Max Speed: 295 mph (475 kmh)
Range: 800 miles (1290 km)
Powerplant: Shvetsov ASL-21
Output: 730 hp (425 kW)

First Flight Date:
1946 (Yak-11)

Surviving Airworthy Variant(s):
Yak-11, LET C.11 and Yak-3UTI

Right: Some of the first Yak-11/C.11s to appear on the civil registers in the West were 41 ex-Egyptian aircraft acquired by French firm Salis Aviation in 1984. This particular aircraft was one of those machines, and it was later sold to Californian airline pilot Joe Haley, who had it restored at Chino in 1989 with a Pratt & Whitney R-2000 1450 hp engine grafted to the front of it! The C.11 subsequently appeared at the Reno air races.

Yakovlev Yak-18/Nanchang CJ-5/6 USSR and China

Type: piston-engined primary training and aerobatics aircraft
Accommodation: two pilots seated in tandem, one pilot (Yak-18PM) or two pilots seated side-by-side and two passengers (Yak-18T)

Derived from the pre-war Yak UT-2, the Yak-18 was built from the outset as a dedicated basic trainer for the Soviet air forces. The first production aircraft entered service in the USSR in 1947. In 1955 the Yak-18U was introduced, the new aircraft featuring a lengthened fuselage and semi-retractable tri-cycle undercarriage. Wing dihedral was also increased, but despite a considerable increase in all up weight, the aircraft still relied on the venerable Shvetsov M-11FR radial engine. The horsepower problem was swiftly addressed with the advent of the Yak-18A in 1957, the new aircraft boasting a 260 hp Ivchyenko AI-14R radial in a revised cowling. Developed alongside the -18A was the single-seat -18P aerobatics aircraft, the first of which flew in 1961. By this time licence-production had begun in China on the CJ-5, followed by the improved CJ-6/6A (total production of the later aircraft came to 1500+). The final Yakovlev-built variant to enter production was the four-seat Yak-18T tourer, which first appeared in 1967 with side-by-side seating for both the pilot(s) and passengers. Production of the original Yak-18 training variant stopped at the end of 1967 after the delivery of 6,760 aircraft, many of which had been exported. Construction of the Yak-18T continued into the late 1980s, by which time over 1,000 had been built. In a surprise move, the now independently run Smolensk Aircraft factory re-commenced Yak-18T production in 1993.

Specification:

Dimensions: (for Yak-18A)
Length: 28 ft 0 in (8.53 m)
Wingspan: 34 ft 9.25 in (10.60 m)
Height: 11 ft 0 in (3.35 m)

Weights:
Empty: 2259 lb (1025 kg)
Max T/O: 2900 lb (1316 kg)

Performance:
Max Speed: 163 mph (263 kmh)
Range: 630 miles (1015 km)
Powerplant: Shvetsov M-11FR (Yak-18/18U), Ivchyenko AI-14R (Yak-18A/P) or AI-14RF (Yak-18PM/PS), VOKBM M-14P (Yak-18T) and Zhuzhou (SMPMC) Huosai 6A (licence-built AI-14RF)
Output: 160 hp (119 kW), 260 hp (193 kW), 300 hp (223 kW), 395 hp (294 kW) and 285 hp (213 kW) respectively

First Flight Date: 1946

Surviving Airworthy Variant(s):
Yak-18/18A/18U/18PM/18T, CJ-5, CJ-6 and CJ-6A

Right: A vast number of surplus Yak-18s have appeared in the West over the past decade as Eastern European air forces and flying clubs have sold off aircraft in the search for hard currency. This aircraft is a French-registered Yak-18U. Chinese-built Nanchang CJ-5/6s have also found their way onto civil registers in Australia, New Zealand, the USA and Canada.

7
F-AZFG

Yakovlev Yak-52

USSR and Romania

Type: piston-engined primary training and aerobatics aircraft **Accommodation:** two pilots seated in tandem or one pilot Yak-50)

Built as the successor to the Yak-18 family by Yakovlev in the mid-1970s, the Yak-52 bore a strong family resemblance to its predecessor despite having been totally redesigned by the manufacturer. Its stressed-skin airframe was derived from the single-seat Yak-50 aerobatics aircraft developed specially for the 1976 World Aerobatics Championship, which was held in Kiev. Production of the Yak-52 was assigned to the IAv factory at Bacau, in Romania, and work commenced on the first aircraft in 1979. Deliveries to the USSR began in 1980, and by mid-1992 over 1,600 had been constructed, primarily for use in the former Soviet Union. The aircraft is fully aerobatic, and one of its unique features centres on its tri-cycle undercarriage, which remains fully exposed when retracted so as to give the fuselage some protection in the event of a wheels-up landing. IAv became Aerostar following the communist overthrow in Romania, and the type remains in production today. A healthy number of ex-Soviet Yak-52s have been acquired by Western pilots during the 1990s, with examples featuring on most European registers, as well as in civilian hands in Australasian and North American.

Specification:

Dimensions: (for Yak-52)
Length: 25 ft 5 in (7.75 m)
Wingspan: 30 ft 6.25 in (9.30 m)
Height: 8 ft 10.25 in (2.70 m)

Weights:
Empty: 2238 lb (1015 kg)
Max T/O: 2877 lb (1305 kg)

Performance:
Max Speed: 223 mph (360 kmh)
Range: 310 miles (500 km)
Powerplant: VMKB (Vedenyev) M-14P
Output: 360 hp (268 kW)

First Flight Date:
1976

Surviving Airworthy Variant(s):
Yak-50/-52 and Aerostar Iak-52

Right: The Yak-52 has become a popular airshow performer in the UK in the past decade, this example being photographed on finals to Popham in September 1995. The aircraft has also proven popular with flying clubs, who appreciate its relatively low operating costs.

G-YAK I
100
ЯK-52

Helicopters

Aérospatiale Alouette II

France and India

Type: light utility helicopter **Accommodation:** pilot and four passengers

Developed from Sud-Est's three-seater SE 3120 of 1952, the Alouette II (then designated the SE 3130) was totally redesigned to incorporate the more powerful Artouste I turboshaft in place of the original helicopters, Salmson 9NH radial piston engine. Flown for the first time in March 1955, the helicopter received its French certification just over a year later and was immediately put into production. The helicopter's designation changed to SE 313B following SNCASE's merger with Sud Aviation, which was in turn absorbed by Aérospatiale in 1970. Re-engining in 1961 saw the introduction of the definitive SA 318C with its Astazou IIA powerplant, this variant being built in considerable numbers, raising overall production to 1,303. The final variant to be built was the 'hot and high' optimised SA 315B Lama, built specifically for the Indian army and combining the Alouette II airframe with the larger powerplant and dynamic components of the Alouette III. Aérospatiale built 407 up to 1989, whilst Indian manufacturer HAL continues low-rate licence production today. The Indian helicopters are known as Cheetahs. Over 50 countries have used the Alouette II in military service, with the German army being the biggest employer with 226 SA 315Bs and 54 SA318Cs. Many still remain in frontline service across the globe today. Aside from the many Alouette IIs built specially for civilian operators, surplus German and French aircraft in particular have also donned civil registrations in Europe over the past decade.

Specification:

Dimensions:
Length: 31 ft 11.75 in (9.75 m)
Rotor Diameter: 33 ft 5 in (10.20 m)
Height: 9 ft 0 in (2.75 m)

Weights:
Empty: 1961 lb (890 kg)
Max T/O: 3630 lb (1650 kg)

Performance:
Max Speed: 127 mph (205 kmh)
Range: 447 miles (720 km)
Powerplant: Artouste IIC6 (SE 313B), Turboméca Astazou IIA (SA 318C) or IIB (SA 315B)
Output: IIC6 and IIA both 360 shp (268 kW) and IIB 870 shp (649 kW) respectively

First Flight Date:12 March 1955

Surviving Airworthy Variant(s):
SE 313B Alouette II, SA 318C Alouette II and SA 315B Lama

Right: This Alouette II is maintained in airworthy condition by the Army Air Corps Historic Flight, based at Middle Wallop.

Bell Model 47/H-13 Sioux

USA, UK, Japan and Italy

Type: light utility and training helicopter **Accommodation:** pilot and two passengers

The world's first truly successful helicopter, the diminutive Bell Model 47 was built to the tune of over 5,000 airframes between the late 1940s and the early 1970s. Production lines were set up in Italy by Augusta, the UK by Westlands and by Kawasaki in Japan. The helicopter can trace its lineage back to the Model 30 of 1943, which the US Army ordered (ten examples) for service evaluation. Following their recommendations for general improvements, Bell created the Model 47 in late 1945, and this became the first helicopter to be certificated by the American Civil Aeronautics Administration (CAA). Military orders followed in 1947, with both the USAAF and the US Navy acquiring examples as the YR-13 and HTL-1 respectively. The US Army followed suit the following year by purchasing 65 H-13Bs. Bell continued to improve its Model 13 as more and more civil and military orders flowed in, and by 1953 it had focused production on the Model 47G. The military H-13 saw widespread use in the medevac role in Korea, assuming this critical mission from the Grasshoppers of World War 2. Numerous other air arms also experienced the versatility of the helicopter for the first time with the Bell 47, and today the type still remains in service albeit in greatly reduced numbers. A large quantity of ex-military Bell 47s have featured on civil registers across the globe, although in recent years a handful have donned pseudo-military marking once again and joined the 'warbird set'.

Specification:

Dimensions:
Length: 32 ft 7 in (11.31 m)
Rotor Diameter: 37 ft 1.5 in (11.31 m)
Height: 9 ft 3.75 in (2.82 m)

Weights:
Empty: 1936 lb (877 kg)
Max T/O: 2850 lb (1293 kg)

Performance:
Max Speed: 105 mph (169 kmh)
Range: 324 miles (521 km)

Powerplant: Franklin 6V-200-C32 (OH-13G/TH-13M), Lycoming VO-435-AIA/AIB/AID (OH-13H/UH-13H) or TVO-435-AIA (OH-13S/TH-13T)
Output: 200 hp (149 kW), 240 hp (179 kW) and 260 hp (193 kW) respectively

First Flight Date: 8 December 1945

Surviving Airworthy Variant(s):
Bell 47G/J, Augusta AB 47G and H-13B

Right: Over 30 Bell 47s are airworthy in the UK, this Redhill-based Westland-built 47G-4A boasting a most appropriate registration!

G-MASH

Bell UH-1 Iroquois

USA, Japan, Taiwan, Germany and Italy

Type: utility and battlefield helicopter **Accommodation:** pilot and up to 14 passengers (UH-1H)

Built in greater numbers than any other military aircraft since World War 2, the UH-1 family of helicopters has also seen service with more air forces than any other type. Developed from the XH-40 prototype, which had been built by Bell in response to a US Army requirement for a general utility and medevac helicopter, the first production HU-1A (Model 204), as it was then designated, entered service in the late 1950s. In 1961 Bell modified the design into the Model 205 through the adoption of a longer fuselage and more powerful engine, and the resulting UH-1D/H went on to become the most popular variant in military service – it remained in production until 1986, with 2,008 D-models being delivered to the US Army alone. The mainstay of the air mobile units during the Vietnam War, the Iroquois was also armed with a variety of gun packs, rocket pods and hand-held machine-guns during the conflict and flown in the helicopter gunship role. Further modifications to the basic design have seen the helicopter fitted with twin engines for naval use, ASW radar for sea search duties, and drastically enlarged so as to be able to carry up to 17 troops – the original HU-1A could accommodate just six. Still in widespread use today, the UH-1 in its many guises will undoubtedly feature in military service well into the 21st century. A substantial quantity of surplus Iroquois have been sold to civilian customers predominantly in the USA, where they have undertaken all manner of work.

Specification:

Dimensions: (for UH-1H)
Length: 41 ft 10 in (12.77 m)
Rotor Diameter: 48 ft 0 in (14.63 m)
Height: 14 ft 5.5 in (4.41 m)

Weights:
Empty: 5210 lb (2363 kg)
Max T/O: 9500 lb (4309 kg)

Performance:
Max Speed: 127 mph (204 kmh)
Range: 318 miles (511 km)
Powerplant: Textron Lycoming T53-L-13
Output: 1400 shp (1044 kW),

First Flight Date:
22 October 1956 (XH-40)

Surviving Airworthy Variant(s):
UH-1B/C/D/H/N and Augusta AB 205

Right: This UH-1H was one of those captured on the Falkland Islands in the wake of the Argentine surrender following the 1982 conflict. Returned to the UK, it was subsequently restored to airworthiness and flown for a number of years on the UK airshow circuit.

G-HUEY
UK

Hiller UH-12 Raven

USA

Type: light utility helicopter **Accommodation:** pilot and two passengers

Adopted as the standard US Army observation helicopter in 1950, the UH-12 was the end product of pioneering helicopter development carried out by Stanley Hiller Jr in 1944. Designated the H-23 by the army, 100 were initially acquired with optional dual controls and associated equipment for carrying two stretcher casualties in external panniers. The USAF ordered five H-23As at the same time, whilst the navy opted for 16 HTE-1s as helicopter trainers, followed by a larger purchase of the quad landing gear or skid-equipped HTE-2. The army re-ordered again with the advent of the H-23B, buying 273 fitted with skids rather than the tri-cycle gear of the of the A-model. These were used predominantly as trainers. The three-seater one-piece canopy H-23C followed (145 built) again for the army, but by far the largest order received by Hiller for the Raven was that placed for the D-model, which had an uprated engine and overhaul life extended from 600 to 1000 hours. No fewer than 483 were acquired, and these served on well into the 1970s. Overseas, the aircraft was used by a number of countries including Britain, Argentina and Egypt, with the latter two nations still having a few in service today. 2000+ UH-12s have been built, and the type still remains in limited production with Hiller Aircraft Corporation. Many ex-US Army aircraft have been flown in the USA over the past two decades, whilst a single HT 2 also remains airworthy in the UK.

Specification:

Dimensions:
Length: 27 ft 9.5 in (8.45 m)
Rotor Diameter: 35 ft 0 in (10.67 m)
Height: 9 ft 9.5 in (2.98 m)

Weights:
Empty: 1816 lb (824 kg)
Max T/O: 2700 lb (1225 kg)

Performance:
Max Speed: 95 mph (153 kmh)
Range: 205 miles (330 km)
Powerplant: Franklin O-335-4 (H-23) and O-335-6 (H-23B, or Lycoming O-540-23B (H-23D onwards)
Output: 178 hp (132 kW), 200 hp (149 kW) and 250 hp (186 kW) respectively

First Flight Date: January 1948

Surviving Airworthy Variant(s):
H-23A/B/C/D and HT 2 (UH-12E4)

Right: Representing the 41 HT 1/2s purchased by the Fleet Air Arm in the 1950s and 60s, this HT 2 (UH-12E4 has been beautifully restored in its original No 705 Sqn colours by PAN Air. This unit operated the helicopter in the training role between 1962-75 at RNAS Culdrose.

ROYAL NAVY
37

Kellett YG-1B

USA

Type: Autogiro pilot-artillery spotter trainer

Accommodation: pilot and passenger seated in tandem

Forerunner to the helicopter, the Kellett family of Autogiros can trace its lineage back to the late 1920s when brothers Rod and Wallace Kellett commenced experimentation with the K-1X. Having realised that their unique concept of using a two-bladed rigid rotor (that looked more like a rotating wing) was inferior to the work carried out by legendary Autogiro manufacturer Cierva, Kellett abandoned the 'flying wing' and fitted its next design with a more conventional hinged four-bladed rotor. By the mid-1930s the company had made such advances with the Autogiro that around 20 K-2/-3s had been sold to both civil and military buyers. The advent of the all-new KD-1 in the mid-1930s attracted much interest across the USA, with the army air corps deciding that it too should evaluate the Autogiro for possible military applications. A single KD-1 was obtained in 1936 and redesignated a YG-1 for USAAC purposes. The following year seven YG-1Bs were also purchased, these differing from the previous Autogiro in having additional radio equipment an reduced fuel capacity. Five of the seven YG-1Bs were placed in a standard training programme for pilot-artillery spotters and liaison duties, whilst the remaining two were bailed back to Kellett for further development work. After comprehensive test, USAAC pilots reported that the YG-1B offered no great advantage over fixed-wing aircraft at the time, and the Autogiros were duly passed on to the US Border Patrol in Texas.

Specification:

Dimensions:
Length: 21 ft 0 in (6.40 m)
Rotor Diameter: 40 ft 0 in (12.19 m)
Height: 10 ft 3 in (3.13 m)

Weights:
Empty: 1315 lb (596 kg)
Max T/O: 2250 lb (1020 kg)

Performance:
Max Speed: 120 mph (192 kmh)
Fuel Capacity: 30 USgal (113 l)
Powerplant: Jacobs L-4MA
Output: 225 hp (167 kW)

First Flight Date:
mid-1930s

Surviving Airworthy Variant(s):
YG-1B

Right: Astoundingly, one of the seven YG-1Bs survived border patrol work, followed by several years of private use and then several decades of storage, to be acquired by the Yanks Air Museum of Chino and restored to airworthiness. It was unveiled in mid-1997.

Piasecki (Vertol) HUP/H-25 Retriever USA

Type: utility, support, casevac and rescue helicopter **Accommodation:** two-man crew and five passengers

Piasecki's response to a US Navy Bureau of Aeronautics requirement issued in 1945 for a helicopter designed specifically for operations at sea, the HUP was designed to be both compact enough to fit aboard a variety of ships, yet capable of performing vertical replenishment, casevac, rescue and plane-guard duties. Known for its work with tandem rotor designs, it therefore came as no surprise when Piasecki adopted just such a layout for the HUP, which was placed into series production in 1948 following receipt of an order for 22 (later increased to 32) HUP-1 Retrievers. Crewed by two pilots and with space for five seated passengers or three stretchers, the HUP-1s made their fleet debut in early 1949. Continued development work by Piasecki resulted in the Sperry autopilot-equipped HUP-2, of which 165 were delivered (some of which were kitted out with ASW equipment, being duly designated HUP-2S). Army interest in the navy helicopter saw the company produce the H-25A, which had boosted flight controls and a strong cargo floor. Seventy were constructed alongside the final navy order for fifty HUP-3s (three of which were supplied to the Canadian navy). Surviving HUP-2/3s remained in US Navy/Marine Corps service long enough to be redesignated UH-25B/Cs respectively in 1962, although they were finally retired soon after. Today, two or three later model HUPs have been restored to flying condition in the USA, whilst a handful of others can be found on static display in various museums across North America (including Canada).

Specification:

Dimensions:
Length: 31 ft 10 in (9.7 m)
Rotor Diameter: both 35 ft 0 in (10.67 m)
Height: 13 ft 2 in (4.01 m)

Weights:
Empty: 3938 lb (1782 kg)
Max T/O: 6100 lb (2767 kg)

Performance:
Max Speed: 108 mph (174 kmh)
Range: 340 miles (547 km)
Powerplant: Continental R-975-34 (HUP-1) or R-975-42/-46A (remaining variants)
Output: 525 hp (391 kW) and 550 hp (410 kW) respectively

First Flight Date: March 1948

Surviving Airworthy Variant(s):
HUP-2/3 and H-25A

Right: This HUP-2 (BuNo 128596) has been restored and put on display at the MCAS El Toro museum in California, the helicopter having spent the final years of its military career at the base serving in the SAR role.

MARINES
596
DANGER

Piasecki (Vertol) H-21 Shawnee/Work Horse USA

Type: transport, assault and rescue helicopter

Accommodation: two-man crew and up to 20 armed troops (H-21B)

A vastly improved version of the metal-framed and fabric-covered Piasecki HRP-1 'Flying Banana' of the late 1940s, the HRP-2 was the result of a US Navy order in 1948 for a replacement design featuring an all-metal fuselage. The new helicopter was a totally revised design which saw the cockpit altered to seat the two-man crew side-by-side rather than in tandem, as well as the diameter (and length) of the fuselage appreciably increased. The smoother exterior finish made possible by the metal skinning also improved the helicopter's flight performance. Despite these modifications, the navy ordered only a handful of HRP-2s, and it was left to firstly the USAF, who acquired 18 YH-21s, followed by 38 H-21A Work Horses and 163 H-21Bs (with more powerful engines), and the army, with a massive purchase of 334 H-21C Shawnees, to make the most of this pioneering Piasecki design. The air force used a vast number of their H-21s in the utility role over the frozen wastes of Alaska in support of various bases and radar sites being built in the area, whilst the army sent 33 H-21Cs to South Vietnam as early as December 1961, making the Shawnee one of the first US military aircraft to arrive in-theatre. More than 90 of these obsolescent utility helicopters would eventually see action over Vietnam up to their final retirement in 1969. As with the smaller HUP, several H-21s have recently been restored to flying condition in the USA.

Specification:

Dimensions: (for H-21C)
Length: 52 ft 4 in (15.98 m)
Rotor Diameter: both 44 ft 6 in (13.56 m)
Height: 15 ft 1 in (4.6 m)

Weights:
Empty: 8700 lb (3946 kg)
Max T/O: 13 500 lb (6124 kg)

Performance:
Max Speed: 130 mph (209 kmh)
Range: 300 miles (482 km)
Powerplant: Wright Cyclone R-1820-103
Output: 1425 hp (1062 kW)

First Flight Date:
1949

Surviving Airworthy Variant(s):
H-21B/C

Right: HU-21B 53-4326 has been meticulously restored in its original USAF scheme by the team at the March AFB museum, the helicopter having been acquired through the local US Marshall's Office some years before.

U.S. AIR FORCE
326
34326

Saro (Saunders-Roe) Skeeter UK

Type: air observation post and training helicopter **Accommodation:** pilot and one passenger

Originally designed by pre-war Autogiro specialists Cierva, the W 14 Skeeter 1 completed its initial flight trials powered by a Jameson FF-1 engine. This rather limited horsepower engine was soon replaced by the Gipsy Major 10, with the resulting powerplant/airframe combination being designated the Skeeter 2. Other changes incorporated at this time included a larger-diameter main rotor and a boom of circular rather than triangular section. Cierva was acquired by Saunders-Roe in 1951, and development continued on the Skeeter through Mks 3 to 6, all of which utilised more powerful engines. The Mk 5 was the first free of ground resonance problems, and used the definitive Gipsy Major 200 Mk 30 engine. Further refinement produced the Mk 6, and four of these were delivered to the army for service evaluation – three Skeeter AOP 10s a one dual-control T 11 trainer. After a thorough trial, the army purchased 64 AOP 12s, of which a handful were subsequently supplied to the RAF for training purposes as T 12/13s with CFS Helicopter WIng. Entering service with the newly-formed Army Air Corps in 1957, the Skeeter flew in a variety of utility roles until given the tasking of immediate battlefield support in place of the fixed-wing Auster AOP 9 in 1961. However, performance deficiencies with the Skeeter meant that the AOP 9 remained in service until 1966. Fifteen Skeeters were also acquired by the German government and used by the Portuguese air force. All surviving British Skeeters were replaced by the Westland Sioux in 1968.

Specification:

Dimensions:
Length: 26 ft 6 in (8.08 m)
Rotor Diameter: 32 ft 0 in (9.75 m)
Height: 7 ft 6 in (2.31 m)

Weights:
Empty: 3938 lb (1782 kg)
Max T/O: 2200 lb (998 kg)

Performance:
Max Speed: 101 mph (161 kmh)
Range: 215 miles (344 km)
Powerplant: de Havilland Gipsy Major 200 Mk 30
Output: 200 hp (149 kW)

First Flight Date:October 1948

Surviving Airworthy Variant(s):
AOP 12

Right: A number of Skeeters were purchased for private use following the type's withdrawal from service, with this AOP 12 (XM553) being amongst the first. Only a handful remain airworthy today, with the Army Air Corps operating a solitary example as part of its Historic Aircraft Flight at Middle Wallop.

DANGER
G-AWSV

Sikorsky S-55/Westland Whirlwind USA, Japan and UK

Type: multi-role helicopter **Accommodation:** two-man crew and eight to twelve passengers

Few designs advanced the cause of rotary-winged flight as much as the Sikorsky S-55, which was built in previously unseen numbers for a helicopter: over 1,700 in the USA, UK and Japan. Constructed with the cabin directly beneath the rotor hub to avoid centre of gravity problems with varying payloads, the S-55 had its engine fitted in the nose behind two clamshell doors. The drive produced by the powerplant was relayed to the gearbox beneath the rotor hub via a diagonal shaft. Positioned above the fuselage was the cockpit, with the pilots seated on either side of the driveshaft. Used by all three services and the Coast Guard in the USA, the first production examples (HO4S-1s) were issued to the US Navy in late December 1950. Subsequent detail changes to the tail boom and stabilisers resulted in the USAF H-19B being produced, this variant also utilising the more powerful Wright Cyclone in place of the Wasp engine. Built as the H-19D Chickasaw for the army, the HO4S-3 and the HRS-3 for the Marines, it was this version of the helicopter which formed the bulk of the type's huge production run. Westland helicopters produced their first licence-built Whirlwind in 1952, and over the decade more than 400 were delivered to the RAF and Fleet Air Arm (FAA) in a handful of versions. Easily the best of these was the turboshaft-powered HAR 9 (FAA) and 10 (RAF), which remained in service into the late 1970s.

Specification:

Dimensions:
Length: 42 ft 3 in (12.88 m)
Rotor Diameter: 53 ft 0 in (16.16 m)
Height: 13 ft 4 in (4.07 m)

Weights:
Empty: 5250 lb (2381 kg)
Max T/O: 7900 lb (3583 kg)

Performance:
Max Speed: 112 mph (180 kmh)
Range: 360 miles (578 km)
Powerplant: Pratt & Whitney R1340-40/-57 Wasp, Wright R-1300-3 Cyclone, Alvis Leonides Major 755 (Whirlwind Series 2) or Rolls-Royce Gnome H 1000 (Whirlwind HAR 10)
Output: 600 hp (447 kW), 800 hp (596 kW), 750 hp (559 kW) and 1050 shp (783 kW) respectively

First Flight Date: 10 November 1949

Surviving Airworthy Variant(s):
H-19, HO4S and Whirlwind HAR 2 and 10

Right: One of three Whirlwinds currently flying in the UK, HAR 10 XJ729 has been operated by Austen Associates since mid-1994 after undergoing a thorough restoration. A number of Sikorsky-built S-55s also remain current on the US civil register too.

RAF
RESCUE
XJ729
ROYAL AIR FORCE
RESCUE

Sikorsky CH-54 Tarhe

USA

Type: heavy crane helicopter **Accommodation:** three-man crew and jump seats for two loader/technicians

Built specifically as a crane helicopter, the CH-54 Tarhe started life in the late 1950s as the first of its type built with the fuselage replaced by a slim beam, which was left as unobstructed as possible so as to allow bulky loads to be carried centrally. The helicopter was operated by a three-man crew (with two additional jump seats available), one of whom faced aft at all times in order to watch the load and operate the hooks and winches. Sikorsky built six YCH-54A pre-production aircraft in 1962-63, of which five were issued to the army for evaluation at Fort Benning. An order for 54 A-models was soon received by the company, and the first of these entered army service in late 1964. A further 37 CH-54Bs were subsequently delivered, these improved Tarhes having uprated engines and twin-wheel gears. A series of purpose-built Universal Military Pods were also acquired by the army from Sikorsky, these containers being configured either for the carriage of 46 troops or 24 stretchers. Others were kitted out as mobile command posts. communication centres or surgical hospitals. The Tarhe saw considerable use in Vietnam, operating with the 478th Aviation Company in support of the First Cavalry Division (Airmobile). They were used to lift M114 howitzers, armoured vehicles, bulldozers, troops and more 380 damaged aircraft during their time in combat. Finally retired from Army National Guard service in the early 1990s, most have appeared on the US civil register as general utility helicopters.

Specification:

Dimensions:
Length: 70 ft 3 in (21.41 m)
Rotor Diameter: 72 ft 0 in (21.95 m)
Height: 25 ft 5 in (7.75 m)

Weights:
Empty: 19 234 lb (8724 kg)
Max T/O: 42 000 lb (19 050 kg)

Performance:
Max Speed: 126 mph (203 kmh)
Range: 230 miles (370 km)
Powerplant: two Pratt & Whitney T73-1 (CH-54A) or T73-700 (CH-53B) turboshafts
Output: 9000 shp (6711 kW) and 9600 shp (4563 kW) respectively

First Flight Date:
9 May 1962

Surviving Airworthy Variant(s):
CH-54A/B and S-64E

Right: A considerable number of Tarhes have been converted into precision waterbombers (designated S-54Es) by companies like Hawkins & Powers and Erickson Air-Crane. These have proven to be so popular that 'new' aircraft have also been constructed using stockpiles of army spare parts.

ERICKSON AIR-CRANE
N6962R
S64E

Westland AH 1 Scout

UK

Type: multi-role tactical helicopter **Accommodation:** pilot and four passengers

The AH 1 Scout started life in 1956 as Saunders-Roe light helicopter proposal P.531, with work commencing on the first two prototypes two years later. Following the company's acquisition by Westland, work continued on the helicopter to the point where the Army Air Corps ordered a batch of pre-production aircraft. The first of these was delivered in August 1960, and was followed just a month later by the first of several production orders. Christened the Scout AH 1, the helicopter commenced army service at Middle Wallop in early 1963: 150 helicopters were eventually delivered, these machines subsequently being used for all manner of roles ranging from straight forward utility taskings to the anti-tank mission. Scouts saw action in the Falklands War, being employed primarily in liaison and medevac roles. The final examples in army service were retired in 1994, although two are maintained in airworthy condition by the Historic Flight at Middle Wallop. A naval version of the Scout, known as the Wasp, was also built in significant numbers (133), and served with distinction aboard numerous Royal Navy vessels for over 25 years. Fitted with four castoring wheels in place of the fixed skids, the Wasp also saw action in the Falklands War. Today, just a handful remain in service with the Indonesian and Malaysian navies, the Royal New Zealand Navy having retired their last examples in early 1998. No Wasps are presently operating in civilian hands.

Specification:

Dimensions:
Length: 30 ft 4 in (9.24 m)
Rotor Diameter: 32 ft 3 in (9.83 m)
Height: 11 ft 8 in (3.56 m)

Weights:
Empty: 3232 lb (1465 kg)
Max T/O: 5300 lb (2404 kg)

Performance:
Max Speed: 131 mph (211 kmh)
Range: 314 miles (505 km)
Powerplant: Rolls-Royce Nimbus Mk 101/102
Output: 1050 shp (783 kW)

First Flight Date:
20 July 1958

Surviving Airworthy Variant(s):
AH 1 Scout

Right: This Scout is seen fully armed up with SS 11 wire-guided anti-armour missiles on its stub weapons pylons. XW280 was not one of those AH 1s that survived military service.

DANGER
XW 280
ARMY

Index

A
A-1 (see Douglas Skyraider)
A-3 (see Douglas Skywarrior)
Aermacchi MB-326 **238**
Aero L-29 Delfin**240**
Aero L-39 Albatros **242**
Aeronca O-58 and L-3/-16 Grasshopper **106**
Aerospace Airtrainer CT-4 **244**
Aérospatiale Alouette II **424**
Airacobra (see Bell)
Albatros (see Aero)
Albatross (see Grumman)
Alouette (see Aérospatiale)
Anson (see Avro)
Antonov An-2 **246**
Argosy (see Armstrong-Whitworth)
Armstrong-Whitworth Argosy **248**
Auster (see British Taylorcraft)
Auster AOP 6/9/11 **250**
Avenger (see Grumman)
Avro 504 **12**
Avro Anson **42**
Avro Lancaster **108**
Avro Shackleton **252**
Avro Tutor **40**

B
B-17 (see Boeing)
B-24 (see Consolidated)
B-25 (see North American)
B-29 (see Boeing)
BAC Buccaneer **258**
BAC Jet Provost **254**
BAC Strikemaster **256**
Bearcat (see Grumman)
Beaver (see de Havilland)
Beech Model 18 **112**
Beech T-34 Mentor **260**
Beech UC-43/GB-2 Traveller **110**
Bell Model 47/H-13 Sioux **426**
Bell P-39 Airacobra **114**
Bell P-63 Kingcobra **116**
Bell UH-1 Iroquois **428**
Birdog (see Cessna)
Blenheim (see Bristol)
Boeing B-17 Flying Fortress **118**
Boeing B-29 Superfortress **120**
Boeing C-97 Stratofreighter/Stratotanker **262**
Boeing Model 100 (F4B-1) **44**
Boeing-Stearman Model 75 **46**
Boomerang (see CAC)
Bristol Blenheim IV/Bolingbrooke IVT **122**
Bristol F2B **14**
British Taylorcraft Auster I-V **124**
Bronco (see North American/Rockwell)
Buccaneer (see BAC)
Bücker Bü 131 Jungmann/CASA 1.131E **48**
Bücker Bü 133 Jungmeister/CASA ES-1 **50**
Bücker Bü 181/Zlin C.6/C.106 **126**
Buckeye (see North American T-2)

C
CAC CA-12 Boomerang **134**
CAC CA-25 Winjeel **264**
CAC Wirraway **132**
Camel (see Sopwith)
Canberra (see English Electric)
Caribou (see de Havilland)
CASA 2.111/Heinkel He 111H **128**
Catalina (see Consolidated)
Cavalier F-51D Mustang Mk 2 **266**
Cessna Model 185/U-17 Skywagon **272**
Cessna Model T-50 **130**
Cessna O-1 Birdog **268**
Cessna O-2 Super Skymaster **270**
Chipmunk (see de Havilland)
Consolidated B-24 Liberator **138**
Consolidated PBY Catalina **136**
Consolidated PB4Y-2 Privateer **140**
Convair C-131 **274**
Corsair (see Vought)
Culver PQ-14 **142**
Curtiss C-46 Commando **146**
Curtiss JN-4 Jenny **16**
Curtiss O-52 Owl **52**
Curtiss P-40 Warhawk **144**
Curtiss SB2C Helldiver **148**
Curtiss SNC **54**

D
Dassault MD.311/312 Flamant **276**
de Havilland Canada DBC-2 Beaver **286**

de Havilland Canada DHC-1 Chipmunk 284
de Havilland Canada DHC-4 Caribou 288
de Havilland Devon/Sea Devon 282
de Havilland DH 82 Tiger Moth 56
de Havilland DH 89 Dominie 58
de Havilland Mosquito 150
de Havilland Vampire 278
de Havilland Venom/Sea Venom 280
Dewoitine D 26 60
Douglas A-1 Skyraider 290
Douglas A-3 Skywarrior 296
Douglas A-4 Skyhawk 292
Douglas A-20 Havoc 158
Douglas A-26 Invader 160
Douglas B-23 Dragon 62
Douglas C-47 Skytrain 154
Douglas C-54 Skymaster 156
Douglas C-133 Cargomaster 294
Douglas R4D-8 298
Douglas SBD Dauntless 152
Draken (see Saab J 35)

E
English Electric Canberra 300

F
F-4 (see McDonnell Douglas)
F-5 (see Northrop T-38/F-5)
F-86 (see North American)
F-100 (see North American)
F-104 (see Lockheed)
Fairchild Argus 162
Fairchild C-119 Flying Boxcar 302
Fairchild C-123 Provider 304
Fairchild PT-19/-23/-26 Cornell 64
Fairey Firefly AS 5/6 306
Fairey Gannet 308
Fairey Swordfish 164
Fiat G.46 310
Fiat G.59 312
Fieseler Fi 156 Storch/Morane Saulnier 500 166
Fleet Finch 66
Fleet Fort 168
Focke-Wulf Fw 44 Stieglitz 68
Fokker S.11 Instructor 314
Folland Gnat T1 316
Fouga CM178 Magister 318
Freedom Fighter (see Northrop T-28/F-5)

G
Gannet (see Fairey)
Gloster Gladiator 70
Gloster Meteor 320
Gnat (see Folland)
Grasshopper (see Aeronca)
Grumman AF-2 Guardian 324
Grumman Albatross 328
Grumman F3F 74
Grumman F4F Wildcat 170
Grumman F6F Hellcat 176
Grumman F7F Tigercat 178
Grumman F8F Bearcat 322
Grumman F9F Panther 326
Grumman G-21A Goose 76
Grumman G-44 Widgeon/Super Widgeon 172
Grumman JF/J2F Duck 72
Grumman OV-1 Mohawk 332
Grumman S-2 Tracker/C-1 Trader 330
Grumman TBF/TBM Avenger 174

H
Harvard (see North American)
Havoc (see Douglas)
Hawker Fury/Sea Fury 334
Hawker Hind 78
Hawker Hunter 338
Hawker Hurricane 180
Hawker Sea Hawk 336
Heinkel He 111 (see CASA)
Helio AU-24 Stallion 340
Helldiver (see Curtiss)
Hispano HA-200/-220 Saetta/Super Saetta 344
Hispano HA-1112 BuchSaetta/SHuey (see Bell UH-1 Iroquois)
Hunting Percival Provost 346

J
J 32 (see Saab)
J 35 (see Saab)

Junkers Ju 52/3m/CASA 352L 80

K
Kingcobra (see Bell)
Klemm Kl 35 82

L
L-29 (see Aero)
L-39 (see Aero)
Lancaster (see Avro)
Liberator (see Consolidated)
Lockheed B-34/PV Ventura/Harpoon 186
Lockheed C-69/C-121 348
Lockheed F-104 Starfighter 354
Lockheed Model 18 Lodestar 184
Lockheed P-2 Neptune 352
Lockheed P-3 Orion 356
Lockheed P-38 Lightning 182
Lockheed T-33/Canadair CL-30 350
LVG C.VI 18

M
Magister (see Fouga)
Martin B-26 Marauder 188
Martin JRM-3 Mars 358
Max Holste M.H.1521M Broussard 360
McDonnell Douglas F-4 Phantom II 362
Mentor (see Beech)
Messerschmitt Bf 108 Taifun/Nord Pingouin 84
Messerschmitt Bf 109G 190
Miles Hawk Magister III/M 14 86
Miles M 38 Messenger 192
Mikoyan-Gurevich MiG-15/-15UTI 364
Mikoyan-Gurevich MiG-17 366
Mikoyan-Gurevich MiG-21 368
Mitchell (see North American)
Mitsubishi A6M Zero-Sen 194
Mohawk (see Grumman)
Morane-Saulnier MS.230 88
Morane-Saulnier MS.760 370
Morane-Saulnier Type AI 20
Mustang F-51D (see Cavalier)
Mustang P-51 (see North American)

N
Naval Factory N3N 90
Navion (see North American L-17A)
Neptune (see Lockheed)
Nieuport 10.C1 22
Nieuport 28.C1 24
Noorduyn UC-64 Norseman 196
North American A-36/P-51A Mustang 202
North American B-25 Mitchell 200
North American BT-9/-14/Yale I 92
North American NA-50/-68 and P-64 94
North American (Rockwell) OV-10 Bronco 378
North American P-51C/D Mustang 204
North American T-6 Texan/Harvard 198
North American Aviation F-86 Sabre 372
North American Aviation F-100D/F Super Sabre 374
North American Aviation L-17 Navion 382
North American Aviation L-17A Navion 382
North American Aviation T-2 Buckeye 380
North American Aviation T-28 Trojan/Fennec 376
Northrop T-38/F-5 384
Northrop T-38 Talon/F-5 Freedom Fighter 384

P
P-3 (see Lockheed Orion)
P-39 (see Bell Airacobra)
P-51 (see North American)
P-63 (see Bell Kingcobra)
Panther (see Grumman)
Percival Pembroke/Sea Prince 388
Percival Prentice 386
Percival Proctor 206
Phantom (see McDonnell Douglas)
Piaggio P.149D 390
Pilatus P-2 394
Piper O-59/L-4/L-19 Grasshopper 208
Polikarpov Po-2 210
Privateer (see Consolidated)
Provider (see Fairchild)

Provost (see Hunting Percival)
Pup (see Sopwith)
PZL-104 Wilga **396**
PZL TS-11 Iskra **398**

R
Raven (see Hiller UH-12)
Republic (Seversky) AT-12 Guardsman **98**
Republic P-47 Thunderbolt **212**
Royal Aircraft Factory SE5A **26**
Ryan PT-16/-22 and NR-1 Recruit **96**

S
Saab B17A 214
Saab J 29 Tunnan **400**
Saab J 32 Lansen **402**
Saab J 35 Draken **404**
Saab 91 Safir **406**
Sabre (see North American)
Scottish Aviation Twin Pioneer **408**
SE5A (see Royal Aircraft Factory)
Shackleton (see Avro)
Shorts Skyvan 3M **410**
Sioux (see Bell Model 47)
Skyraider (see Douglas A-1)
Skywarrior (see Douglas A-3)
Soko G2A Galeb **412**
Sopwith Camel 32
Sopwith Pup **28**
Sopwith Triplane 30
Spad 13.C1 **34**
Spitfire (see Vickers-Supermarine)
Stallion (see Helio)
Stampe SV4 **100**
Starfighter (see Lockheed F-104)
Stinson AT-19 Reliant **216**
Stinson O-49/L-1 Vigilant **218**
Stinson O-62/L-5 Sentinel **220**
Strikemaster (see BAC)
Superfortress (see Boeing B-29)
Supermarine (see Vickers-Supermarine)
Swordfish (see Fairey)

T
Taylorcraft O-57/L-2 Grasshopper **222**
Thomas-Morse S-4 **36**
Thunderbolt (see Republic P-47)

V
Vampire (see de Havilland)
Venom (see de Havilland)
Ventura (see Lockheed)
Vickers-Supermarine Spitfire (Griffon) **226**
Vickers-Supermarine Spitfire (Merlin) **224**
Vickers-Supermarine Spitfire Mks XVIII and XIX **414**
Vought F4U/Goodyear FG-1 Corsair **228**
Vultee BT-13/-15 and SNV-1/-2 Valiant **102**

W
Westland Lysander **230**
Widgeon (see Grumman)
Wildcat (see Grumman)
Winjeel (see CAC)
Wirraway (see CAC)

Y
Yakovlev Yak-3UA **232**
Yakovlev Yak-9UM **234**
Yakovlev Yak-11 **416**
Yakovlev Yak-18/Nanchung CJ-5/6 **418**
Yakovlev Yak-52 **420**

Picture credits

Dave Davies: 19, 33, 51, 87, 89, 207, 437, 443

Tony Holmes: 15, 29, 31, 79, 109, 123, 133, 137, 165, 181, 191, 231, 251, 301, 335, 409, 433, 435

Peter March: 13, 21, 27, 41, 49, 57, 61, 67, 69, 83, 91, 97, 101, 107, 125, 127, 159, 163, 167, 185, 193, 211, 255, 259, 273, 277, 279, 281, 283, 299, 311, 315, 325, 337, 343, 361, 371, 381, 391, 393, 401, 403, 405, 407, 413, 419, 423, 425, 429, 439

Norman Pealing: 215, 265, 399

Michael O'Leary: 37, 45, 47, 53, 55, 63, 65, 71, 73, 75, 77, 81, 85, 93, 95, 99, 103, 111, 113, 115, 117, 119, 121, 129, 131, 135, 139, 141, 143, 145, 147, 149, 151, 153, 155, 157, 161, 169, 171, 173, 175, 177, 179, 183, 187, 189, 195, 197, 199, 201, 203, 205, 209, 213, 217, 219, 221, 223, 225, 227, 229, 233, 235, 239, 241, 243, 247, 249, 253, 257, 261, 263, 267, 269, 271, 275, 287, 289, 291, 293, 295, 297, 303, 305, 307, 309, 313, 317, 319, 321, 323, 327, 329, 331, 333, 339, 341, 345, 347, 349, 351, 353, 355, 357, 359, 363, 365, 367, 369, 373, 375, 377, 379, 383, 385, 387, 389, 395, 397, 411, 415, 431, 441

Mike Vines: 17, 23, 25, 35, 43, 59, 285, 417, 427

Jim Winchester: 245